9-99 ✓

- b

Britain's modern
ROYAL NAVY

As part of ongoing market research, we are always pleased to receive comments about our books, suggestions for new titles, or requests for catalogues. Please write to: The Editorial Director, Patrick Stephens Limited, Sparkford, Near Yeovil, Somerset, BA22 7JJ.

Britain's modern
ROYAL
NAVY

Paul Beaver

Patrick Stephens Limited

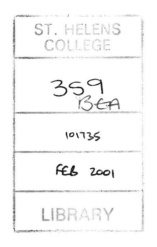
First published in 1996

British Library Cataloguing-in-Publication Data:
A catalogue record for this book
is available from the British Library.

ISBN 1 85260 442 5

Library of Congress catalog card no. 95 79129

Patrick Stephens Limited is an imprint of
Haynes Publishing, Sparkford,
Nr Yeovil, Somerset, BA22 7JJ

Typeset by G&M, Raunds, Northamptonshire
Printed and bound in Great Britain by
Butler & Tanner Ltd of London and Frome

Contents

HMS Cardiff. (Jeremy Flack/Aviation Photographs International)

Introduction

THIS BOOK HAS been a long time in the writing. The Royal Navy has changed significantly since the end of the Cold War and this presentation is designed to reflect those changes – for better or for worse.

The Royal Navy is not what it was in the 1980s, but there are good, clear indications that the professionalism and standards have not dropped. Instead, there is a small question mark over morale in some areas, notably the Submarine Service, and of course, there are less warships.

The First Sea Lord 1993–95, Admiral Sir Benjamin Bathurst, was the architect of the warship number reductions and many believe that he did an outstanding job considering the cost restraints which the British Government placed on him – at the same time as giving him increasing commitments, like Yugoslavia. He had to make the fateful decision to pay off the world's most advanced diesel-electric submarines and yet saw into service the latest nuclear-powered submarines, the Trident-carrying 'Vanguard' class.

His successor, Admiral Sir Jock Slater, will have the task of slimming down the Senior Service, especially at the top. There is always criticism when a naval service has more admirals than front-line warships and Sir Jock is determined to continue many of Sir Ben's reforms.

Training and professionalism count even more in a slimmed-down Royal Navy. The co-educational nature of naval training is working well and the integration of Wrens at sea appears to me to be better than the popular press would have us believe. In early 1995, it was decided to reduce the number of warships carrying female sailors, to concentrate them into larger complements, and so remove the 'uniqueness' of women aboard ship, which was proving to be a problem in some warships.

There are clear signs also that the British Government understands the changing nature of the warships which are required. By the time this book reaches bookshops, there should be orders for a new class of amphibious assault ship, follow-on nuclear-powered attack submarines and more Type 23 frigates. Project Horizon is just around the corner and the Merlin helicopter should enter service within months.

I am confident that the Modern Royal Navy is a worthy successor to the Fleet of the past; the men and women who serve are amongst the best trained and have the finest motivation in the world.

Paul Beaver
London, January 1996

HMS London *and a Lynx helicopter.* (Jeremy Flack/Aviation Photographs International)

Acknowledgements

DURING THE PREPARATION of this book I have received a huge amount of assistance from the Royal Navy and from the industry which supplies and supports it. I would like to single out the following for their continued help. There are of course many others and if I have missed you out, please accept my apologies for the omission.

Admiral Sir Benjamin Bathurst, Captain Christopher Beagley, Captain Charles Style, Captain Chris Esplin-Jones, Commander Duncan Fergusson, Major Simon Haselock, Captain Bob Fanshawe, Lt Cdr Simon Brown, Lt Cdr Alistair McLaren, Lt Cdr Tim Reynolds, Lt Paul D'Arcy, Lt Sue Barrett, Lt Simon Pink, WO Paul Wellings, CSgt Dieter Lorriane, CPO Stu Antrobus and the ships' companies of HMSs *Campbeltown*, *Dolphin*, *Norfolk*, *Plover*, *Tamar* and *Vanguard*.

Leslie Burgess, David Carey, Lorraine Coulton, James Gee and Michael Hill made significant contributions to the book. Thanks also to Mike Bryant, Peter Nicholson and John Sulman.

In industry: Charles Carr and Mark Ritson (British Aerospace), Chris Loney and Mike Peters (Westland), the public relations teams at Racal, Loral-ISIC, Vickers Shipbuilding & Engineering and Vosper Thornycroft.

From the world of naval illustrations, this book could not have been completed without the assistance of David Reynolds of Photo Press, Ian Sturton and Robin Walker. The official Royal Navy photographs are Crown Copyright.

To you all, thanks! But as usual, the errors and omissions are mine alone.

CHAPTER ONE

The Royal Navy and the Cold War

ONCE THE WORLD'S largest and most powerful naval force, the UK Royal Navy is now in the second division as regards number of warship hulls, but has still managed to maintain its position as number one in training, personnel and professionalism. The challenge for the modern Royal Navy, as it moves towards the 21st century, is to maintain that credibility in the face of defence cuts and changing commitments.

As 1994 drew to a close, the Royal Navy made plans to lay off 2,400 officers and ratings under a fourth round of redundancies which were a result of Front Line First, the Defence Costs Study announced in the previous July.

Like most sections of British society, the Royal Navy (RN) has not been quite the same since the end of the Second World War. That great conflict saw such widespread changes in the Navy, its ideas, its equipment, its ships, but most of all in its men, that it can truly be said to have changed out of all recognition from the inter-war period.

The greatest single factor was the sheer increase of manpower, the influx of the Royal Naval Volunteer Reserve (RNVR) – the temporary gentlemen of the *Cruel Sea* saga. Mainly seconded to small ships and the Air Branch – the Fleet Air Arm, as it was popularly if a little inaccurately known – RNVR officers and ratings had provided the backbone of the world's second largest fleet when the war ended in 1945. That year saw many – the vast majority in fact – demobbed (demobilized or returned to civilian life), and many of the warships in which they had served so gallantly, paid off. Most arms of the Royal Navy were pared down to the bare minimum, from Coastal Forces to battleships, and even the new capital ships, the aircraft carriers, were rapidly taken out of service.

The war had seen the eclipse of the battleship and the rise of the carrier and, by August 1945, the Royal Navy could boast over 50 of the latter;

Britain's top sailor – the First Sea Lord, Admiral Sir Jock Slater KCB LVO, pictured as the Commander-in-Chief Fleet in 1994. (Crown Copyright)

Sea power – the surface warship plays a vital part in the projection of sea power. The Type 23 frigate, equipped with the Lynx HAS 8 helicopter, will be the mainstay of the surface escort force well into the next century. (HMS Osprey)

sadly, postwar austerity and a general rush, 'hell for leather', into peace saw the rapid decline of the 'flat-top'. By 1947, only three remained active – *Implacable*, *Ocean* and *Triumph*.

The naval scene world-wide was changing rapidly, although it would be only half a decade before the Cold War would begin in earnest, leading to a rapid rebuilding plan in the seafaring nations of the West, or the Free World as it was becoming known. Before this could take place, there were changes in the everyday life of the Navy. Despite the demobilization of the RNVR and other temporary personnel, the minority who stayed were quickly commissioned into the regular Royal Navy – the 'Andrew' as many call naval service. This led to an amazingly self-defeating

idea to segregate officers into a 'wet' and 'dry' list: those on the former were assured, all things being equal, of gaining command at sea; their counterparts on the 'dry' list, however, were destined never to command a ship. This came as a savage blow to many war-experienced naval officers. Their ability to command men and organize fighting units could not have been questioned judging by wartime records.

So, as Empire gave way to Commonwealth, the Royal Navy began to adopt a new role, that of fulfilling the obligations established by the large number of treaties drawn up postwar and the covering of the numerous guerilla wars in colonies seeking independence.

The foremost of these treaty obligations derived from the North Atlantic Alliance or NATO (North Atlantic Treaty Organization). The growing tension in South-East Asia following the assistance given by the Allies to the communist-led 'popular' resistance movements led to growing discontent in former colonial territories. The Royal Navy played a major part in the liberation from Japanese hands of many areas, particularly Hong Kong, Indo-China and Dutch East India. Many thousands of British and Commonwealth prisoners of war (POWs) were evacuated in various warships, including aircraft carriers, of the British Pacific Fleet.

Besides POWs, there were a large number of internees from the prewar civilian populations to be released, but the jubilation of liberation did not last long in the Far East. Not only did pirates have a new freedom to operate on the civilian sea traffic which suddenly multiplied, but many former resistance fighters became 'Freedom' fighters.

By far the most serious area of tension was China, where there was all-out civil war. Although the country was, in theory, one of the big five allies, the internal problems which followed the Japanese surrender led to a communist take-over. Britain, like many Western nations, had considerable commercial interests in China prewar and when the situation became too risky for UK citizens to remain in the towns and cities, being caught between the warring factions, the Royal Navy went to assist evacuation. In 1949, the frigate *Amethyst* was moving along the Yangtze River to take regular supplies to the British Embassy at Nanking (now Nanjing).

On 20 April the warship was fired upon by People's Liberation Army artillery and forced aground. There then followed three months of protracted negotiations with the communist authorities who were just a few months away from total victory and the formation of the People's Republic of China. Despite the fact that the initial Chinese assault had cost the lives of 17 of the ship's company, the Commanding Officer,

Lieutenant Commander John Kearns, RN, decided to try and break for the high seas, 140 nm (259 km) away. The *Amethyst* reached open water on July 8; her signal on the occasion has gone down in history as a proud moment for Britain's Senior Service: 'Have rejoined the Fleet. No damages or casualties. God Save the King.'

Without doubt this action boosted morale at an important time because, within twelve months, the Royal Navy was again in action in that troubled area with a Communist government. On 24 June 1950, the North Koreans crossed the 1945 frontier line into South Korea, taking almost everyone by surprise. Within 24 hours, British naval forces in the Far East were put at the disposal of the United Nations, or rather for practical reasons, the United States government. The Royal Navy's largest warship in the area was the light fleet carrier *Triumph,* which had just begun passage from Japan to the United Kingdom. In addition there were cruisers and destroyers at several locations, including Hong Kong.

This was to be the beginning of a sustained Royal Naval presence in Korea which lasted for the next three years, during which the naval blockade of the Korean coast was maintained in all weathers by various navies, including those of Australia, Canada and the United States. Britain's main contribution was a light fleet carrier stationed permanently offshore, apart from when re-storing, to operate air strikes against ground and sea targets. The carriers involved were *Theseus*, *Ocean*, *Glory* and *Sydney* (Royal Australian Navy). The main task of the naval blockade, to prevent coastal shipping moving men and materials for the other side, worked well and, following the peace treaty in 1953, the RN maintained warships in the area to monitor the peace for several years.

On the technological side, the Korean War did not hamper the developing Fleet, but rather accelerated certain aspects of it. Nowhere were the innovations more obvious than in the naval aviation field. The advent of the jet aircraft in carriers, following the successful trials of Lieutenant Commander (later Captain) Eric Brown in December 1945, paved the way for jet air squadrons. Progress was slow at first until two amazing inventions made the whole concept of carrier flying a thousand times safer.

The angled-deck principle, invented by Captain (later Rear Admiral) Dennis Campbell and Mr Lewis Boddington of the Royal Aircraft Establishment Farnborough, was the first of these. It allowed the free take-off and landing of aircraft without the need to protect parked aircraft with a crash barrier. To assist the actual landing, Commander (later Rear Admiral) Nick Goodhart invented the mirror deck landing sight which allowed an incoming pilot to line himself up on the flight deck and then execute a safe landing without need of external assistance.

The first operational jet squadron was 800 (commanded by Lieutenant Commander, later Captain George Baldwin), which commissioned the Supermarine Attacker aircraft into service in 1951. The first helicopter, a Sikorsky R-4B, had already been successfully landed on the frigate *Helmsdale* in 1946 by the man who later founded the world's largest commercial helicopter operating company, Lieutenant Alan Bristow RN. Slowly the aircraft carrier fleet and naval aviation was built up again. The RNVR Air Branch was reactivated until 1957 when the government of the day thought that manned aircraft would soon be totally replaced by missiles. It was during this period that the two most famous postwar carriers were launched and commissioned – *Eagle* (1952) and *Ark Royal* (1955). Reserve aviators are now back in service, with the Royal Naval Reserve Air Branch.

At sea, the last of the cruisers were still on station in the Far East, Mediterranean and Caribbean. With no major rivals afloat except in the US Navy, the Royal Navy decided that most of the cruiser force could be discarded. By 1950, there were only about ten left in commission and although three new hulls were under construction their completion had been suspended in 1946. Off Korea, cruisers like the *Belfast* had been used most successfully as flagships and to provide bombardment of shore areas. Their traditional scouting role had, of course, been taken over by radar and naval aircraft. The last of the conventional cruisers were the 6-in (152 mm) gun 'Tiger' class, of which two were converted into anti-submarine warfare cruisers during 1965 and the third was scrapped in 1975. Although the Royal Navy has continued to build and commission cruiser-size warships, they have long been reclassified as destroyers.

Destroyers themselves continued to evolve, the most outstanding in the early postwar years being the 'Darings'. Originally, because of their size, they were classified as fleet escorts but later the term destroyer was applied. They were truly beautiful 2,800-ton warships which first appeared with the Fleet in 1952, designed as leaders but quite capable of independent operations, especially in the Far East. By 1954 there were eight of them and they were sovereigns of the seas. Their main armament was the then-new 4.5-in (114 mm) dual-purpose gun which, being 'radar controlled', put them in a different class to their wartime forbears. The 'Darings' were tasked primarily with cruiser-type reconnaissance and anti-submarine defence of a task force or convoy; their impressive gun armament was also a useful anti-surface vessel (ASV) weapon.

Destroyers were in action during Korea, but before that in October 1946 *Suamarez* and *Volage* were severely damaged by Albanian offensive mines placed in international waters off Corfu – this was the period of the Greek Civil War following liberation from German occupation.

The anti-air warfare (AAW) side of naval operations was still the province of the small-calibre gun in the immediate postwar years, but the increasing use of aircraft led to a number of destroyers being converted into radar pickets – an idea originally developed by the United States Navy (USN) in the Pacific at the end of 1945 to combat the Japanese 'Kamikaze' raiders. The main feature of these conversions was the conspicuous Type 965 air warning radar on the main mast – the 'bedstead' radar scanner. The first conversions to 'Weapons' class warships were originally completed in 1958–59. The earlier 'Battle' class destroyers – beautiful ships which clearly represented the peak of traditional destroyer design – were also converted into radar pickets in 1962. The latter carried the double-bedstead Type 965 radars but, unlike the 'Weapons', they were positioned on the foremast. The radar only passed from service in the 1980s.

The last true destroyer in the Royal Navy, *Cavalier*, one of the numerous 'C' class of war emergency construction, was neither converted nor sold after the war and her only allowance to modern warfare is the Seacat surface-to-air missile (SAM) launcher and director installed aft. Built in 1944 and eventually paid off at Chatham in 1972, she represents the last British warship to see action in the Second World War.

On 15 June 1953, the newly-crowned Queen Elizabeth II reviewed her combined Fleet at Spithead. It was indeed an 'armada', with 197 RN warships being present, including the last British battleship *Vanguard* and eight aircraft carriers. For the first time, the flypast included jets and helicopters (led by the late Rear Admiral Walter Couchman). On the warship side, this review was remarkable because specialist landing craft were present for the first time. The most numerous of the surface combat ships were the smaller warships, including 62 'Ocean' minesweepers and 47 frigates. It is these latter types which were the mainstay of the Fleet in the postwar period, in numerical terms at least.

Just as the destroyer had migrated postwar into the cruiser tonnages, so the frigate continued to increase its size. Initially, the type had been revitalized during the war with the need to provide anti-submarine warfare (ASW) escorts for the Atlantic convoys. In the later 1940s, the Admiralty reclassified most of its escorts as frigates. Most suited to work in the majority of theatres from 1945, the frigate made its own the

role of peacekeeper and 'flag shower' in the Far East, Mediterranean and West Indies. In warmer climes, such as the Gulf, the 'Loch' and 'Bay' classes were well employed dealing with British interests, including the suppression of pirates. Displacing about 1,575 tons, both classes were very similar, although the 'Bays' retained four 102 mm guns whilst the armour of the 'Lochs' was generally pared down to two. By the late 1950s, these two classes had been downgraded into the Reserve or transferred into the embryo navies of the emerging Commonwealth.

Some destroyers, notably the War Emergency 'R-Z' classes and the famous 'Hunts', were fully converted to fast anti-submarine frigates. Mainly used for training and experimental purposes, these warships provided the Royal Navy with a much-needed ASW capability in a time of gathering threat from classes of Soviet submarine.

The first specialist frigates designed for the Royal Navy were initiated during the major Western rearmament programmes caused by the Korean conflict. These were the 'Whitby' class, completed 1956–58, with their characteristic forecastle allowing better seakeeping than their predecessors. A further nine which followed were known as the 'Rothesay' class, 1960–61, under the 1954–55 programme; in 1966–68, *Rothesay*, the name ship of the class, was converted to operate ASW helicopters and the Seacat surface-to-air missiles.

Specialist frigates were also designed and built for anti-aircraft duties and for aircraft direction as well. The former were used with the Fleet and known as the 'Big Cats' or 'Leopard' class (1953–59), being equipped with 114 mm Mk 6 guns and Type 965 radar. The latter purpose-built radar pickets were ordered during the same period and the last, *Lincoln*, was completed in 1960. Their radar fit was far more extensive as they were designed primarily for the direction of carrier-based aircraft such as the Scimitar and the Sea Vixen, or their shore-based counterparts. More utilitarian but still worthy of a place in British postwar naval history is the 'Blackwood' class of second-rate ASW frigates, built 1955–58.

By the middle of the 1950s, the need to have specialized frigates in the Royal Navy had been rethought by the Admiralty planners and this led to the most famous class of all postwar frigates – the 'Leanders'. There were originally 28 of the class and they served in all theatres and on all commitments with the Royal Navy until 1993. The last 'Leander' was *Andromeda* which was paid off in 1994. The class was originally considered in the 1955–56 Naval Estimates.

The Submarine Service, like the Fleet Air Arm, an elite group within an elite organization, began postwar operations with a large number of diesel-

Deterrent force – for nearly 30 years, the United Kingdom has claimed an independent nuclear deterrent force of Polaris missile-carrying submarines. Vanguard *approaches the Clyde Submarine Base for the first time.* (HMS *Neptune*)

powered patrol submarines of the 'A', 'S' and 'T' classes. For several years, four midget submarines of the 'XE' class were retained for training duties, together with a new postwar 'improved' midget design. By 1950, there were 61 submarines of all types in commission, under refit or being used in experimental work with propulsion or sonar gear for the new era. The 'A' class continued in service until 1974, when *Andrew*, completed in 1948, retired. One of her claims to fame was the first submerged crossing of the Atlantic, in 1953. Some years later the whole class was reconstructed with streamlined conning tower and deck guns removed. With the capture of so many former U-boats in 1945, it was possible for the Royal Navy to carry out trials with hydrogen peroxide-powered Walter-type submarines (e.g. *Meteorite*, ex-*U-1407*). Later, in the 1950s, two Vickers-built submarines tested the propulsion system. Although amongst the fastest submarines in the world, they were overshadowed by the development of nuclear power.

Postwar conventional types have been confined to two classes – the 'Porpoise' and 'Oberon' classes. It is undoubtedly in the Submarine Service that the Royal Navy has seen one of its greatest changes; for not only is the submarine in its Fleet role the capital ship of the 1980s and 1990s (succeeding the carriers in the 1970s), but

it also represents the independent deterrent to aggression from unfriendly powers. The revolution which has caused this change is, of course, nuclear power.

The birth of the nuclear submarine fleet was planned during the days of the Cold War (in the 1950s) but the technology was not available to allow the Royal Navy to build a nuclear-powered submarine for some time. The first such boat, although British-constructed, relied on a US-designed reactor and was commissioned in April 1963 as *Dreadnought* – an apt name for the first of a new generation of warships, like the *Dreadnought* of the battleship era. She cost a staggering £18.5 million which, although it compares well with the £250 million for a modern nuclear-powered attack submarine, stretched the defence budget at the time.

Unaffected by the Defence Cuts of the 1960s, the submarine force grew for the last two decades of the Cold War. There are two types of nuclear boat – the hunter-killer Attack or Fleet type (SSNs) and the nuclear-powered ballistic missile-carrying boats (SSBNs). The first all-British SSN was *Valiant*, launched in 1965. The new submarines, with their modern technology, heralded a new era in crew comfort and amenity and for the first time provided submarines with unlimited fresh water, air and power. Morale was boosted by the provision of separate messes for junior and senior rates whose meals can be provided at cafeterias, such is the internal space available. These first-generation submarines have now been paid off and replaced by the 'Swiftsure' and 'Trafalgar' classes.

The Anglo-American Accord known as the Nassau Agreement led to the replacement of the nuclear strike V-bombers of the Royal Air Force (RAF) with a small, yet powerful, fleet of submarines. Developing the technology used in the early SSNs, Vickers Armstrong and Cammell Laird produced four large (7,500-ton) submarines in the period 1966–68. These craft each carry 16 American-built Polaris medium-range ballistic missiles. The first nuclear-armed boat, *Resolution*, left on her first top secret deterrence patrol in 1967; she had cost £52 million to build and equip. The Polaris missile boats are now close to being paid off; in January 1995, there were only two left in commission and the first Trident boat, *Vanguard*, had begun its first three-month patrol.

Conventional submarines – no longer part of the Royal Navy's order of battle, despite the fact that the 'Upholder' class had been in commission less than two years. (Paul Beaver)

The most important development for the Royal Navy in the 1990s was the decision to pay off the 'Upholder' class of latest-generation conventional diesel-electric submarines after only months of service. The decision almost wrecked the morale of the Submarine Service and can be blamed directly on the government of the day. The 'Upholders' could well be sold to Canada or another friendly nation, but they represented an early opportunity for young submariners to achieve responsibility, including command.

Changes were made in other branches of the Royal Navy afloat during the 1960s. The converted aircraft carrier or Commando Carrier, equipped only to fly helicopters but with a full Royal Marines (RM) Commando, had been developed. Its origins can be traced directly to the Suez police action for intervention in November 1956, when an Anglo-French fleet attempted to mediate between Israel and Egypt and thus secure the future of the recently nationalized Suez Canal.

Political ineptitude and US pressure effectively hamstrung the Royal Navy's effort, yet very good use was made of carrier-based aircraft including helicopters. Several assaults and casualty evacuations (casevacs) were flown by the latter, manned by aircrew from the Joint Services Trials Unit based in *Ocean* and *Theseus*. It was these operations, coinciding with more powerful aircraft, such as the Wessex helicopter, being available, which opened the way for Commando Carrier operations.

The Royal Navy was thereby given the capability of flexible response to minor, brushfire wars. In addition, the smaller carriers were becoming too small for big jet operations. Ironically, it was Suez veterans *Bulwark* and *Albion* which were converted, followed in 1971–73 by the last conventional carrier to enter service, *Hermes*. The first test of the idea came in 1961 when the Kingdom of Kuwait was threatened by its larger neighbour, Iraq; *Bulwark* was already in the Gulf of Oman and steamed at top speed into the Gulf, arriving off Kuwait within hours of the Ruler's plea for assistance.

Britain had at that time a defence agreement with the Kingdom and so disembarked 42 Commando (Cdo) in Whirlwind HAS 7 helicopters of 848 Naval Air Squadron. Despite unfavourable flying conditions, a full Commando was deployed in position and the situation was stabilized.

With the withdrawal from Empire, the Commando Carrier also looked to new horizons and concentrated on the NATO flanks, specifically Norway. By the mid-1970s, the need was more pressing in the ASW role and so the LPHs (NATO parlance for Commando or Helicopter Carriers) became joint LPH/CVS (anti-submarine warfare carrier) ships. The election of 1966 saw the beginning of the end of the conventional aircraft carrier with its ASW helicopters and so it was important that they should still be afloat whether in a CVS or helicopter-carrying cruiser (CCH) role, like *Tiger* and *Blake*. This time the Defence Cuts axed the new generation of aircraft carrier, CVA-01 and her class, rather than postponing the programme; thus, when *Ark Royal* decommissioned in 1978, she was the last fixed-wing conventional aircraft carrier.

In more peaceful waters, the Royal Navy began to turn its attention more and more to specialist surveying and hydrography. The ocean sciences not only benefit the navies of the world, but the merchant fleets as well. Britain, under the Hydrographer to the Navy, has always led the world in chart making and recording; now there was the new horizon of Antarctica as well. In addition, the new generation of deep-diving SSNs and SSBNs need more detailed oceanographic data to fight and survive in the modern undersea environment.

In 1950, the Royal Navy laid down a specialist survey ship at Chatham; named the *Vidal* on launching in 1951, she was the first of her type to be equipped with a flight deck and helicopter. This enables independent survey parties to operate away from the ship and thus cover a greater area. She also has a place in the heart of all sailors of that era because she was the first warship to be designed to operate cafeteria messing (hammocks went out with the introduction of *Ark Royal* in 1955; these improvements to the lot of the average sailor were greatly appreciated).

Several 'Bay' class frigates were modified for survey duties but it was not until 1964 that the next new class of hydro-oceanographic survey ship was ordered. The 'Cook' class survey ships of the immediate postwar period carried out much initial survey work off the coast of the frozen southern continent. In the mid-1950s, the Ice Patrol Ship *Protector* spent some time in the South Atlantic and Antarctic following rather anti-social claims by Argentina. Designed to operate as a Falkland Islands' guardship, survey vessel and transport for Royal Marine detachments, she remained in service until replaced by *Endurance* in 1968. *Endurance* herself was paid off in 1990 and replaced by the former *Polar Circle*, again taken up and bought from trade.

The Hydrographer's ships are still working on a daily basis to update and improve nautical charts. More than 50 per cent of the world's maritime traders rely on an Admiralty chart, making an important contribution to the UK's balance of payments.

The serious problems created by mines in the Second World War, and to a certain extent during the Korea conflict, led the Royal Navy to build a sizeable fleet of 54 minesweepers (later known as mine countermeasures vessels or MCMVs). These vessels of the 'Ton' class, displacing 360 tons, were only recently paid off, the last leaving service in 1993.

The Royal Navy launched and commissioned the world's first glass-reinforced plastic (GRP) warship in July 1973 and she was paid off in 1994. This development led to the highly successful 'Hunt' class which were operational in the South Atlantic and the Islamic Gulf in the 1980s and early 1990s. The Royal Navy is rated as the world leader in mine warfare and proved the claim in the Gulf conflict with Iraq, by being the provider of the Coalition's mine warfare expertise.

The Coastal Forces, traditionally the forte of the then Royal Naval Volunteer Reserve, were to see the development of the Fast Patrol Boat (FPB) in Britain with the 'Dark' and 'Brave' Classes, which are both now sadly out of service, several having been expended as targets. In the Royal Navy's NATO role, the use of the FPB has ended although several overseas navies buy British designs from British shipbuilders.

Specialist vessels for the Royal Fleet Auxiliary Service (RFA) and the Royal Marine Auxiliary Service (RMAS) – which includes the Port Auxiliary Service – have abounded since the war. Both organizations have modern and large fleets of craft designed for many tasks. The latter did possess many wartime-constructed craft through until a building boom in the 1965–80 period, and today most of the old steam-powered craft have disappeared.

The art and skill of provisioning and refuelling at sea was learnt the hard way during the Pacific campaign in 1944–45, but since then the RFA has perfected the art to such a degree that it now leads the world in replenishment at sea (RAS). Four fleet oilers were completed in 1945–46 to form the 'Wave' class and these craft bore the brunt of early RASing exercises and operations; in 1954–58, the class was augmented by the 'Tides', and later in 1965–66 by the 'Ol' class. Both 'Wave' and 'Tide' classes are no longer in service. With the new range of weapons and aircraft carried by ships of the RN, the RFA ordered and manned a new type of ammunition, food, explosives and stores (AFES) carrier of several classes.

A new one-stop design was developed in the late 1980s, mainly to provide a service to the new Type 23 frigates; two of these ships are now in commission.

The non-naval manned supplies and transportation facets of the RN were run as almost separate organizations until the appointment of the then Vice Admiral Lord Louis Mountbatten as Fourth

Plastic warships – the Royal Navy pioneered the use of glass-reinforced plastic warships for mine warfare during the Cold War. This is the 'Hunt' class MCMV Cottesmore. *(Photo Press)*

Sea Lord in 1950. With a special responsibility for this part of the Navy, Mountbatten set about reorganizing the stores, victualling and armament supplies of the Fleet. A decade later Mountbatten, by then Chief of the Defence Staff, began to put his ideas into action and began the creation of the unified defence command – the Ministry of Defence.

The scheme was much opposed at first, but with the backing of Prime Minister Macmillan and later Wilson, the Admiralty was merged with the other two Services. The merger was not as complete as in Canada in the same period, and thus none of their unfortunate problems have occurred in Britain. Mountbatten will be remembered with great affection by the Royal Navy for his tireless efforts on its behalf during the postwar era.

The postwar years have seen a dramatic change in the Navy's overseas commitments and of the

The Rock – Gibraltar is no longer a naval dockyard and now rarely sees more than one British warship at a time. The base is still important to NATO as a communications centre and commands the sea areas which wash the shores of an increasingly militant North Africa. (Paul Beaver)

traditional Royal Navy's Dockyards abroad; only Gibraltar remains as a base. There are limited facilities in Hong Kong, although the Royal Navy moved from Tamar in September 1994 in readiness for the reversion to China in 1997. Ceylon (now Sri Lanka) was abandoned in 1956, Singapore in 1971 and finally Malta in 1979.

Jolly Jack was rarely seen in whites until the early 1980s and this is somewhat ironic considering just how efficient the laundry service aboard a modern warship has become! The increase in tension, then fighting, in the Islamic Gulf, first between Iran and Iraq and then following the Iraqi invasion of Kuwait, have caused the change of dress.

During the Cold War, the Royal Navy developed into a primary anti-submarine warfare force for operational duties in the Eastern Atlantic (known as Eastlant to NATO). With the demise of the Soviet Union but the increased emphasis on peacekeeping, that has changed little.

The Royal Navy of the next century will still depend on the individual sailor, now a professional man or woman, a volunteer with a higher educational standard than ever before. The sending of women to sea in the late 1980s caused some inevitable problems of accommodation and harassment. The Admiralty Board is said to be reviewing the role of women, especially following the abandonment of WRNS as a separate service. By 2005, there will probably be a female commanding officer of a major warship.

Vast changes have also occurred in the systems which these men and women have to operate. Naval weaponry is more effective, less manpower intensive and more lethal. Although the wartime sailor would be able to recognize the smaller-calibre, general-purpose machine-guns still fitted to destroyers, frigates, patrol vessels and the like, he would probably be completely bemused by the guided weapons and their computerized directors. Both Oerlikon 20 mm and Bofors 40 mm guns can still be found in the same mountings as wartime users, but the newer 20 and 30 mm mountings are rapidly replacing them. The Gatling-type Phalanx and Goalkeeper systems are also present on all high-value warships.

The guided missile did not replace the larger-calibre gun as many predicted in the early 1980s. The Falklands conflict showed the need for the naval gun and resulted in the Type 22 Batch 3 frigates being redesigned to accommodate the standard 114 mm Mk 8 mounting.

The guided missile has however been the major weapon system of the last two decades. Initial sea trials took place aboard *Girdle Ness*, the former Fleet Maintenance Ship, in October 1963 and July 1965. At first, missiles – Short Seacat and Seaslug – were designed for the anti-aircraft role,

Naval gunnery – after the Falklands conflict, the naval gun was deemed vital for any new class of warship. The resultant Type 22 Batch 3 (this is Campbeltown) *has been described as the best class of British warship in 50 years.* (Paul Beaver)

to combat high-speed aircraft at both close and medium ranges. They have been replaced by the Sea Dart for area air defence and the Seawolf for short-range defence; the gun is still the close-in weapon system of choice.

In the torpedo field, the Second World War role for this weapon has gone, as have the tubes aboard destroyers and the motor torpedo boat. The submarine still uses the weapon as its primary armament but since 1945 guidance systems, either by wire or internally, have meant that success is almost guaranteed. The new generation Spearfish, now operational in *Vanguard*, has taken ten years to develop but is the most lethal conventional heavyweight torpedo in the world. By 1998, all British submarines are destined to be armed with Spearfish.

Seawolf – a world-class self-defence missile system which achieved fame in the Falklands and is now fitted to British warships in the vertical-launch configuration. (BAe)

Submarine sonar, both passive and active, is now computer-assisted and can classify the sound of another ship's screws, a facet of naval design in which the Royal Navy has often led the world in the postwar era. Both SSNs and SSBNs have been fitted with the passive, ultra low frequency towed array sonar which allows them to listen to a ship's noise many hundreds of nautical miles away in certain sea conditions.

In the late 1960s the SLAM (submarine-launched air missile) was experimented with and operationally fired under trial conditions in *Aeneas*, but the programme was cancelled in late 1972. Yet, in 1994, it was announced that the Royal Navy will acquire the US Navy's Tomahawk submarine-launched land attack missile for the 'Improved Trafalgar' and 'Swiftsure' class submarines.

In the modern naval environment, the radar array of modern warships could be more of a hindrance than a help, particularly in the opening gambits of conflict. So, although much effort has been put into the development of better and better radar in the period since 1945, the so-called Mark One Eyeball still has a place in the Royal Navy. Aircraft are now equipped with far better radar and other sensors than in the past, especially in the anti-submarine role.

The introduction of helicopters in this role in 1957 (Westland Whirlwind HAS 7) and the improved range and weapons delivery of the Wessex (in 1961) have been important. Small ships' flights were established in the early 1960s for operation, initially aboard the 'Tribal' class general-purpose frigates which served in the West Indies, Far East and Gulf as independent units, showing the flag and being available to support the local friendly powers in time of national emergency.

In the latter part of the present decade, the Royal Navy is destined to receive the Merlin HAS 1 helicopter for its Type 23 frigates and other warships. This helicopter, although designed for the Cold War, has a serious of features which will make it adaptable to the post-Cold War period. It is a flying command, control and weapon centre – the closest yet to the flying frigate envisaged in the 1960s.

Not only has the Royal Navy's organization afloat changed, with the only sea-going Commander-in-Chief (CINCFLEET) residing in a 'stone frigate' at Northwood, and thereby contracting the warships of the Royal Navy into one Fleet of operational warships in the Surface Flotilla, where before there were Atlantic, Home, Far East and Mediterranean Fleets. There is also Naval Support Command with a decreasing number of Royal Naval establishments.

With each round of defence cuts, the number of establishments grows smaller; the emphasis is now on bringing everything together to three key centres: Faslane (submarines and patrol craft), Plymouth (destroyers, submarines, frigates and sea training) and Portsmouth (aircraft carriers, mine warfare, destroyers and frigates). CINCFLEET's facilities at Northwood are to be the national crisis centre for joint operations, Rosyth is now a forward operating base, and the Fleet Air Arm will lose Portland in 1998.

By the early 1980s, the Women's Royal Naval Service was under the Naval Discipline Act, and the Wrens no longer had the luxury of their own

Touchdown – the next-generation Merlin comes aboard Norfolk, *the first Type 23 frigate, in Portland harbour. Merlin, a child of the Cold War, will grow up in a period of even greater uncertainty.* (Westland)

training establishment (*Dauntless* closed in 1981, transferring recruit training to *Raleigh*). Several other naval branches now have shared accommodation and resources with the other Services. The Royal Navy's nursing service, the QARNNS, have now also been brought under the Naval Discipline Act and service is open to male or female recruits.

With the end of naval National Service, the 'bull' of the Royal Navy has decreased and in recent years it has been possible for ratings to buy their way out of the Service with ease. Dress regulations have been relaxed and several of the old uniform patterns have gone. New material and fabrics have helped here. The Rum Ration – the Tot – was dispensed with in 1971, although on

Clyde Submarine Base – home to the Royal Navy's nuclear missile-carrying submarines. Faslane is assured of its future as the premier Scottish naval base. (Paul Beaver)

very special occasions it is still possible to 'splice the mainbrace' at the sovereign's command.

Naval rig, although superficially the same since the end of the last world war, has changed with the invention of modern materials, and the needs of modern warships with automatic washing facilities. 'Square rig' has been maintained but modernized with the retention of essential features. In 1971, a new idea in dress was put to trials and competition and in 1975 the Queen approved a new jumper and a new suit of worsted serge, with velcro fastenings for the collar, while separate black silk, lanyard and tapes were dispensed with in favour of an integral trimming. The bell-bottomed trousers were declared obsolete in 1994.

Women's Royal Naval Service uniform also changed in the mid-1970s when the rough serge rig began to be phased out. The whole naval kit went through a transformation, including the issue of slimmer-fit raincoats, new shirts to replace the existing No 8 and easy care white drill items. At the same time an orange working jacket had been

Royal Yacht will leave service in 1997 (after hand-over of Hong Kong). The Britannia *never put to sea in her war role of hospital ship, even during the Falklands (Malvinas) conflict.* (Photo Press)

introduced for greater safety, but this was found to be unworkable as it quickly picked up the dirt, and the waterproof/windproof jacket was changed to navy blue in colour, which has proved far more serviceable.

In the 1990s, the female rank structure was amended to conform with the Royal Navy and the Women's Royal Naval Service eventually disbanded. There is now equal opportunity in all but front-line combat roles for women in the Royal Navy, with over 600 female sailors and nurses serving at sea.

Between 1950 and 1980, nine overseas bases were closed: Bahrain, Bermuda (a small presence is retained), Colombo, Hong Kong (no dockyard facilities), Malta, Mauritius, Simonstown, Singapore and Trincomalee, as well as Sheerness in the United Kingdom.

The Fleet Air Arm lost its fixed-wing aviation during the Cold War when *Ark Royal* was paid off in 1978. Since then, there has been considerable development of the short take-off and vertical landing capability with the Sea Harrier force.

After the war, it was decided that Commandos were needed for tasks demanding special skills in amphibious operations and the Royal Marines were given the task of providing these troops. Since 1945, the Commandos of the Corps of Royal Marines (all Royal Marines are now Commando-trained except the Band Service, the RM sea service men coming ashore in the early postwar period) have taken part in operations in the following countries: Palestine, Egypt, Malaya, Korea, Cyprus, Kuwait, Aden, Tanganyika, Brunei, Borneo, Falkland Islands and Northern Ireland. Warships still carry detachments of Royal Marines, although this was reduced in 1978, and they have carried out numerous landings abroad to assist the civil power in a number of ways, including disaster relief.

The most important series of operations undertaken in the Cold War period, yet ironically against a former ally, was in the South Atlantic. A Task Force under Rear Admiral 'Sandy' Woodward, First Officer First Flotilla, fought to liberate the islands during April, May and June 1982. On 2 April, a strong force of Argentine commandos and regular troops invaded the British Crown Colony of the Falkland Islands and the British Dependency of South Georgia, in the South Atlantic. British defence forces were limited to Naval Party 1009 (about company strength) and the Ice Patrol Ship *Endurance* (on her last patrol before disposal). The result of the invasion was a foregone conclusion.

Although politically caught 'on the hop', the British were able to assemble a Task Force, led by the carrier *Hermes*, within five days and warships, replenishment ships and requisitioned merchant ships sailed from Portsmouth, Rosyth and Plymouth. The immediate result was the postponement of the rundown of Portsmouth and Chatham, and also at Gibraltar where much work was carried out on vessels 'going south'. Using Ascension Island as a base, the task group of warships, Royal Marines (with British Army support) and aircraft of the Fleet Air Arm deployed to war stations. The initial operations were concerned with the retaking of South Georgia, which was accomplished by the weekend of 24–25 April. Prominent in this attack were the guided missile destroyer *Antrim* (and her Wessex HAS 3 helicopter) and the frigates *Plymouth* and *Brilliant*, plus associated landing ships and craft.

The main purpose of the powerful Task Force was the blockade by air and sea of the Falkland Islands. British nuclear-powered Fleet submarines were operational in the areas closest to Argentina because of the latter's powerful air force and fleet air arm. On 2 May, one submarine, *Conqueror*, torpedoed the Argentine cruiser *Belgrano*, but the Royal Navy suffered a major loss two days later when the Type 42 destroyer *Sheffield* was hit and sunk by a single air-launched Exocet missile in its sea-skimming mode.

Perhaps the greatest lesson learned by the Royal Navy during the 11-week operation was the power of the Exocet and the vulnerability of warships without fleet airborne early warning. Later that month, *Sheffield*'s sister ship *Coventry*, and the requisitioned container ship *Atlantic Conveyor*, were sunk, the latter by the same means during a resupply operation to the Task Force's operating base at Port San Carlos on East Falkland. In addition, the Type 21 frigates *Antelope* and *Ardent* were lost to aerial bombing whilst covering the ground forces in San Carlos Water and Falkland Sound.

The lesson learned here was that neither was equipped with a viable point defence missile system, such as Seawolf, and this meant that, despite the superb performance of Sea Harriers on Combat Air Patrol (CAP), the area missile defence of Sea Dart-equipped warships, plus the older Seacat and Seaslug systems, a single wave of attackers getting through only had 20 mm and 40 mm guns to contend with in the target area. In addition to the losses, the warships *Broadsword*, *Argonaut*, *Glasgow*, *Glamorgan*, *Alacrity* and *Plymouth* were damaged by air and land attacks.

Of the Royal Fleet Auxiliaries with the Task Force, *Sir Galahad* and *Sir Tristam* were caught in an unprepared situation on the south coast of East Falkland and were hit by attacking Argentine aircraft. As was the case in all the other attacks, the courage of those on board and that of the helicopter pilots involved in rescue operations was magnificent. Undoubtedly, but for the cool of the British Servicemen, there would have been more fatalities.

The intense air and sea and land pressure on the Argentine forces (which outnumbered the Royal Marines and British Army units) led to a steady series of successes on the road to Port Stanley, the Islands' capital. On 15 June, the Argentine forces surrendered and the Union Jack was restored to the Colony. But the lessons learned are still being analysed in the corridors of the Ministry of Defence and will undoubtedly shape the Fleet in years to come.

Just as the Cold War appeared to be drawing to a close and the threat of Soviet naval power receded, a new threat appeared on the horizon. It should have been anticipated but in August 1990, Saddam Hussein invaded Kuwait, a state with which the United Kingdom had defence and other ties.

The Royal Navy was already active in the Islamic Gulf and the Armilla Patrol, so was reinforced as the US-led, United Nations-mandated coalition forces were brought into being.

The Royal Navy, Royal Marines and Royal

Sea Skua – responsible for the destruction of the majority of Iraqi naval craft in the Gulf conflict of 1991, the missile is carried here by a Lynx helicopter. (BAe Defence)

Fleet Auxiliary Service were tasked with keeping the Iraqi Navy and the newly acquired patrol craft of the Kuwaiti Navy bottled up. In the event, the Royal Navy was involved in providing the coalition's defence against Iraqi mines and coastal defence missiles. The Sea Dart missile again proved its worth in defending US and other coalition warships, but most striking were the successes of the Lynx/Sea Skua combinations against Iraqi and captured patrol craft.

In the civil war in Bosnia-Herzegovina, the Royal Navy's commando helicopters have been actively involved in mercy missions to rescue refugees and to support the UN Protection Force on the ground. Sea King HC 4s are based at Split in Croatia and at sea the Royal Navy has deployed an aircraft carrier and escorts to the region since 1993. The Royal Fleet Auxiliary provides a Landing Ship Logistic (LSL) for base facilities at Split, and the various task groups are supported by tankers and replenishment ships of the Royal Fleet Auxiliary.

Fleet Air Arm Sea Harrier operations have been conducted over Bosnia and in support of UN/NATO air strikes and close air support operations. In April 1994, one Sea Harrier FRS 1 was destroyed by an Igla-1E (SA-16) surface-to-air missile and others have been targeted and attacked by Dvina (SA-2) missiles. Another Sea Harrier FRS 1 was lost on a training flight over the Adriatic on 15 December, the same day as a Sea King HC 4, due to transport UN Bosnia commander, Lieutenant General Sir Michael Rose, was hit by ground fire near Mount Igman, Sarajevo.

At sea in the Adriatic, there is always a Royal Navy frigate or destroyer on Operation Sharp Guard, to prevent illegal cargoes reaching the republics of former Yugoslavia.

Elsewhere in the world, the Royal Navy has warships deployed to the West Indies, the Islamic Gulf, the South Atlantic and North Atlantic waters.

The sad fact is that the Royal Navy now pays off ten warships for every new one entering service. The present government policy of operating about 35 frigates and destroyers cannot be sustained into the next century unless some more orders are placed. Research shows that at the present rate of pay-offs, the Royal Navy will have only 25 surface escort combat ships by the end of the decade.

Concern was also expressed about the paying-off of the conventional submarines to save about

Bosnia – the Fleet Air Arm, land-based, is providing the UN Protection Force with a vital service in former Yugoslavia. Sea Harrier strike and reconnaissance fighters return to their carrier in the Adriatic. (RN)

£8 million a year, when the boats cost nearly £1 billion to build. There will be a gap of a decade between nuclear-powered submarine commissionings even at the current programme speed, let alone if there are any further defence cuts.

Major events in the Royal Navy since 1945

1945 First jet landing aboard a carrier; demobilization
1946 RN operations off Palestine
1947 Palestine operations cease
1948 Walter-powered submarine experiments; Flogging abandoned (suspended in 1897)
1949 Yangtze Incident; Britain joins NATO
1950 Korean War begins; first RN helicopter squadron formed; cafeteria messing introduced
1951 First jet fighter squadron formed; 'wavy navy' stripes abolished
1952 'Darings' enter service
1953 Coronation Fleet Review; Korean War ends
1954 Withdrawal from Canal zone (Egypt)
1955 *Ark Royal* commissioned; Mountbatten appointed First Sea Lord
1956 Suez landings; RN leaves Ceylon; guided missile trials begin
1957 First RN operational ASW helicopter squadron
1958 Nuclear strike aircraft for RN
1959 Mountbatten appointed Chief of Defence Staff; Commando Carriers
1960 First nuclear-powered submarine launched; Sheerness closed
1961 Last cruiser commissioned (*Blake*); last midget submarine paid off; Kuwait Crisis; Nore Command ceased to exist
1962 Indonesia Confrontation; first guided missile destroyer (*Devonshire*)
1963 ASW helicopters embark in frigates; 'Leander' class enters service; VTOL trials in *Ark Royal*
1964 Ministry of Defence created
1965 *Beira* patrol
1966 Confrontation ends; drastic defence cuts; *CVA-01* cancelled
1967 *Torrey Canyon* affair; first SSBN patrol
1968 First supersonic jets for FAA (Phantoms);

last warship built at Devonport launched
1969 Torbay Fleet review; last 'T' class SSK paid off
1970 *Hermes* begins LPH conversion
1971 Withdrawal from Far East; rum ration finished
1972 Last wartime destroyer paid off; SLAM trials
1973 Cod War with Iceland; Exocet missile refits
1974 First Group Deployment out of NATO area; RNR/RNVR review
1975 Cod War with Iceland
1976 QARNNS put under Naval Discipline Act; Silver Jubilee Review; Devonport frigate complex opened
1978 First WRNS course at Dartmouth; *Ark Royal* decommissioned
1979 Last aircraft and last cruiser paid off
1980 First 'Invincible' class carrier accepted; Sea Harriers enter service
1982 Falkland Islands conflict
1984 Evacuation of Beirut
1987 Minesweeping in Islamic Gulf
1990 Armilla Patrol strengthened as Iraq invades Kuwait
1991 Warships and Lynx helicopters in action against Iraqi patrol craft and missiles; mine warfare in the Gulf; Women go to sea
1992 Deployments in support of UN operations in Cambodia
1993 Blockade of Yugoslavia; Operation Sharp Guard
1994 Fleet Air Arm team came third in World Helicopter Championships (705 Squadron, Gazelles); Last conventional submarine, last 'Leander' and Type 21s pay-off; Royal Navy leaves Victoria (Hong Kong); Royal Marines sent to Kuwait (October); *Vanguard*'s first operational patrol
1995 Junior rates permitted wine in place of beer at sea; RNAS Lee-on-Solent closes (December)
1997 Royal Navy leaves Hong Kong
1998 RNAS Portland and the Naval Base closes

CHAPTER TWO

The role
and operations

DEFENCE ROLE

There has been considerable debate and review of the role of the Royal Navy since the demise of the Soviet Union in late 1991. As a result of various studies, some of which are still continuing, the UK government has given the Royal Navy three roles:

Defence Role One: to ensure the protection and security of the United Kingdom home base and the dependent territories overseas, even when there is no major external threat.

In this role, the Royal Navy patrols and guards UK territorial waters, provides the independent nuclear deterrent force of ballistic missile-carrying submarines, supports the civil power in Northern Ireland, provides the Hong Kong Patrol Squadron and Fishery Protection vessels and, with the Royal Air Force, assists with Search & Rescue operations.

Defence Role Two: to insure against any major external threat to the United Kingdom and her allies.

This role typifies the naval commitment to NATO, including the various standing naval forces and rapid reaction forces.

Defence Role Three: to contribute to promoting the United Kingdom's wider security interests through the maintenance of international peace and stability.

In support of this role, the Royal Navy assists with arms control and proliferation matters, supports United Nations operations, the Five Power Defence Arrangements in the Far East and the Armilla Patrol in the Islamic Gulf.

The UK Ministry of Defence has broken down the three roles into more than 50 military tasks of current commitments and possible contingency. Most of these tasks are joint service and remain classified.

The Royal Navy has developed its own response to these roles and has developed the thesis of three major platforms to support the roles: nuclear-powered submarines, aircraft carriers and amphibious capability.

Nuclear-powered submarines

Although the UK Ministry of Defence has cut the four conventionally-powered submarines from the Royal Navy's order of battle, there are planned to be 12 nuclear-powered attack submarines in service. These warships provide a deterrent force by their very presence or the threat of their presence, as in the early days of the Falklands conflict.

The UK national strategic deterrent, a nuclear missile, is carried by the remaining 'Resolution' class and the new 'Vanguard' class nuclear-powered ballistic missile submarines. This is the United Kingdom's only strategic nuclear weapon platform.

Aircraft carriers

The major surface ship assets of the Royal Navy are the three 'Invincible' class aircraft carriers *Invincible*, *Illustrious* and *Ark Royal*, which, together with their frigate and destroyer escorts, make up the major conventional strike capability. The Royal Navy has a policy of having two carriers operational at any one time, the other being in refit or reserve.

In his July 1994 statement on the Defence Cost Studies, the UK Secretary of State for Defence, Malcolm Rifkind, said that there will be about 35 frigates and destroyers in service at any one time. Critics point to the mid-1990s' order and building rate, which appears to show that there will be less

Quiet menace – the first Trident missile-equipped nuclear-powered submarine, Vanguard, *prepares for her first active service patrol in December 1994.* (Paul Beaver)

than that figure in service by the year 2000. A new area air defence frigate will be jointly built with the French and Italian navies, and later a new aircraft carrier design will be needed, probably after 2010.

The carrier battle groups of the Royal Navy are usually attended by a nuclear-powered attack submarine and a collection of Royal Fleet Auxiliary replenishment ships.

Amphibious shipping

The two assault ships which provide landing and

Amphibious shipping – Intrepid *will probably never put to sea again and the Royal Marines are eagerly awaiting a replacement.* (Photo Press)

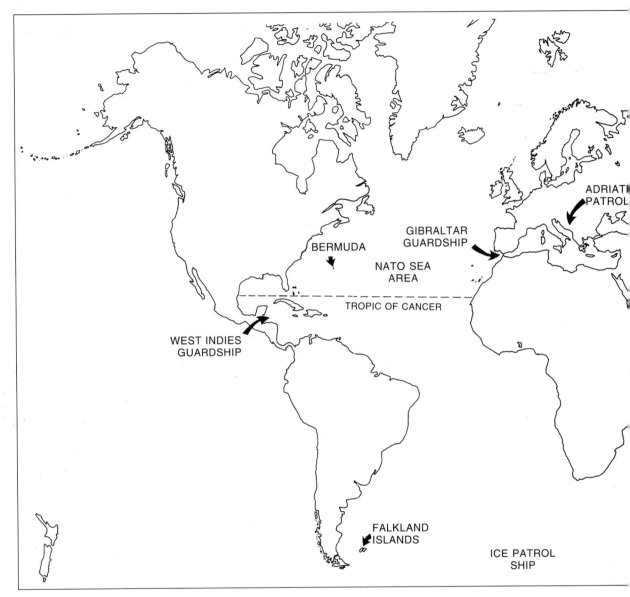

ADRIATIC
PATROL

GIBRALTAR
GUARDSHIP

BERMUDA

NATO SEA
AREA

TROPIC OF CANCER

WEST INDIES
GUARDSHIP

FALKLAND
ISLANDS

ICE PATROL
SHIP

docking facilities for the Royal Marine Commandos are now more than 30 years old. *Intrepid*, currently in reserve, is very unlikely to put to sea again, except perhaps to go to the breaker's yard, so replacements are vital if Britain is to keep two major amphibious ships available.

The UK government has launched a new helicopter carrier, *Ocean*, and the Ministry of Defence is expected to order two replacements for the assault ships in 1995 or 1996. In addition, there are five landing ships manned by the Royal Fleet Auxiliary and there is always provision to take up ships from trade. The so-called STUFT vessels worked reasonably well in the Falklands conflict, but it is widely thought that ro-ro ferries

and container ships would not make adequate frontline ships in wartime.

OPERATIONS

Surface Flotilla

Although the Royal Navy's frigates and destroyers maintain the more traditional tasks of patrolling the North Atlantic under NATO auspices, they have also been operational in pursuit of national commitments.

Operationally the Flag Officer Surface Flotilla is a Vice Admiral (the Royal Navy having combined the First and Third Flotillas in the early

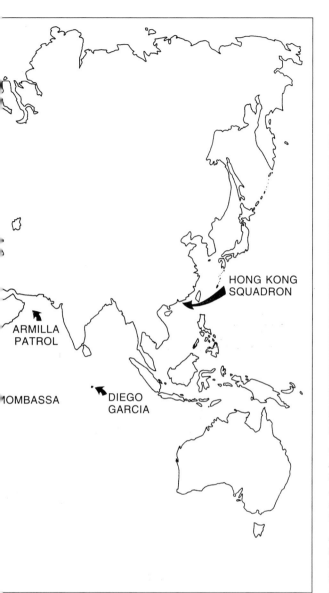

Gulf patrol – despite the defeat of Iraq, the Royal Navy and other coalition navies keep warships in the Islamic Gulf. Here, Nottingham's Lynx HAS 3S *is equipped with multi-spectrum jammer (port) and GIAT/FN machine-gun pod (starboard).* (HMS *Osprey*)

Patrol – the British frigates Campbeltown *(nearest camera) and* Coventry *(F98), both Type 22s, refuel from the German naval auxiliary tanker* Spessart *during Operation Sharp Guard in the Adriatic Sea.* (Paul Beaver)

1990s). He is described as the type commander for the major surface vessels (aircraft carriers, destroyers, frigates, assault ships, the ice patrol ship and survey ships).

Subordinate to him are Rear Admirals appointed as Flag Officer Sea Training (FOST) and Commander UK Task Group (COMUKTG). The UK Task Group was set up to provide a rapid reaction group for national commitments, including the provision of a flagship and escorts for the NATO/WEU maritime sanction force for Operation Grapple in support of the United Nations in former Yugoslavia.

Armilla Patrol

Another national commitment is the patrol in the Islamic Gulf which was formed in 1980 and now consists of two escorts, most recently two Type 42 destroyers. With tension in the area moderated since the end of the Gulf conflict in 1991, the warships of the Armilla Patrol have been exercising in the Far East as well.

In 1993, HMSs *Southampton*, *London* and *Cornwall* were deployed to exercise with the warships of two Five Power Defence Agreement states, Singapore and Malaysia.

Caribbean Guard Ship

Co-operation with the US Coast Guard is the hallmark of the international duties of the West Indies Guardship (WIG). These are mainly in support of anti-narcotics operations, targeted against drug runners from central and South America. WIGs also carry out national duties, including support in the event of natural disasters and for the regional security system for the Lesser Antilles and UK dependent territories. Bilateral exercises are also held with the Royal Netherlands and French navies.

Hong Kong

In the countdown to China regaining sovereignty of the Crown Colony of Hong Kong, there have been numerous changes in the role of the British Forces there, although the Royal Navy remains firmly committed to protecting the territorial integrity of the Territory until midnight on 30 June 1997.

From 1874 until 1994, the Royal Navy was established on Hong Kong Island in the Central District, also known as Victoria. The Victoria Basin, abandoned to developers in 1994, was originally built between 1909 and 1914. In the late 1970s, the Hong Kong government agreed to meet the costs for the landward developments of the British Forces and this has included funding 75 per cent of the construction of a new class of patrol vessel, the 'Peacocks'.

In 1993, the Royal Navy began the active development of Stonecutters' Island, the former hovercraft base and government ammunition dump. This is now connected by reclaimed land to the Kowloon peninsula, forming part of the busiest and largest container port in the world. HMS *Tamar*, the Hong Kong shore establishment, moved from Victoria to Stonecutters' on 18 May 1993 and the three Royal Navy warships *Peacock*, *Plover* and *Starling* became permanently based there in 1994.

The Royal Navy and Royal Marines have 329 personnel in Hong Kong, including 172 locally-enlisted personnel (LEPs) from the local Chinese (mainly Cantonese) community.

The role is security and law enforcement, to ensure that the Chinese People's Liberation Army warships do not infringe Hong Kong's territorial waters, and to prevent smuggling and illegal immigration. There is concern that PLA Navy operations have increased in recent years; even

Hong Kong Squadron – the three 'Peacock' class patrol craft of the Royal Navy's HK Squadron alongside at Stonecutters', the new naval base in the Colony. (Paul Beaver)

after 1997, there will still be a need to retain the 'one country, two systems' principle, so patrols continue every day. The smuggling of cars and electrical goods decreased from a value of HK$29 million confiscated in 1993 to HK$8 million in 1994. The illegal immigrant situation has also stabilized so the emphasis is on anti-smuggling operations, mainly by fast boats called *dai fie* (five engines) or *chung fei* (three engines) which are operated by well-organized and often armed groups from the Chinese mainland.

The Royal Navy's response has been to operate one patrol vessel at sea within the 'square boundary' of Hong Kong waters at all times. These craft carry two Watercraft Fast Pursuit Craft, with Royal Marines coxswain and Royal Naval boarding parties. These operations are co-ordinated with the Anti-Smuggling Task Force and the Royal Hong Kong Police Small Boats Unit.

Unlike commanding officers of other Royal Naval warships, the COs of *Peacock*, *Plover* and *Starling* have the legal right to board and search all merchant ships within the Hong Kong territorial boundaries, even if the craft is exercising its right to free passage under the UN Law of the Sea Convention.

South Atlantic
The Royal Navy maintains a presence in and around the Falkland Islands and South Georgia. During the southern hemisphere summer, the Ice Patrol Ship *Endurance* patrols this area and she is often supported by a destroyer or frigate, with its attendant Royal Fleet Auxiliary.

In addition, a 'Castle' class patrol craft operates in the inshore fishery protection and anti-smuggling role, and it is usual for a Royal Navy frigate to patrol the outer limits of the Falkland Islands exclusive economic zone.

Adriatic Sea
Reacting to the civil war in Bosnia-Herzegovina, the Royal Navy has deployed warships, fleet auxiliaries, naval aircraft and personnel to the Adriatic Sea under the NATO auspices of Sharp Guard.

Operation Sharp Guard is a joint North Atlantic Treaty Organization/Western European Union operation which includes elements of the Standing Naval Force Atlantic and the Standing Naval Force Mediterranean, as well as the mines countermeasures standing force. It began operational duties on 15 June 1993. The United Kingdom usually contributes a frigate and a destroyer to Sharp Guard; both ships have embarked helicopters and Royal Marines.

Royal Naval ships, under the auspices of UN Security Council Resolution 820, can enter Yugoslav and Croatian territorial waters to board and inspect merchant ships. The normal boarding party is six Royal Marines for protection and ten members of the Royal Navy ship's company who actually carry out search operations.

In addition, to support the British Army's operations under the auspices of the NATO Implementation Force, the Royal Navy has a task group operating at sea, including an aircraft carrier with Sea Harrier F/A 2 STOVL aircraft to police the Bosnia air exclusion zone. There is also a deployed flight of Sea King HC 4 helicopters at Split (Croatia). Alongside at Split there is a Landing Ship Logistic from the Royal Fleet Auxiliary which provides the accommodation for 200 naval and British Army personnel.

The Royal Navy and NATO
NATO has been the cornerstone of the Royal Navy's maritime strategy for nearly 30 years, since the then Labour government began with the withdrawal from East of Suez.

NATO appointment – Admiral Sir Hugo White KCB CBE, NATO's Commander-in-Chief Channel and Commander-in-Chief Eastern Atlantic. (Crown Copyright)

With the ending of the Cold War and the demise of the Soviet Union as a major threat to the United Kingdom and the Alliance, there has been a complete reappraisal of the role of NATO.

In 1993, the turf was cut for the new Headquarters for Allied Forces North Western Europe (AFNORTHWEST) at High Wycombe, Buckinghamshire. This organization took over from Allied Command Channel in 1994, when the former HQ of Allied Forces Northern Europe in Norway ceased to function.

The Royal Navy provides three vice admirals (NATO three star), one as Deputy SACLANT at Norfolk, Virginia, at the Headquarters of Supreme Allied Command Atlantic (SACLANT, another is SACLANTREPEUR) and the other as Chief of Staff to Commander Naval Forces South (COM-NAVSOUTH) at Naples. There is also a rear admiral (NATO two stars) as Assistant Chief of Staff (Policy & Requirements) at Supreme Headquarters Allied Powers Europe (SHAPE) at Mons in Belgium. Commander British Forces Gibraltar automatically wears the NATO hat of Commander Gibraltar– Mediterranean Sub Area (COMGIBMED). The Royal Marines will share a new brigadier (NATO one star) post with the British Army at Jaatta (Stavanger), Norway.

At sea, NATO naval forces have changed considerably since the North Atlantic Council meeting in Rome in November 1991. The Council pledged to keep two major NATO commands extant: Supreme Allied Commander Atlantic (SACLANT), an American admiral at Norfolk, Virginia, and Supreme Allied Commander Europe (SACEUR), an American general at Mons, Belgium. NATO headquarters remains at Brussels, where the Secretary-General and his staff co-ordinate the political developments within the Alliance.

The former Commander-in-Chief (CINCHAN) headquarters at Northwood, near London, will be disbanded and the Royal Navy will lose its only major NATO command slot. However, the Royal Navy's CINCFLEET will remain a major subordinate commander as Commander-in-Chief Eastern Atlantic (CINCEASTLANT). He is also a Principal Subordinate Commander of AFNORTH-WEST as COMNAVNORTHWEST.

The Council created the Immediate Reaction Force (IRF) concept whereby naval forces are kept at very short notice to deploy to troublespots as the crisis develops. They are multi-national and have rotating national command:

STANAVMINFOR
Standing Naval Mine Countermeasures Force is a mine warfare group which re-emerged in 1994 from the previously disbanded Standing Naval Force Channel (STANAVFORCHAN).

STANAVFORLANT
Standing Naval Force Atlantic (SNFL) is made up of escorts from the navies of Canada, Germany, the Netherlands, the UK and others.

STANAVFORMED
Standing Naval Force Mediterranean (SNFM), which was created out of the On-Call force in the early 1990s, began Yugoslav embargo operations in the autumn of 1992, following the June 1992

Northwood – the national Joint Command headquarters for all future military operations and a major NATO headquarters. (RN)

Channel force – the NATO Standing Naval Force Channel approaching Lisbon (Portugal) in May 1993. (RN)

Oslo meeting when NATO decided to authorize peacekeeping operations. NATO has since combined its operations with the Western European Union in the Adriatic Sea under the auspices of Operation Sharp Guard. There are three task groups, for which SNFL and SNFM have provided warships: one is off Montenegro to stop all traffic in or out of Yugoslav ports, another patrols the Otranto Strait to check all vessels entering or leaving the Adriatic, and a third task group is

Mediterranean force – Commander, Standing Naval Force Mediterranean flies his flag in the British frigate Campbeltown. (Paul Beaver)

Flagship – use of the Royal Navy's aircraft carriers as flagship is central to the role of the Commander, Anti-Submarine Warfare Strike Force, a NATO appointment in war. (Photo Press)

training or alongside. Between 1993 and 1996, the Royal Navy has maintained a carrier task group in the Adriatic Sea in support of this operation and the British Army ashore with the United Nations Protection Force (UNPROFOR). Sea King HC 4 helicopters of 845 Naval Air Squadron also operate in support of UNPROFOR and there has been considerable submarine activity in the area.

The next layer down is the Rapid Reaction Force which is available at short notice, has an enhanced war fighting capability and is made up of more substantial forces: NATO On-Call Task Groups (NTG), NATO On-Call Task Forces (NTF) and NATO Expanded Task Forces (NETF). These are equivalent to the Allied Command Europe's Rapid Reaction Corps.

War-role naval groups will include:

COMASWSTRIKFOR

This is a NATO two stars afloat headquarters, which is traditionally a Royal Navy responsibility and can include an 'Invincible' class aircraft carrier, amphibious forces, maritime patrol aircraft and submarines. It can be configured to command a NATO Task Force, which is now considered to consist of a carrier battle group with amphibious forces attached. Command of this group is a wartime role for the Commander UK Task Group (COMUKTG), who took over such duties from Flag Officer Surface Flotillas (FOSF) in January 1994.

Royal Navy NATO appointments

UK appointments	NATO appointments
CINCFLEET	CINCEASTLANT (Commander-in-Chief Eastern Atlantic)
FOSNI	Commander Nore Sub Area & Commander Northern Sub Area, Eastern Atlantic
Flag Officer Submarines	COMSUBEASTLANT (Commander, Submarines Eastern Atlantic)

In addition, the Commander British Naval Staff Washington acts as the UK National Representative to SACLANT and the Commander British Forces Gibraltar is also COMGIBMED (Commander Gibraltar–Mediterranean Sub Area).

Sea Commands of the Royal Navy, 1995–96

First Frigate Squadron
Beaver, Boxer, Brave, Coventry (F1), *London, Sheffield*

Second Frigate Squadron
Campbeltown, Chatham, Cornwall (F2), *Cumberland*

Third Destroyer Squadron
Birmingham, Edinburgh, Glasgow, Liverpool, Nottingham, York (D3)

Fourth Frigate Squadron
Marlborough (F4), *Westminster, Lancaster, Iron Duke, Richmond*

Fifth Destroyer Squadron
Cardiff, Exeter (D5), *Manchester, Newcastle, Southampton, Gloucester*

Sixth Frigate Squadron
Argyll, Northumberland, Monmouth, Montrose, Norfolk (F6)

Note: the () suffix to a warship's name indicates the squadron leader and the command of the squadron commander, usually a Captain RN. The commanding officer of a large warship is generally a Commander RN and smaller craft, including patrol vessels, are commanded by the Lieutenant Commander RN.

First Submarine Squadron
Vanguard, Victorious, Resolution, Sceptre, Spartan, Splendid, Superb, Sovereign

Second Submarine Squadron (SM2)
Talent, Tireless, Torbay (SM2), *Trenchant, Triumph, Turbulent*

Note: Unicorn, Unseen and *Ursula* paid off before the end of 1994; each squadron is commanded by a Captain RN. Captain SM1 is subordinate to Flag Officer Scotland, Northern England and Northern Ireland, the operational commander of the Clyde Submarine Base at Faslane.

Hong Kong Squadron
Peacock, Plover, Starling

Note: the Senior Officer Hong Kong Squadron (SOHKS but pronounced 'socks') is a Lieutenant Commander RN; he is directly subordinate to the Commanding Officer of HMS *Tamar* (a Commander RN), the Hong Kong shore establishment, who in turn is subordinate to the Commander British Forces (a Major-General), through the Senior Naval Officer Hong Kong (a Captain RN).

Northern Ireland Squadron
Blackwater, Itchen, Spey, Arun

Fishery Protection Squadron
Alderney, Anglesey, Bicester, Dumbarton Castle, Guernsey, Leeds Castle, Lindisfarne, Orkney, Shetland

Note: the Senior Officer is Captain Fishery Protection

Hydrographic Flotilla
Hecla, Herald, Gleaner

First Mine Countermeasures Squadron
Berkeley, Brocklesby, Chiddingfold, Dulverton, Ledbury, Middleton (MCM1), *Quorn*

Second Mine Countermeasures Squadron
Atherstone (MCM2), *Bicester, Brecon, Cattistock, Cottesmore, Hurworth*

Third Mine Countermeasures Squadron
Bridport, Cromer, Inverness, Sandown (MCM3), *Walney*

Commodore, Royal Yachts

The Admiralty Board

Chief of the Naval Staff & First Sea Lord	Adm Sir Jock Slater (from July 1995)
Commander-in-Chief Fleet	Adm Sir Peter Abbott
Controller of the Navy	Vice Adm Sir Robert Walmsley
Chief of Fleet Support	Vice Adm Sir Toby Frere
Second Sea Lord	Adm Sir Michael Boyce
Asst Chief of Naval Staff	Rear Adm J.J. Blackham

Fleet Flag Officers

Deputy Fleet Commander	Vice Adm J.J.R. Tod
Surface Flotilla (FOSF)	Vice Adm John Brigstocke
Naval Aviation (FONA)	Rear Adm Terry Loughran
Submarines (FOSM)	Rear Adm J.F. Perowne
Sea Training (FOST)	Rear Adm P.M. Franklyn
Commandant Gen Royal Marines	Maj Gen D.A.S. Pennefather
Commander UK Task Group	Rear Adm A.W.J. West
Training & Recruiting	Rear Adm J.P. Clarke

Area Flag Officers

Flag Officer Plymouth	Vice Adm Sir Roy Newman (until 1996)

Flag Officer Scotland & Northern Ireland (FOSNI)	Vice Adm C.C. Morgan
Flag Officer Portsmouth	Rear Adm Neil Rankin (until 1996)

* The appointments of Flag Officers Portsmouth and Plymouth lapse in April 1996 and are to be replaced by Naval Base Commanders.

The Central Staff

Under the tri-Service approach to running the British armed forces, there are a number of very senior officers regarded as 'purple'. That means that they serve the joint staff rather than their own branch of service.

The Prime Minister's senior military adviser is the Chief of the Defence Staff. In March 1994, General Sir Peter Inge (formerly Chief of the General Staff) replaced Marshal of the Royal Air Force Sir Peter Harding.

In December 1995, the Central Staff in the Ministry of Defence had the following naval appointments:

Deputy CDS (Systems)	Vice Adm J.H. Hunt
Assistant CDS OR* (Sea Systems)	Rear Adm J.A. Trewby
Surgeon General	Vice Adm A.L. Revell
Cmdt Joint Service Defence College	Rear Adm N.J. Wilkinson
Head of British Defence Staff (Washington)	Rear Adm D.A.J. Blackburn
Senior Naval Member Royal College of Defence Studies	Rear Adm J.H.J. Armstrong

Assistant CDS (Programmes)	Rear Adm N.R. Essenhigh

* Operational Requirements

These positions may change service designation from appointment to appointment, but generally the Royal Navy has seven to eight very senior staff appointments in the 'Centre'.

The Naval Staff

To administer, plan and organize the modern Royal Navy along the lines of policy directed by the Admiralty Board requires a considerable staff effort, even in the mid-1990s. The following appointments at Director-General (DG) level were held in early 1996:

DG Submarines/Deputy Controller	Rear Adm R. Walmsley
Hydrographer to the Navy	Rear Adm J.P. Clarke
DG Naval Personnel Strategy & Plans	Rear Adm N.J. Wilkinson
DG Fleet Support	Rear Adm P. Spencer
DG Aircraft (Navy)	Rear Adm D.J. Wood
Naval Secretary	Rear Adm F.M. Malbon
Chief Strategic Systems Executive	Rear Adm P.A.M. Thomas
Medical DG (Navy)	Surg Rear Adm A. Craig
DG Naval Chaplaincy	The Ven M.W. Bucks
COS to CINCNAVHOME	Rear Adm R.B. Lees
DG Surface Ships	Rear Adm F.P. Scourse

CHAPTER THREE

The warships of the modern Royal Navy

WITH THE CHANGING political climate and redefining of the United Kingdom's foreign policy commitments, the size and shape of the Royal Navy's active fleet has changed.

In the last few years there has been considerable debate, particularly by members of the House of Commons Defence Select Committee on Defence, about the composition of the surface escort fleet of destroyers and frigates. The UK government continues to claim that there will always be 'about 35 surface escorts' available, but the reality could be a smaller number unless some of the 'invitations to tender' are not converted into firm orders in the latter half of the decade.

Even the Submarine Service, for so long the most important element of the Fleet, has not been exempt from cuts and policy changes. In 1995, for the first time in almost a century, the Royal Navy is without a single conventional, diesel-electric submarine in commission.

The four 'Upholder' class submarines, described by many as the 'most advanced conventional submarines in the world', were paid off within months of commissioning. As a budget-saving measure, the class was paid off in 1994 and then put up for sale. By late 1995, it appeared that Canada would not take the four boats and that Chile, Portugal or Malaysia could be the eventual owner. The class does require the expertise of a first division navy to operate it.

The Royal Navy still commands a position in the top five navies of the world in terms of numbers of combat surface ships, but defence cuts have seen the force reduced to a point where Japan's Maritime Self-Defence Force and Maritime Safety Agencies possess a greater number of high-technology surface escorts.

The trend towards cheaper and more cost-effective (particularly in manpower terms) warships will continue, although there is some doubt about the continued, long-term presence of WRNS personnel at sea. Technology is continually improving and hull design is following the same route, albeit more slowly.

New generations of surface escorts are likely to be designed, built and equipped in conjunction with the United Kingdom's European allies, making programmes like the Anglo-French-Italian new generation air defence ship of particular importance.

All three major UK political parties continue to pledge support to keeping the Trident ballistic missile submarine fleet in commission, although everyone is now convinced that there is a sub-strategic role for the boats, carrying a reduced destructive power to make the weapon system more suitable for regional conflicts.

The strength of the modern Royal Navy
Official figures released in December 1995 indicated that the strength of the Royal Navy on 1 December 1995 was:

Submarines 15 (Trident SSBN: 2, Polaris SSBN: 1; attack SSN: 12)
Frigates 23 (Type 23: 10; Type 22: 13) (7 in refit)
Destroyers 12 (all Type 42)
Aircraft carriers 3 (1 in refit)
Assault ships 2 (1 in refit)
Survey ships 6 (3 in refit)
Royal Yacht 1
MCMVs 8
Patrol craft 50 (6 in refit)
Ice patrol ship 1

In the eight months from April 1994, the Royal Navy paid off one SSBN, one SSN, four SSKs, two Type 21s, the 'Leander', and four MCMVs. Four Type 23s and *Vanguard* were commissioned in the same period.

Definitions

Net tonnage This is the measurement of the net capacity of a ship, excluding engine, boiler, crew, stores and working compartments.

Gross displacement This is the measurement of the total cubic capacity of a ship.

Standard displacement This is the total weight of the ship with everything aboard less the weight of fuel and reserve feed water for the boilers. This is the international standard for quoting warship displacement.

Full displacement This is the total weight of the ship fully loaded and is particularly used for auxiliaries.

Light displacement This is the weight of the fabric of the ship.

hp horsepower

Invincible saw action in the Falklands (Malvinas) conflict and has been at sea off former Yugoslavia. (Photo Press)

bhp brake horsepower
ihp indicated horsepower
shp shaft horsepower
CIWS close-in weapons system
CM countermeasures
SAM surface-to-air missile
SLBM submarine-launched ballistic missile
SSBN nuclear-powered ballistic missile submarine (ship submersible ballistic nuclear)
SSN nuclear-powered attack submarine (ship submersible nuclear)
STWS Shipborne Torpedo Weapon System

AIRCRAFT CARRIERS (CVSG)

Class: 'Invincible'

Name *Invincible*; **Pennant Number** R05; **Flight deck code** N; **Standard displacement** 16,000 tons; **Full displacement** 20,600 tons; **Length** 209.1 m overall; 192.6 m waterline; **Beam** (flt deck) 36.0 m; (waterline) 27.5 m; **Draught** 8.0 m; **Propulsion** 4 x RR Olympus TM3B gas turbines (97,200 shp) driving two shafts; **Range** 5,000 nm at 18 kt; **Speed** (maximum) 28 knots; (cruising) 18 knots; **Complement** 60 officers, 625 ratings (ship's company including 100 women); 80 officers, 286 ratings (air group); **Armament** 1 x 2 Sea Dart SAM launcher, 3 x 30 mm Goalkeeper CIWS, 2 x 20 mm Oerlikon GAM-B01, 2 x SRBOC CM launchers, 2 x Corvus CM launchers, 2 x Sea Gnat CM dispensers, 1 x Prairie Masker noise suppression; **Sensors** 2 x 1007 navigation, 2 x 909 fire control, 1 x 996 surface search, 1 x 1022 air search radar; UAF and 2 x Type 675 electronic warfare and direction finding equipment, SCOT; ADAWS 10, Link 10/11/14 data link, VHF SATCOM, Marisat; **Sonar** 1 x 2016 hull-mounted active; **Aircraft** 21 maximum, usually 9 x Sea Harrier FRS 1, 9 x Sea King HAS 6, 3 x Sea King AEW 2A; **Builders** Vickers Shipbuilding & Engineering (Barrow); **Laid down** 20 July 1973; **Launched** 3 May 1977; **Accepted/Completed** 19 March 1980; **Commissioned** 11 July 1980; **Refits** 1982, 1987–89 (major modernization); 1994–95.

Name *Illustrious*; **Pennant number** R06; **Flight deck code** L; **Builders** Swan Hunter; **Laid down** 7 October 1976; **Launched** 1 December 1978; **Completed** 18 June 1982; **Formally accepted** 12 June 1982; **Re-dedicated** 30 March 1983; **Refit** 1988, 1991–94 (major modernization).

Name *Ark Royal*; **Pennant number** R07; **Flight deck code** R; **Length** 209.1 m overall; **Beam** 35 m (flt deck); **Armament** 2 x 30 mm Oerlikon CGM; **Sensors** 1 x 992R surface search radar;

Illustrious *entering Portsmouth Harbour in 1994 after refit, with the RMAS tug* Powerful *in attendance.* (Paul Beaver)

Builders Swan Hunter; **Laid down** 14 December 1978; **Launched** 2 June 1981; **Completed** October 1984; **Accepted** 1 July 1985; **Commissioned** 1 November 1985; **Refit** 1994–96; **Reserve** 1996–2000.

The first aircraft carrier to be designed, ordered and built after the Second World War started life as an anti-submarine cruiser design with the express purpose of taking a large number (up to ten) of medium anti-submarine helicopters to sea and acting as a command and control ship for a naval task group. The original plan was for a 12,500-ton ship with a hangar in the island structure. By the late 1960s, the design had changed to that of 'through deck cruiser' at 17,500 tons, carrying 12 Sea King-type helicopters and mounting Seawolf as well as the Sea Dart area defence missile system.

By April 1973, when the first 'cruiser' was ordered from Vickers, the design changes had included the abandonment of the Seawolf system, with the future ships of the new class relying on the air defence of escort destroyers instead. Another new factor was the possibility of carrying vertical take-off and landing (VTOL) aircraft, thus requiring a full-length flight deck, hangar below the flight deck and eventually a 7° ski-jump-type take-off ramp for'ard. The Sea Harrier was considered part of the ship's complement from May 1975.

Invincible commenced builder's sea trials in April 1979 and the first Royal Naval acceptance trials were completed in the winter of 1980–81,

allowing the ship to deploy to the Western Atlantic in 1981. It was a brief spell of action in 1982 which provided the ship and the concept with its greatest and totally unforeseen test, following the Argentine invasion of the Falkland Islands and South Georgia. In 1975–76, plans were made to allow the ship to carry a Royal Marine Commando group for quick-dash and use was made of this facility during Operation Corporate.

The Royal Navy's Falklands Task Force was led by the aircraft carrier *Hermes* (decommissioned in 1984), with *Invincible* providing slightly less than 50 per cent of the Sea Harrier air defence force. During the conflict, the ship spent 166 continuous days at sea, steaming 51,660 nm and spending 273 hours at action stations. The nine Sea King HAS 5 helicopters embarked flew 4,700 hours and the eight Sea Harriers (three additional to the peacetime complement) were airborne for 1,580 hours. The ship remained in the South Atlantic until relieved by *Illustrious* in August, both ships meeting for the first time in the Falkland Islands Protection Zone (FIPZ).

After a post-operational refit, which included the fitting of the US Vulcan-Phalanx 20 mm close-in weapon system and other self-defence equipment, *Invincible* was made ready to be the flagship of the 1983–84 Far Eastern Deployment, called Orient Express. The remainder of 1984 was spent on exercise and flag-showing and in 1985 *Invincible* undertook six major NATO exercises. In January 1986 the ship was redesignated as the Dartmouth Training Ship, with her air group being embarked in her sister ship *Ark Royal*, and

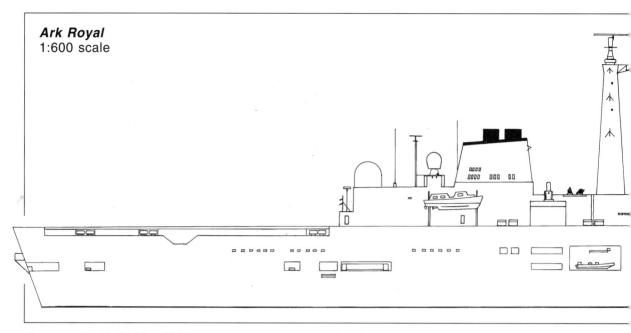

Ark Royal
1:600 scale

she entered refit in May 1986.

The refit included the upgrading of the crew and aircraft accommodation, new sensors and communications gear, and provision to carry Sea King AEW 2A airborne early warning helicopters. The Phalanx was replaced by Goalkeeper CIWS and a 12° ski-jump.

When *Invincible* came out of a 27-month refit in January 1989, she was also fitted to take 21 aircraft and had better passive self-defence systems. Like *Ark Royal* and *Illustrious*, *Invincible* is fitted for a Flag Staff and has accommodation for an enlarged air group.

Second of the 'Invincible' class CVSs, *Illustrious* had a remarkable early life, being completed by the shipbuilders for service nearly a year ahead of schedule in order that she be ready to operate in the South Atlantic. A rapid series of sea trials and shake-down followed her departure from Tyneside in June 1982, including the fitting of the Phalanx CIWS at Portsmouth. Aircraft were embarked and the ship declared operationally ready by 2 August, with her air complement including two hastily converted Sea King helicopters equipped with the Thorn EMI Electronics Searchwater airborne early warning radar.

When *Illustrious* emerged from her 1991–94 modernization, her shape and appearance had been altered considerably, making her, in late 1994, the most technologically advanced of the three aircraft carriers.

Illustrious was deployed to the South Atlantic between August and December 1982, actually leaving the FIPZ in late February and returning via exercises with the US Navy off Florida. 1983

and 1984 were spent on exercises with NATO forces (during which time a Sea Harrier from the ship successfully completed an emergency landing on a Spanish coaster), and in 1985, the first front-line AEW in the Fleet Air Arm for nearly seven years was embarked. In July 1986, the ship set out on the around-the-world group deployment as flagship. She is scheduled for refit to *Ark Royal* standard in 1998, although her CIWS system may be upgraded before then.

Originally to have been named *Indomitable*, *Ark Royal(V)* was completed four and a half months ahead of schedule, although the gun armament was added at Portsmouth, the warship's base port. The full work-up was undertaken in the spring of 1986 and it is recorded that Plessey Type 996 radar will be fitted in due course. Because of the lack of a third carrier air group, the Sea Harrier and Sea King group from *Invincible* embarked in April 1986, together with a newly formed flight of Sea King AEW 2 helicopters.

In 1990, it was confirmed that only two CVSGs would be in commission at any one time. In 1993, the Royal Navy deployed a CVSG to the Adriatic Sea to act as a headquarters ship for the British contingent to the UN Protection Force (UNPROFOR) in former Yugoslavia. During 1994, when *Ark Royal* was on station, her embarked Sea Harrier FRS 1 fighter aircraft were employed carrying out reconnaissance over the Bosnian-Serb-occupied areas of Bosnia-Herzegovina; during one operation in April a Sea Harrier was shot down by an Igla-1E shoulder-launched surface-to-air missile, but the pilot survived and was rescued. By

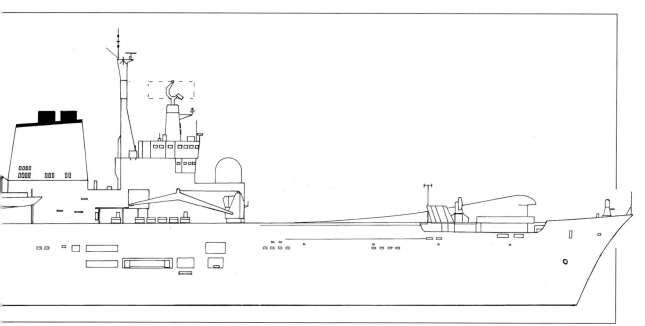

late 1994, *Ark Royal* had returned from active service in the Adriatic Sea and had been replaced by *Illustrious*. *Invincible* was the duty aircraft carrier off Bosnia during the November air strikes against the Bosnian-Serbs in the Bihac enclave.

Design work has begun within the Ministry of Defence to consider a replacement aircraft carrier for around 2010. It is possible that a fixed-wing

Ark Royal, *the third of the Royal Navy's light aircraft carriers, enters Portsmouth in 1985. Since then she has been refitted and now awaits further improvements.* (Robin Walker)

super carrier may be acquired from the US Navy, but it is more likely that a pan-European design will be examined for political reasons.

Sea Harrier FRS 1 was replaced by Sea Harrier F/A 2 with advanced radar and missiles in 1995. The first squadron, 801, embarked in *Illustrious* in January when the aircraft carrier sailed to the Adriatic to relieve *Invincible*. Since 1993, one aircraft carrier has been on station to support the UNPROFOR mission; each deployment is for six months, with the embarked Sea Harrier and Sea King aircraft flying patrols under NATO control for Operation Deny Flight. Sea Harrier F/A 2 strike fighters, flying from *Invincible* took part in a number of operational sorties against Bosnian Serb targets during the NATO air strikes of August/September 1995.

THE ROYAL NAVY'S SUBMARINE FORCE

During the Cold War, the nuclear-powered submarine became the capital ship of the modern Royal Navy, but even the submarine service has not been safe from the government's defence cuts since 1990.

There are currently two distinct types of submarine in service:

Ballistic missile submarine (SSBN) The nuclear-powered ballistic missile-carrying submarine provides the UK notionally independent nuclear deterrent with Polaris and increasingly Trident missiles. There is one boat of the 'Resolution' or 'R' class based at the Clyde Submarine Base, Faslane, in Scotland. In December 1994, the first of the new-generation Trident ballistic missile-carrying 'Vanguard' class of submarines departed from Faslane on its first operational patrol. The Royal Navy plans to commission four 'Vanguard' class nuclear-powered submarines to deploy the US Trident 2D5 ballistic missile. *Vanguard* and her sister ships have several important advantages over the 'R' class, including the use of better sonar systems, the Spearfish anti-ship/submarine torpedo and a ship's company of 17 less. As *Vanguard*, *Victorious*, *Vigilant* and *Vengeance* (ex-*Valiant*) enter service (1994–97), the remaining Polaris-carrying submarine will be paid off, following *Revenge* which left service in May 1992, earlier than previously planned. *Resolution* was paid off in June 1994.

Nuclear attack submarine (SSN) The nuclear-powered but conventionally armed boats of the 'Swiftsure' and 'Trafalgar' class have been described as the best anti-submarine weapons available.

Following the 'Options for Change' and 'Front

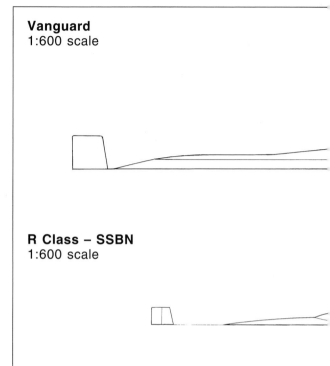

Vanguard
1:600 scale

R Class – SSBN
1:600 scale

Line First' white papers, the Royal Navy will operate 12 nuclear-powered attack submarines at any time, the five 'Swiftsure' boats being steadily replaced by the Improved 'Trafalgar' class from 2001 onwards. It is expected that the existing 'Trafalgars' will be refitted to extend their service lives to 2005–2010. During the Cold War, the plan had been to continue operating four conventional submarines and *between* 15 and 18 SSNs. To counter the reduction in the submarine force and to replace the roles, especially the coastal and covert operational tasks of the 'Upholder' class, the 'Trafalgars' in particular have been training in confined waters and shallow seas. Unlike conventional submarines, even the latest 'Trafalgar' class cannot undertake all the roles of the defunct 'Upholder' class, in that they cannot sit on the sea bottom for surveillance and covert operations. The roles and tasks of the 'Trafalgars' and, in the future, the Improved 'Trafalgars' will be greatly increased as a result of the decision to pay off the 'Upholders' early. In the future, the Royal Navy's SSN fleet will be equipped with the Tomahawk conventionally armed cruise missile.

Ballistic missile submarines (SSBN)

Pressurized water reactor
The Rolls-Royce pressurized water reactor

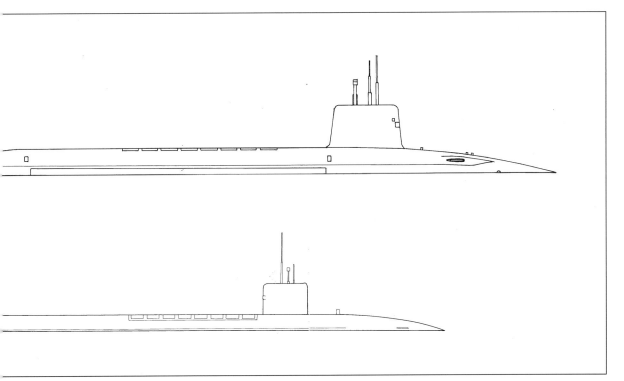

(PWR) is situated in the after end of the nuclear-powered submarine, in a specially designed, lead-shielded reactor compartment. It is normally out-of-bounds to all but duty staff from the Engineering Department aboard. Much of the machinery and control systems are classified.

The PWR is based on primary and secondary circuits. Water coolant travels round the primary circuit, through the reactor pressure vessel, where it is heated by the nuclear fuel elements, then on through tubes in the steam generator. A high pressure is maintained in the primary circuit to prevent the coolant from boiling, which would be potentially disastrous.

In the steam generator, the heat from the primary coolant is used to convert water outside the tubes into steam, which is used to drive the main turbine engines. From there, a system of clutches, gearing and propulsion systems transmits the torque (power) to the sea, pushing the boat through the water. Steam is used to drive turbo-generators which also supply the submarine with electricity for driving the weapon systems and the life support aids, including the air-cleaning system.

The nuclear reactor and the steam-generating facilities are operated through an array of automatic and manual controls, with a network of electronic and mechanical sensors and fail-safe devices to monitor the PWR's performance and safety.

Considerable energy is stored in the uranium fuel rods of the PWR. As a rule of thumb, about 1 tonne of fissionable uranium releases the same amount of energy as 2.5 million tonnes of coal

Class Vanguard

Name *Vanguard*; **Full displacement** 15,900 tons; **Length** 149.9 m overall; **Beam** 12.8 m; **Draught** 12 m; **Propulsion** 1 x Rolls-Royce & Associates PWR 2 pressurized water reactor, rated at 27,500 hp, driving a single shaft; also a pump jet propulsor and an auxiliary retractable propulsion motor; **Speed** 25 knots (dived); **Armament** 5 x 53 cm forward torpedo tubes for Spearfish torpedoes only, 16 x Trident 2D5 SLBM with up to 96 warheads; SSE Mk 10 CM launchers; **Sensors** 1 x 1007 navigation radar, UAP 3 electronic warfare suite; **Sonars** 1 x 2054 composite hull-mounted, 1 x 2046 towed array, 1 x 2043 hull-mounted active/passive, 1 x 2082 passive intercept/range-finder; **Builders** Vickers Shipbuilding & Engineering Limited (Barrow); **Ordered** 30 April 1986; **Laid down** 3 September 1986; **Launched** 4 March 1992; **Named** 30 April 1992; **Completion** 1992; **Commissioned** 14 August 1993.

Aboard HMS *Vanguard*

Britain's first Trident ballistic missile-equipped submarine patrol departed the Clyde Submarine Base in mid-December 1994, after HMS *Vanguard* had completed loading with live warheads at RNAS Coulport, on Loch Long.

Commanded by Cdr Peter Wilkinson, captain of the port crew, HMS *Vanguard* completed final first-of-class trials in late November 1994. Amongst the final items on the checklist was the acceptance of the Spearfish torpedo. Such anti-submarine/anti-surface ship torpedoes would be used for self-defence and for the unlikely event that HMS *Vanguard* had fired all 16 Trident missiles, when she would revert to an attack submarine role.

The main weapon system aboard HMS *Vanguard* remains the US-developed Trident 2D5 ballistic missile with a range of about 6,000 nm. The Royal Navy will not say exactly how far a single Trident warshot will fly but it is widely believed that the range depends on payload, fuel and targeting data.

There are 16 Trident missiles aboard each of

Vanguard *at sea, just before her first patrol in December 1994.* (HMS *Neptune*)

the four 'Vanguard' class submarines, but the UK government says that the combined destructive power will never exceed that of the Polaris missile submarines which the Trident boats are now replacing.

Whitehall figures indicate that up to 96 individual warheads would be carried in each submarine. The missiles in their individual silos take up most of the amidships section of the submarine; the bulk of the after end is the nuclear reactor and steam generation plant.

Each tube stretches down the submarine's four decks and the complete series of watertight compartments are identical in every respect to the US 'Ohio' class submarines which are already in service with Trident.

The whole submarine is far more spacious than any other which has been commissioned into the Royal Navy. It is almost as big as an 'Invincible' class aircraft carrier, yet has a much smaller crew (about 132 officers and men) than a Polaris boat.

The old practice of hot bedding does not apply any more. Each member of the crew has his own bunk and locker, with the addition of a personal stereo system for off-duty, personal entertainment. Otherwise, there are the latest films, quizzes and even Open University classes to attend.

Walking round HMS *Vanguard*, it is possible to move without bending to accommodate the piping of smaller submarines. There are few crew members in evidence, not because there are not sufficient, but because the submarine is as fully automated as is viewed safe.

The central galley complex is modern and as high-tech as one would imagine for the Royal Navy's latest warship. The food has to be of a high quality if the ship's company are to remain healthy and fit during what could be a three months' submerged cruise.

And where does HMS *Vanguard* go on patrol? That's highly classified, one of the greatest of all naval secrets, as no British ballistic missile submarine has ever been traced by the Soviet, Russian or any other navy, the Royal Navy claims. The answer could be anywhere in the world's oceans, but at a sedate 3 kt and always in range of the primary targets.

In the state-of-the-art control room, there is a great similarity between HMS *Vanguard* and a Type 23 frigate. The first thing which strikes a visitor is that the periscopes, themselves the very latest Barr & Stroud systems, the most advanced in the world, do not block the captain's view.

The two 'scopes are at the after end and are generally viewed using a video camera system

Aboard Vanguard – *a rare sight indeed: nuclear-powered submarines spend most of their time at sea submerged. Here Cdr Peter Wilkinson is on the tiny bridge with his Navigating Officer.* (HMS Neptune)

which displays on TV monitors in several places in the control room and in the captain's cabin. If there is a need to check the view visually, a junior officer is generally sent up a deck to use the periscopes in the conventional manner. Above deck, the fin is much further forward than one would expect, again to accommodate the 16 Trident missile tubes.

The tubes are apparent on close examination. In fact to board the submarine, it is necessary to walk across them.

Sixteen large doors are set into the deck on the casing which covers the upper side of the submarine's main pressure hull. These doors are lifted by hydraulic rams for loading, servicing and perhaps firing the missiles.

Unlike early generation nuclear missile submarines in the US and Soviet navies, the 'Vanguard' class does not have to surface to launch its Trident missiles. The mechanical procedure involves the missile chambers being filled with water to stabilize the submarine and an explosive charge which creates superheated steam actually propels the missile to the sea's surface where the rocket booster cuts in to carry the vehicle into space. There is, however, a complex procedure to be gone through in the submarine's control room and in several other compartments before the missile is actually launched.

Although the whole procedure remains classified, it is known that two officers aboard are responsible for receiving and decoding the numerical coded signals from the headquarters of Commander-in-Chief Fleet at Northwood, Middlesex, north-west of London. The transmission is made via the ultra low frequency transmitters at Rugby in the English Midlands and relayed to the submarine through the oceans' water.

The captain and the weapon engineering officer (WEO) are responsible for the missile launch. They would receive the signal by teleprinter and confirm the digits with a pre-set series in a safe in the captain's cabin. At no time do the coordinates signify to the crew the exact target, but it is widely understood that one of the Trident's multiple, independently targeted re-entry vehicles – nuclear warheads – could destroy a major city the size of St Petersburg, Kiev or Baghdad. Of course, that is only speculation.

The launching procedure includes the call to all hands to assume action stations and the final act is for the WEO (pronounced 'Wee O' in naval parlance) to pull a trigger not unlike that of a Colt 45 pistol. Incidentally, hanging next to the safe in which the firing pistol grip is housed is a naval policeman's truncheon, described as 'civilization's last hope'.

The captain wears a key around his neck with which he can stop the launch procedure at any time. What happens if someone goes mad aboard? That remains a closely guarded secret, but there appear to be significant checks and balances.

Name *Victorious*; **Ordered** 6 October 1987; **Laid down** 3 December 1987; **Launched** 29 September 1993; **Completed** July 1994; **Commissioned** 26 January 1995.

Name *Vigilant*; **Ordered** 13 November 1990; **Laid down** 16 February 1991; **Launched** 13 October 1995; **Commissioned** 1996.

Name *Vengeance*; **Ordered** 7 July 1992; **Laid down** 1 February 1993; **Launched** 1996; **Completed** 1997; **Commissioned** 1997.

Design work for the 'Vanguard' class was shared with the US Navy and American contractors, with the missile compartment taken as an entity from the US Navy's 'Ohio' class of ballistic missile submarine design. The strategic weapon system was designed by General Dynamics Electric Boat Division with additional inputs from the Atomic Weapons Establishment at Aldermaston, Hampshire.

The submarine's structure is a single hull of stainless steel, covered with elastomeric acoustic tiles to reduce water noise and absorb certain sonar frequencies.

The 'Vanguard' class has been designed to carry ballistic missiles, unlike the 'Resolution' boats which were a development of the earlier 'Valiant' class SSNs. The class incorporates a selection of successful design features from other British submarines, also designed by VSEL, including a state-of-the-art nuclear propulsion system, based on a Rolls-Royce design, and an advanced tactical weapons system from a design by BAeSEMA.

The tactical weapons system aboard 'Vanguard' is the Submarine Command System (SMCS) which is very similar to that fitted to the new Type 23 frigates of the Royal Navy.

'Vanguard' is the only class to be fitted with the new Type 2054 composite multi-frequency hull-mounted sonar system, which has an array of hydrophones and transducers twice the size of any in service elsewhere in the Royal Navy. There is also a towed array passive sonar system aboard.

Another striking feature of the 'Vanguard' design is the forward position of the fin and conning tower. The control room, resembling that of a modern frigate, is placed forward to the missile compartment suite. The 'Vanguard' features two

Victorious on contractor's sea trials. (Crown Copyright)

optronics masts with optical, television, thermal imaging and infra-red sight facilities. There are also new-generation electronic countermeasures and navigational antennas, some with a characteristic stealth shape when raised.

Because of the larger Trident ballistic missiles, the 'Vanguard' class is longer and deeper than the Polaris missile boats. There is a fourth deck which gives the ship's company more spacious living quarters and better working conditions.

The mess space is deemed comfortable by the ship's company. There is even an exercise room. There is normally plenty of water aboard and smoking is permitted only in designated areas. The health physics and safety of the submarine means that aerosols, lighter fuels and shoe polish are banned aboard.

The heart of the submarine is the Trident missile compartment suite. The weapon has a range of between 4,000 and 6,000 nm with an accuracy 'measured in metres'. A three-stage solid-fuel rocket, each missile is about 13 m long, over 2 m in diameter and weighs around 60 tonnes at launch.

The Trident missile is technically capable of delivering up to 12 multiple, independently targeted re-entry vehicles (warheads or decoys) which enables a single missile to be able to attack a number of different targets simultaneously. It is current UK government policy to restrict the 'Vanguard' class to carry no more than 96 warheads. Each UK Trident warhead can yield the equivalent of 100,000 tonnes of TNT and each missile can carry eight such warheads.

Vanguard and her sister ships are lowered into the water after building in the Devonshire Dock Hall at Barrow-in-Furness. VSEL has concentrated on designing a class of submarines with availability, reliability and maintainability in mind. Extensive tests have been carried out in *Vanguard*, the first-of-class, to establish the boat's reliability and ease of maintenance. It became clear in earlier boats that to design in the concept of 'management of maintenance' rather than to accept maintenance on demand.

Vanguard began sea trials in October 1992. The contract for 'Vanguard' class refits from about 1997 has already been awarded to Devonport Dockyard at Plymouth, although the Rosyth Naval Dockyard maintains the capability. *Victorious* completed contractor's sea trials in January 1995 and began sea training work-up the following month.

Operational The 'Vanguard' class may form the 10th Submarine Squadron (SM10). Each boat has two crews (although there will be only six ship's companies in total), each commanded by a Commander; SM10 is commanded by a Captain, with SSBN command experience.

Aboard a 'bomber' – the control room with the planesmen 'driving' the submarine. Note the modern lines and the aircraft-type controls. (HMS *Neptune*)

Repulse – one of the last Polaris boats in the Clyde. (RN)

Costs The Trident programme cost £11,631 million, including £4,191 million for the four submarines, £2,654 million for the Trident system, £965 million for the tactical system, £1,328 million for the construction of the shore facilities, £114 million for the dockyard projects and £2,379 million for the warheads and contingencies.

Victorious was accepted as operational on 4 December 1995 and began its first patrol only days later.

Class: 'Resolution'

Name *Repulse*; **Pennant number** S23; **Surface displacement** 7,500 tons; **Full displacement** 8,400 tons (dived); **Length** 129.5 m overall; **Beam** 10.1 m; **Draught** 9.1 m; **Propulsion** 1 x pressurized water nuclear reactor and geared turbines (15,000 shp), 1 x shaft; **Speed** 25 knots (dived), 20 knots (surfaced); **Complement** 13 officers and 130 ratings (port and starboard crew); **Armament** 16 x Polaris SLBM, 6 x 53 cm bow torpedo tubes; **Sensors** 1 x 1006 navigation radar; **Sonar** 1 x 2001 hull-mounted active/passive, 1 x 2007 hull-mounted passive, 1 x 2046 towed array passive, 1 x 2019 passive intercept (to be replaced by 2082); **Builders** Vickers Shipbuilding & Engineering (Barrow); **Laid down** 12 March 1965; **Launched** 4 November 1967; **Completed** 1968; **Commissioned** 15 November 1968.

The 'R' boats – known as 'bomber boats' to their crews – were designed to take the British independent nuclear deterrent to sea, as a result of the Nassau Convention and the British government's decision to transfer the strategic nuclear role to the Royal Navy from the Royal Air Force's V-bomber force. The four boats in commission have the duty of maintaining the 16 American-built A3 Polaris missiles with their British-built warheads ready to fire in the event of attack on the United Kingdom.

The Polaris missiles are launched beneath the water and the guidance requirements of each missile are calculated by two high-speed computers; to ensure that they are correct, the target information is fed into one and the other checks it for accuracy in 30 milliseconds; the missile still requires the Captain's permission to fire before the boat's weapons engineering officer can actually fire a missile.

Like its American and French counterparts, a British SSBN has two complete crews, the Port and Starboard, who take the submarine to sea alternately on a patrol which can last about three months; when not aboard, the spare crew takes leave or works in the Clyde Submarine Base at Faslane in Scotland.

Navigation is by means of the submarine inertial navigation system (SINS), dead reckoning, Decca Navigator, satellite navigation (Global Positioning System) and perhaps the use of underwater signal buoys. Communications when on patrol can be achieved by trailing a long-line radio antenna for ultra low frequency radio transmissions.

This system would be used in wartime to pass the Prime Minister's decision to use a ballistic missile. 'R' boats come under command of CINCFLEET (Commander-in-Chief Fleet) at Northwood, near London. The Trident missile boats have an almost identical system of command and control.

In 1982, *Renown* became the first SSBN to become operational with the Polaris warhead update, known as Chevaline, tests having been carried out on the US Eastern Atlantic test range in January 1982. Chevaline is an interim update with two 60 kt MRV (Multiple Re-entry Vehicles) and one decoy. There were, in December 1994, a maximum of 70 missiles and 50 warheads remaining in the UK stockpile at ARE Burghclere (near Newbury) or at RNAD Coulport, Loch Long, Strathclyde.

Besides the Polaris missiles, the 'R' class submarines were armed with Mk 8 and Mk 24 Tigerfish torpedoes for self-defence and perhaps even offensive action should it be necessary.

Considerable effort has been taken to ensure that the living accommodation aboard the boats is of a high standard, bearing in mind the patrol routine and time spent at sea. Various onboard entertainment, study and recreational facilities have been designed into the boats. Accommodation was better than most submarines for much of the class's life, but not as good as most surface principle combat ships.

Disposals *Revenge* was paid off in May 1992, *Resolution* in June 1994 and *Renown* in 1995.

ATTACK SUBMARINES (SSN)

Class Improved 'Trafalgar' (Batch 2)

Name *Warspite*; **Propulsion** 1 x Rolls-Royce PWR 2 pressurized water reactor; **Armament** Will include Tomahawk cruise missile, Spearfish homing torpedo, UGM-84D-2 Sub-Harpoon anti-ship missile, SSE Mk 10 CM launchers; **Sensors** 1 x 1007 navigation radar, WSC-3 SATCOM, Link 11 data link; **Sonar** Will include 1 x 2057 tower array, 1 x 2076 hull-mounted passive/active, 1 x 2077 short range classification, UAP electronic warfare system.

The government has announced that up to five (previously six) Improved 'Trafalgar' class attack submarines will be ordered for the Royal Navy from VSEL in July 1996. Full details of the design have not been confirmed, but it is unlikely that the so-called 'W' class will differ externally from the current Batch 1 'Trafalgar' class.

In late 1991, the MoD awarded VSEL a study contract for the most cost-effective definition of Batch 2 'Trafalgar' class; it was completed in early 1993. Following the 'Front Line First' defence cuts, the MoD formally issued the invitation to tender which will lead to a competition for a prime contractor for the development, building, delivery and life-cycle support of the class.

The projected in-service date for the Batch 2 Trafalgar boats is now 2003 and it is expected that the hulls will be built by GEC-VSEL at Barrow-in-Furness.

Class 'Trafalgar' (Batch 1)

Name *Trafalgar*; **Pennant number** S107; **Surface displacement** 4,730 tons; **Full displacement** 5,200 tons (dived); **Length** 85.4 m; **Beam** 9.83 m; **Draught** 9.5 m; **Propulsion** 1 x Rolls-Royce PWR 1 pressurized water reactor, 2 x General Electric steam turbines (15,000 shp), 1 x pump jet propulsor, 2 x Paxman auxiliary diesels (4,000 shp), 1 x emergency drive motor, 1 x shaft, 1 x retractable auxiliary propeller; **Speed** 32 knots (dived); **Armament** 5 x 53 cm forward torpedo tubes for UGM-84B/C Sub-Harpoon or Mk 24 Mod 2 Tigerfish or (by 1996) Spearfish torpedoes, 20 torpedoes carried, 2 x SSE Mk 68 CM launchers; **Sensors** 1 x 1006 (or 1007) navigation radar, UAC/CXA (or UAP) electronic warfare system; WSC-3 SATCOM;

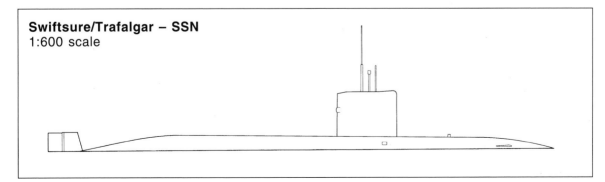

Swiftsure/Trafalgar – SSN
1:600 scale

The current generation of nuclear-powered attack submarines remains on patrol despite the end of the Cold War. This is Trafalgar. *(Photo Press)*

Sonar 1 x 2007 (or 2072) hull-mounted passive, 1 x 2020 (or 2074) hull-mounted active/passive, 1 x 2026 (or 2046 or 2057) passive towed array, 1 x 2019 (or 2082) passive intercept, 1 x 2077 short-range classification (to be fitted);
Complement 12 officers and 85 ratings;
Builders Vickers (Barrow); **Laid down** 1979; **Launched** 1 July 1981; **Completed** 1983; **Commissioned** 27 May 1983. *Note:* Trials ship for the Spearfish torpedo.

Name *Turbulent*; **Pennant number** S87; **Laid**

down 1980; **Launched** 1 December 1982; **Completed** 21 November 1983; **Commissioned** 28 April 1984. *Note:* Trials ship for the Type 2057 tower array sonar.

Name *Tireless*; **Pennant number** S88; **Laid down** 1981; **Launched** 17 March 1984; **Completed** 1985; **Commissioned** 5 October 1985.

Name *Torbay*; **Pennant number** S90; **Laid down** December 1982; **Launched** 8 March 1985;

Turbulent in the Solent – not the most usual place to find the cream of the Royal Navy's submarine force. (Robin Walker)

Completed August 1986; **Commissioned** 7 February 1987.

Name *Trenchant*; **Pennant number** S91; **Laid down** April 1984; **Launched** 3 November 1986; **Completed** 1988; **Commissioned** 14 January 1989; *Note:* Trials ship for UGM-84D Sub-Harpoon. Visited Hong Kong and South-East Asia in 1995.

Name *Talent*; **Pennant number** S92; **Laid down** 1986; **Launched** 15 April 1988; **Completed** 1989; **Commissioned** 12 May 1990.

Name *Triumph*; **Pennant number** S93; **Laid down** 1987; **Launched** 16 February 1991; **Completed** 1991; **Commissioned** 12 October 1991; *Note:* The first Royal Navy SSN to visit the Islamic Gulf.

The nuclear-powered (but not nuclear-armed) attack or Fleet submarine is the modern equivalent of a battleship or battlecruiser; it is the main striking power of the modern Royal Navy.

It is also the single most effective anti-submarine unit in service and is continually being improved. The attack submarine's main wartime role is to find and destroy enemy submarines and surface ships, but it is also capable of conducting an ocean-wide surveillance task using the sonar systems, linked to the onboard computers.

Operating at depths below 500 m, boats of the 'Trafalgar' class are able to detect, track, identify and if necessary engage contacts before the enemy has had the opportunity to identify the presence of a submarine. The class is fitted with conformal anechoic noise reduction tiles. The forward diving planes are retractable for under-ice operations and the fin has been strengthened to allow the submarine to surface through the ice cap, as the Arctic Ocean remains an important operating environment for the class.

Weapons include the Mk 24 Mod 2 Tigerfish wire-guided torpedo and the McDonnell Douglas UGM-84A Sub-Harpoon.

When *Trafalgar* was commissioned, the class was reckoned to have the quietest nuclear-powered submarines in service anywhere. By the time that *Turbulent* entered service even more attention was paid to her silent running and noise reduction to keep the class at the leading edge of technology.

Operational All 'Trafalgar' class (known in the submarine service as 'T boats') are based at Devonport as the Second Submarine Squadron (SM2).

Planned improvements During the 1990s, the class will be progressively refitted to improve the sonar suite and all seven boats will have the Type 2076 sonar system (replacing Types 2074, 2046 and 2082), integrated with the SMCS (from the 'Vanguard' class) and SSE Mk 10 countermeasures. At the same time, the GEC-Marconi Type 2077 short-range classification sonar will be fitted. Tomahawk cruise missiles will also be acquired.

Class 'Swiftsure'

Name *Sovereign*; **Pennant number** S108; **Surface displacement** 4,400 tons; **Full displacement** 4,900 (dived); **Length** 82.9 m; **Beam** 9.8 m; **Draught** 8.2 m; **Propulsion** 1 x Rolls-Royce PWR 1 pressurized water reactor, 2 x General Electric steam turbines (15,000 shp), 2 x Paxman diesels (4,000 shp), 1 emergency motor; **Speed** 30+ knots (dived); **Complement** 13 officers and 103 ratings; **Armament** 5 x 53 cm forward torpedo tubes for UGM-84B Sub-Harpoon anti-ship missile and/or Mk 24 Mod 2 Tigerfish torpedo, 20 reloads, 2 x SSE Mk 6 CM launchers; **Sensors** 1 x 1006 navigation radar, 1 x UAC or UAP(1) electronic warfare; **Sonar** 1 x 2001 (or 2020 or 2074) hull-mounted active/passive, 1 x 2007 hull-mounted, 1 x 2046 towed array, 1 x 2019 passive intercept/range-finder (to be replaced by 2082); **Builders** Vickers Shipbuilding & Engineering (Barrow); **Laid down** 17 September 1970; **Launched** 17 February 1973; **Completed** 1974; **Commissioned** 11 July 1974. **Refit** 1979–82.

Name *Superb*; **Pennant number** S109; **Laid down** 16 March 1972; **Launched** 30 November 1974; **Completed** 1976; **Commissioned** 13 November 1976; **Refit** 1982–85.

Name *Sceptre*; **Pennant number** S104; **Laid down** 25 October 1973; **Launched** 20 November 1976; **Completed** 1977; **Commissioned** 14 February 1978; **Refits** 1985–87.

Name *Spartan*; **Pennant number** S105; **Sensor** UAP(1) electronic warfare system; **Sonar** 1 x 2046 passive towed array, 1 x 2074 hull-mounted active/passive, 1 x 2082 passive intercept/range finder; **Laid down** 24 April 1976; **Launched** 7 December 1978; **Completed** 1979; **Commissioned** 22 September 1979; **Refits** 1988–89; 1998–2001; *Note:* Fitted for Spearfish; trials ship for a classified mast array.

Name *Splendid*; **Pennant number** S106; **Laid down** 23 November 1977; **Launched** 5 October 1979; **Completed** December 1980; **Commissioned** 21 March 1981; **Refits** 1991–93.

Designed to operate as long-range independent

strike units of the Royal Navy, the 'Swiftsure' class submarines have both anti-submarine and anti-surface vessel warfare roles, particularly with the introduction of the Mk 24 Tigerfish Mod 1/2 and the UGM-84B Sub-Harpoon into service.

The Admiralty changed the design of this class to make the submarines wider, with a longer pressure hull but shorter overall hull length than the previous 'Churchill' and 'Valiant' classes. This has allowed the internal arrangement to be greatly improved and by the use of only five torpedo (now called weapons) tubes, the submarine is presumably allowed to dive deeper. The Royal Navy will only say officially that its submarines are capable of diving to depths in excess of 175 m (575 ft), but most well-informed estimates give depths up to five times that figure.

Accommodation is always cramped in submarines but greater efforts have been made in the nuclear-powered types because the patrol lengths are so long – at least 100 days if the boat is deployed to the South Atlantic, as one regularly is every three months or so. Navigation aids for such long voyages include the Decca Navigator, Submarine Inertial Navigation System (SINS) and the use of satellite navigation systems. Communication underwater can be achieved by the underwater telephone (which is not considered secure) and by ultra low frequency radio transmissions.

The PWR 1 pressurized water reactor system has the same core as earlier, now decommissioned nuclear-powered attack submarines, but the life of the system has been increased and the system generally improved, especially for silent running routines. Three of the class have received an improved core to the nuclear reactor (known as Core Z): *Sceptre* (1987), *Spartan* (1989) and *Splendid* (1993).

Operational All 'Swiftsure' class submarines are based at Faslane as the First Submarine Squadron (SM1).

Planned improvements By 1997, it is planned that all Type 2001 hull-mounted active/passive sonars will be replaced by either Type 2020 (in older boats) or Type 2074. The Thomson-Sintra Type 2019 passive intercept/range-finder will be replaced by Type 2082. All boats, except *Spartan*, will be fitted with GEC-Marconi Type 2077 short-range classification sonar. It is planned to replace the Tigerfish homing torpedo with the GEC-Marconi Spearfish system by 1996 or 1997.

Sovereign – *one of the last-generation nuclear submarines which are being progressively upgraded.* (HMS *Neptune*)

In late 1994, it was still planned to fit the class with the BAeSEMA SMCS to replace the Ferranti/Gresham/Dowty DCB/DCG tactical data handling system. Better operational software for the tactical weapons systems will be introduced by 1996.

Disposals *Swiftsure* was paid off in 1992; *Spartan* was retained in 1994 for special trials, but is destined to be paid off in 1998 for 'extended readiness'.

LARGE AMPHIBIOUS SHIPS

One of the four pillars of the Royal Navy into the next century will be amphibious shipping, not just to provide the traditional maritime assault capability to lift the Royal Marines, but also for peacekeeping and other roles in non-conflict emergencies.

The Royal Navy is planning a fleet of one helicopter carrier and up to two assault ships to replace *Fearless* and *Intrepid*. In addition, there will be five landing ships (LSLs): these are described in Chapter Six (Royal Fleet Auxiliary Service).

Helicopter carrier (LPH)

Class 'Ocean'

Name *Ocean*; **Pennant number** n/a; **Flight deck code** OC; **Standard displacement** 17,000 tons; **Full displacement** 20,000 tons; **Length** 193.0 m overall; **Beam** 32.6 m; **Draught** 6.6 m; **Propulsion** 2 x diesels with two shafts, bow thruster; **Range** 8,000 nm at 15 knots; **Speed** 18 knots; **Complement** 255, 480 Royal Marines, 180 aircrew; **Armament** 3 x 20 mm Vulcan-Phalanx Mk 15 CIWS, 8 x 30 mm GCM, 8 x Sea Gnat CM launchers, UAT and 675(2) electronic warfare systems; **Sensors** 1 x 996 air/surface search radar, 2 x 1007 navigation, helicopter landing system, electronic warfare equipment, radio direction finding, SCOT SATCOM; **Aircraft** Up to 12 Sea King/Merlin helicopters; **Landing craft** 4 x LCVP; **Builders** Vickers Shipbuilding & Engineering/Kvaerner Govan; **Ordered** 11 May 1993; **Laid down** May 1994; **Launched** 11 October 1995; **Completed** 1997; **Commissioned** September 1997.

The helicopter carrier was ordered in 1993 after it became clear that the Royal Navy required a warship of this type for peacekeeping and other amphibious-type operations. It is designed to provide helicopter and assault lift for a Royal Marine Commando group.

Its design goes back to 1987 when five companies were invited to prepare tenders; three were submitted in 1989. After a series of political wrangles, the tenders were allowed to lapse and new tender invitations were issued in 1993. Swan Hunter and VSEL responded and the order was eventually placed with Kvaerner Govan for the hull with VSEL at Barrow providing the naval and military equipment.

The flight deck of *Ocean* has been designed to take six support helicopters, up to Chinook size, for landing operations of company strength in a single lift. There will be accommodation for a Royal Marine Commando group and its equipment.

REPLACEMENT ASSAULT SHIPS

Class Not known

Name Awaited; **Pennant number** n/a; **Flight deck code** n/a; **Full displacement** 13,500 tons; **Length** 168 m overall, 154.7 m waterline; **Beam** 26.5 m; **Draught** 7.0 m; **Propulsion** 2 x diesels with two shafts; **Range** n/a; **Speed** 18 knots; **Complement** 320, 300 troops; **Armament** CIWS; **Sensors** Air/surface search; fire control, electronic warfare equipment, radio direction finding, SATCOM; **Aircraft** Provision for two medium support helicopters; **Landing craft** 4 x LCVP (davits), 4 x LCU (dock).

The long-awaited replacement LPDs were the subject of an invitation to tender in 1994 and are expected to enter service in 2000–03.

It is understood that there will be platforms for two medium helicopters of the EH 101 Merlin or Chinook types. There will be command and control facilities for an amphibious brigade group and accommodation for 70 vehicles, including armour.

Assault ships (LPD)

Class 'Fearless'

Name *Fearless*; **Pennant number** L10; **Flight deck code** FS; **Standard displacement** 11,060 tons; **Full displacement** 12,120 tons (16,950 tons in full ballast); **Length** 158.5 m overall; **Beam** 24.4 m; **Draught** 7.0 m forward/9.8 m aft; **Propulsion** 2 x English Electric turbines (22,000 shp) with two shafts; **Range** 5,000 nm at 20 knots; **Speed** 21 knots; **Complement** 37 officers and 500 ratings, 80 RM for landing craft and beach unit; **Armament** 2 x 4 Seacat launchers, 2 x 20 mm Vulcan-Phalanx CIWS, 4 x 30 mm

GCM-A03, 2 x 20 mm GAM-B01, 2 x Corvus CM launchers; **Sensors** 1 x 994 surface search, 1 x 1006 navigation radars, Mentor A electronic warfare equipment, radio direction finding, SCOT SATCOM; **Aircraft** Provision for four support helicopters; **Landing craft** 4 x LCVP (davits), 4 x LCU (dock); **Builders** Harland & Wolff; **Laid down** 25 July 1962; **Launched** 19 December 1963; **Completed** 1965; **Commissioned** 25 November 1965; **Refit** 1988–90.

Name *Intrepid*; **Pennant number** L11; **Flight deck code** IS; **Armament** 2 x 20 mm Oerlikon GAM-B01 and 2 x 30 mm GCM replace, 4 x Sea Gnat CM launchers; **Builders** John Brown; **Laid down** 19 December 1962; **Launched** 25 June 1964; **Completed** 1966; **Commissioned** 11 March 1967; **Refit** 1984–85.

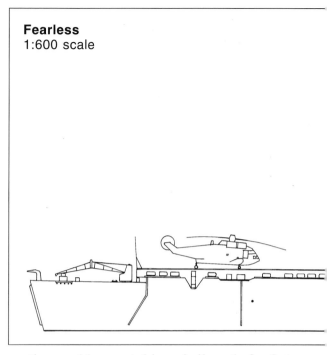

Fearless
1:600 scale

The class was built to provide the Royal Navy with the ability to carry out amphibious operations on either of the NATO flanks and to act as command, control and communications (C3) ships during the landing phase. The class was designed with large vehicle decks and dry dock installations for carrying large landing craft (LCUs); smaller LCVPs are carried on davits. The upper open tank deck was converted to take on the role of helicopter landing deck during the design phase, but there are no undercover facilities for maintaining helicopters.

The two ships of the class are earmarked to support the Royal Marine Commandos in wartime, and have acted in a similar role for Out of Area operations, as during Operation Corporate (1982). The ships are very versatile and have accommodation for up to 700 Royal Marine Commandos, or they can be used for emergency evacuation of civilians and disaster relief. In the late 1980s, one ship acted as Dartmouth Training

Fearless, soon to be replaced – it has been in commission for 30 years. (Photo Press)

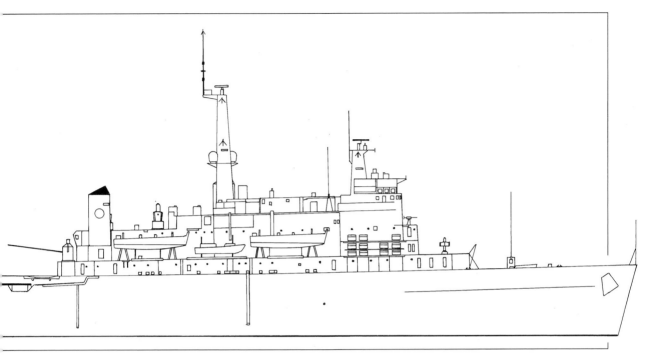

Ship while the other was laid up in refit or reserve. In the 1990s, one ship (currently *Fearless* in 1996) was at sea training and *Intrepid* was in reserve; *Intrepid* is now in a weak condition but could be used operationally in an emergency.

The ships were supposed to have reached the end of their useful lives in 1992 and been replaced, after much discussion and various studies. For example, in October 1986 it was announced that funds of £200 million had been set aside for assault ship development and building. A new design, it was said, would need adequate accommodation for helicopters which operate in support of the embarked Royal Marine Commandos. Project definition studies were completed in December 1992.

Intrepid was used for the first seaborne trials of the SCOT (satellite communications onboard terminal) system for advanced global communications.

GUIDED MISSILE DESTROYERS

Type 42 Batch 1

Name *Birmingham*; **Pennant number** D86; **Flight deck code** BM; **Standard displacement** 3,500 tons; **Full displacement** 4,100 tons; **Length** 125 m overall; **Beam** 14.3 m; **Draught** 5.8 m; **Propulsion** COGOG, 2 x Olympus TM3B (50,000 shp), 2 x Rolls-Royce Tyne RM1C (9,900 hp),

driving two shafts; **Range** 4,500 nm at 18 knots; **Speed** 30 knots; **Complement** 26 officers and 273 ratings; **Armament** 1 x 114 mm Mk 8, 1 x Sea Dart GWS 30, 2 x 20 mm Oerlikon GP, 2 x 20 mm GAM-BO1, 2 x 30 mm GCM (twin), 2 x 20

Type 42 – this class of destroyer should be replaced in 2005 by the first in a new class of air defence frigates, to be built with France and Italy. (Photo Press)

Glasgow – *the Type 42 area air defence destroyer at speed in the English Channel.* (Photo Press)

mm Vulcan-Phalanx, 2 x 3 STWS Mk 3 torpedo tubes, 2 x Corvus CM launchers, 2 x Mk 36 SRBOC CM launchers, 1 x 182 towed decoy; **Sensors** 2 x 909 fire control, 1 x 1022 air search, 1 x 992Q air/surface search (*Birmingham* only), 1 x 1006 navigation, UAA-2, 670 electronic warfare, SCOT SATCOM; **Sonar** 1 x 162M hull-mounted classification, 1 x 2050 hull-mounted active; **Aircraft** 1 x Lynx HAS 3; **Builders** Cammell Laird; **Laid down** 28 March 1972; **Launched** 30 July 1973; **Completed** 1976; **Commissioned** 3 December 1976.

Name *Newcastle*; **Pennant number** D87; **Flight deck code** NC; **Complement** 21 officers and 278 ratings; **Armament** No SRBOC CM launchers; **Sensors** 1 x 996 (replaces 992Q) air/surface search radar; **Builders** Swan Hunter; **Laid down** 21 February 1973; **Launched** 24 April 1975; **Completed** February 1978; **Commissioned** 23 March 1978.

Name *Glasgow*; **Pennant number** D88; **Flight deck code** GW; **Complement** 21 officers and 249 ratings; **Armament** Retains SRBOC; **Builders** Swan Hunter; **Laid down** 7 March 1974; **Launched** 14 April 1976; **Completed** 9 March 1977; **Commissioned** 24 May 1977; **Refits** 1992–93.

Name *Cardiff*; **Pennant number** D108; **Flight deck code** CF; **Complement** 20 officers and 260 ratings; **Armament** Retains SRBOC; **Builders**

Vickers (Barrow); **Laid down** 3 November 1972; **Launched** 22 February 1974; **Completed** 1979; **Commissioned** 24 September 1979.

Sheffield was lost in the South Atlantic on 10 May 1982 after being hit by a missile on 4 May; *Coventry* was lost in the South Atlantic on 25 May 1982 after bombing.

Type 42 Batch 2

Name *Exeter*; **Pennant number** D89; **Flight deck code** EX; **Armament** No STWS, no SRBOC; **Sensors** 1 x 675 electronic warfare; **Sonar** 1 x 2050 hull-mounted classification;

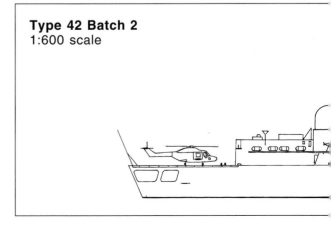

Type 42 Batch 2
1:600 scale

Cardiff – *showing off the characteristic Mk 8 114 mm dual-purpose gun and Sea Dart air defence missile launcher.* (Photo Press)

Builders Swan Hunter; **Laid down** 22 July 1976; **Launched** 25 April 1978; **Completed** 29 August 1980; **Commissioned** 19 September 1980.

Name *Southampton*; **Pennant number** D90; **Flight deck code** SN; **Builders** Vosper Thornycroft; **Laid down** 21 October 1976; **Launched** 29 January 1979; **Completed** 17 August 1981; **Commissioned** 31 October 1981.

Name *Nottingham*; **Pennant number** D91; **Flight deck code** NM; **Builders** Vosper Thornycroft;

Laid down 6 February 1978; **Launched** 18 February 1980; **Completed** 19 November 1982; **Commissioned** 8 April 1983.

Name *Liverpool*; **Pennant number** D92; **Flight deck code** LP; **Builders** Cammell Laird; **Laid down** 5 July 1978; **Launched** 25 September 1980; **Completed** 12 May 1982; **Commissioned** 9 July 1982.

The Type 42s were the first British destroyers to be built with gas turbine propulsion using Rolls-

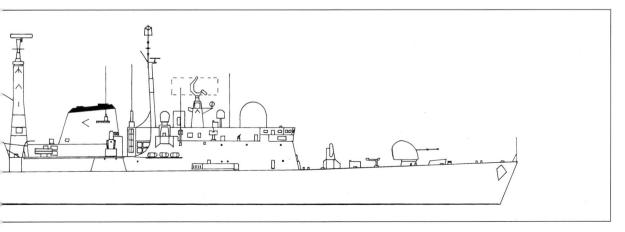

Royce marinized turbines, Tynes for cruising and Olympus for full power which can be reached in about 30 seconds.

The ships need only about 75 per cent of the marine engineering staff of warships of similar size. The ships' role is area air defence, although the lack of quick-reaction surface-to-air missiles, like Seawolf, was shown in the Falklands conflict when the name ship of the class, *Sheffield*, and *Coventry* were lost. Henceforth, the class was not given a class name, but referred to as Type 42. It is thought that Vertical Launch Seawolf is being studied for eventual refit to the class. After returning from Operation Corporate, all Type 42s then in commission were fitted with extra close-in weapons.

The only significant differences between the four Batch 1 destroyers in this class and the four Batch 2 ships is that the latter were built with Type 1022 radar, rather than the Type 965 AKE-2. There were some additional changes to the operations room fit and the data processing facilities.

The ships are highly manoeuvrable and stable and can provide very adequate air defence with Sea Dart GWS 30, which system has the Type 996 air/surface search radar in place of the Type 992Q target acquisition radar in all but *Birmingham*. Sea Dart homing and fuzing systems have been periodically improved.

The air defence facilities aboard the ships include the computer-enhanced Action Data Automated Weapons System (ADAWS 7) in all Batch 2 at building and in the Batch 1 ships on refit. In addition, there is provision for the NATO Link 10, 11 and 14 data link systems.

The embarked Lynx HAS 3 helicopter is equipped to carry Mk 44, Mk 46 and Stingray anti-submarine torpedoes, Mk 11 depth bombs and the British Aerospace Sea Skua anti-shipping missile. The Westland Lynx is fitted with Ferranti Sea Spray radar and Racal Orange Crop ESM. The helicopter's primary role is surface search and anti-ship operations.

Planned improvements From 1996, the STWS (ship torpedo weapons system) Mk 3 is planned to be fitted. All ships to have Sea Gnat CM launchers by 1996.

Type 42 Batch 3

Name *Manchester*; **Pennant number** D95; **Flight deck code** MC; **Standard displacement** 4,100 tons; **Full displacement** 5,350 tons; **Length** 141.1 m overall; **Beam** 14.9 m; **Draught** 5.8 m; **Propulsion** As for Batch 1; **Complement** 26 officers, 69 senior and 178 junior ratings; **Armament** As for Batch 2, but with 2 x Sea Gnat

CM launchers (replacing Corvus and/or SRBOC), DEC laser dazzle sights; **Sensors** 1 x 1022 air search, 1 x 996 air/surface search, 1 x 1006 navigation, 2 x 909 Mod 1 fire control radar, 2100 optronic system, UAA-2 and 675(2) electronic warfare systems, SCOT SATCOM; **Sonar** 1 x 162M hull-mounted classification, 1 x 2016 hull-mounted active; **Aircraft** 1 x Lynx HAS 3; **Builders** Vickers (Barrow); **Laid down** 19 May 1978; **Launched** 24 November 1980; **Completed** 19 November 1982; **Commissioned** 16 December 1982; **Refit** 1992–93 (ADAWS improvement command system).

Name *Gloucester*; **Pennant number** D96; **Flight deck code** GC; **Builders** Vosper Thornycroft; **Laid down** 29 October 1979; **Launched** 2 November 1982; **Completed** November 1984; **Commissioned** 11 September 1985; **Refit** 1993–94 (command system).

Name *Edinburgh*; **Pennant number** D97; **Flight deck code** EB/ED; **Builders** Cammell Laird; **Laid down** 8 September 1980; **Launched** 14 April 1983; **Completed** April 1985; **Commissioned** 17 December 1985; **Refit** 1994 (command system).

Name *York*; **Pennant number** D98; **Flight deck code** YK; **Sensors** 1 x 996; **Builders** Swan Hunter; **Laid down** 18 January 1980; **Launched** 21 June 1982; **Completed** 25 March 1985; **Commissioned** 9 August 1985.

As a result of the experience gained with the first Type 42 guided missile destroyers, it was decided to stretch the design to improve seakeeping and fuel economy. In addition, the later ships were completed after some internal modifications arising from action in the South Atlantic in 1982 had been incorporated. In addition, the beam has been strengthened, adding about 50 tons to the displacement.

Type 42 Batch 3
1:600 scale

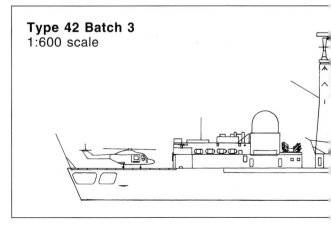

Manchester – *the extended length and improved close-in weapons fit amidships is apparent from this view.* (Paul Beaver)

The fitting of the improved Type 996 radar provides better surveillance facilities and the fully improved Sea Dart missile is carried by the class.

Vulcan-Phalanx CIWS replaced the 30 mm guns in 1987–89 refits. In 1991, the planned refit-

ting of the Vertical Launch Seawolf system was cancelled. *Edinburgh* was fitted with an experimental Phalanx system in 1990.

All Batch 3 destroyers have been fitted with the ADAWS 8 action data automation and have pro-

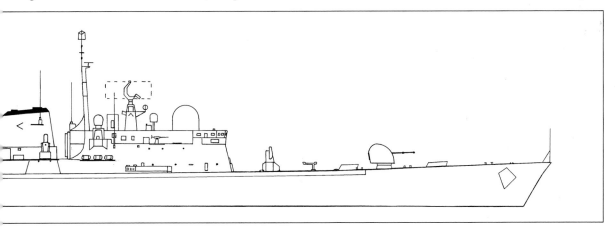

vision for NATO Link 10, 11 and 14 data link systems for the simultaneous passing of information in a task group environment.

FRIGATES

Project Horizon: Common New Generation

Name Awaited; **Pennant number** n/a; **Flight deck code** n/a; **Full displacement** 6,500 tons; **Length** 148.4 m overall; **Beam** 19.9 m; **Draught** 4.8 m; **Propulsion** CODLAG 2 x Rolls-Royce Spey SM1D gas turbines (31,100 hp), 4 x Paxman diesels (8,100 hp), 2 x GEC electric motors (4,000 hp), driving two shafts; **Complement** 200; **Armament** 8 x anti-ship launchers, 1 x VL Aster, 1 x 114 mm Mk 8 dual-purpose gun, 2 x DES 30 mm/75 Mk 1 gun, 4 x fixed torpedo tubes, 4 x Sea Gnat CM launchers, DEC laser dazzle sights, 1 x 182 torpedo decoy, electronic warfare and torpedo decoy systems; **Sensors** 1 x air/surface search, 1 x navigation, 2 x surveillance/fire control radar, optronics, electronic warfare systems, SATCOM; **Sonar** 1 x 2050 bow-mounted active; **Aircraft** 1 x Merlin HAS 1; **Builders** Awaited; **Laid down** n/a; **Launched** n/a; **Completed** n/a; **Commissioned** n/a

Replacing the Type 42 area air defence destroyer with a similar, British-built warship has been deemed too expensive. For budgetary and pan-European political reasons, it was decided to create a new Anglo-French frigate design, using pan-European missiles and sensors. In 1993, the Italian government joined the consortium and a joint project office was formed. The three governments signed a memorandum of understanding in 1994 which covered the design, development and production of the ship, including the combat system. A separate document will be prepared for the Principal Anti-Air Missile System. A design contract was expected in 1995 and the current in-service date is 2002. Full details are awaited.

Type 23

Class 'Duke'

Name *Norfolk*; **Pennant number** F230; **Flight deck code** NF; **Standard displacement** 3,500 tons; **Full displacement** 4,200 tons; **Length** 133 m overall; **Beam** 16.1 m; **Draught** 7.3 m; **Propulsion** CODLAG 2 x Rolls-Royce Spey SM1A gas turbines (31,100 hp), 4 x Paxman

diesels (8,100 hp), 2 x GEC electric motors (4,000 hp), driving two shafts; **Complement** 17 officers, 57 senior ratings and 111 junior ratings; **Armament** 8 x Harpoon GWS 30 anti-ship missile launchers, 1 x VL Seawolf GWS 26 Mod 1 (32 missiles), 1 x 114 mm Mk 8 dual-purpose gun, 2 x DES 30 mm/75 Mk 1 gun, 4 x Cray Marine torpedo tubes, 4 x Sea Gnat CM launchers, DEC laser dazzle sights, 1 x 182 torpedo decoy; **Sensors** 1 x 966(I) air/surface search, 1 x 1007 navigation, 2 x 911 fire control radar, Sea Archer optronics, UAF-1 Cutlass and 675(2) electronic warfare systems, SCOT 1D SATCOM; **Sonar** 1 x 2050 bow-mounted active, 1 x 2031Z passive towed array; **Aircraft** 1 x Lynx HAS 3 (provision for Merlin); **Builders** Yarrow; **Laid down** 14 December 1985; **Launched** 10 July 1987; **Completed** 1990; **Commissioned** 1 June 1990; *Note:* Besides first-of-class trials, first Merlin deck landing in 1990.

Aboard HMS *Norfolk*

When details of the Type 23 frigates were first announced, it was reckoned that they would be cut-price escorts, designed to work as convoy escorts in the North Atlantic – part, in fact, of the Royal Navy's response to the perceived Soviet submarine threat to the resupply routes from North America to Europe. The design evolved, however, into a radical, highly sophisticated warship with a stand-alone capability – almost a stealth warship. In 1990, it became clear from seeing *Norfolk* for the first time at Portland that the frigate design would allow the ship to operate alone, unescorted, in the northern Norwegian Sea.

In those days of the Cold War, the major 'selling point' of the design was the Type 23's ability to operate with a passive towed array sonar to detect Soviet nuclear-powered and increasingly quiet-running submarines leaking out from the Barents Sea bastions.

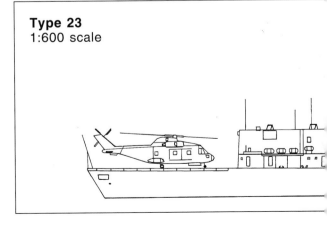

Type 23
1:600 scale

Norfolk – *the first of the Type 23, 'Duke' class frigates with combined gas turbine and electric motor power. The primary role is anti-submarine warfare.* (Paul Beaver)

Aboard Norfolk – *on the starboard bridge wing are (left to right) the Officer-of-the-Watch, the Chief Yeoman of Signals and two Communications ratings manning the signal lamp.* (Paul Beaver)

The main long-range anti-surface weapon system, Harpoon, bought from the Americans, was and still is regarded as a highly effective anti-ship system. For many observers, the large flight deck was an important contribution to the other long-range weapon, the naval helicopter. Although it was not confirmed until 1992, the Type 23 will receive the Merlin HAS 1

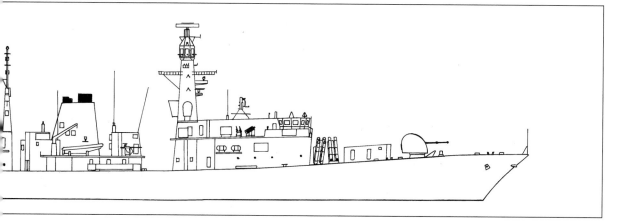

when it enters service in 1998.

The most important impression that the Type 23 gives even the most casual observer is the shape of the superstructure. The sharp edges have gone from earlier designs, the weapon systems are well positioned, and *Norfolk* and her sister ships of the 'Duke' class look like frigates which will see the Royal Navy well into the next century.

Below decks, the accommodation is better than that of any other warship of similar size. Senior ratings live in four- or six-berth cabins, with separate messes for eating and relaxation. Junior rates have less space, but still have a separate recreational area. The Royal Navy has introduced mixed gender crews and ensured that accommodation is flexible so that the problems encountered with filling the places on the Type 42 destroyers are not present. In *Norfolk* and the other Type 23s, there is not the same need to have fixed ratios of female/male ratings.

One former Sea Harrier pilot, who commanded a Type 23 in the Caribbean, amongst other places, describes command of the ship as like having a cruiser, frigate and fast patrol boat rolled into one.

Compared to the Type 22 Batch 3 frigates which immediately preceded the Type 23, the 'Duke' class have almost 100 fewer personnel, such has been the progress with automation and design. The ship's machinery, weapon systems and sensors are fully computerized,

allowing a ship's company of 17 officers, 57 senior ratings and 111 junior rates.

To fight the ship, the captain, his principal warfare officers and the command team has a wide array of sensors, including the Type 996 long-range, three-dimensional radar which videos information to the Operations Room. In the Operations Room, there are two divisions – the Radar Division which mans the radar displays and electronic warfare systems and the Communications Division which keeps everyone in touch with what is developing, as well as ensuring that the ship can communicate with the outside world.

Name *Argyll*; **Pennant number** F231; **Flight deck code** AY; **Builders** Yarrow; **Laid down** 20 March 1987; **Launched** 8 April 1989; **Completed** 1989; **Commissioned** 31 May 1991.

Name *Lancaster*; **Pennant number** F229 (ex F232); **Flight deck code** LA; **Builders** Yarrow; **Laid down** 18 December 1987; **Launched** 24 May 1990; **Completed** 1992; **Commissioned** 1 May 1992.

Name *Marlborough*; **Pennant number** F233; **Flight deck code** MA; **Builders** Swan Hunter; **Laid down** 27 October 1987; **Launched** 21 January 1989; **Completed** 1989; **Commissioned** 14 June 1991.

Name *Iron Duke*; **Pennant number** F234; **Flight**

Iron Duke *alongside at Gibraltar during sea trials.* (Paul Beaver)

deck code IR; **Builders** Yarrow; **Laid down** 18 December 1988; **Launched** 2 March 1991; **Completed** 1993; **Commissioned** 20 May 1993; *Note:* Carried out Merlin trials.

Name *Monmouth*; **Pennant number** F235; **Flight deck code** MM; **Builders** Yarrow; **Laid down** 1 June 1989; **Launched** 23 November 1991; **Completed** 1993; **Commissioned** 24 September 1993.

Name *Montrose*; **Pennant number** F236; **Flight deck code** MR; **Propulsion** Rolls-Royce Spey SM1C replaces SM1A in *Montrose* and subsequent ships; **Builders** Yarrow; **Laid down** 1 November 1989; **Launched** 21 July 1992; **Completed** September 1993; **Commissioned** June 1994; *Note:* Initial Lynx HAS 8 trials in December 1994.

Name *Westminster*; **Pennant number** F237; **Flight deck code** WM; **Sensors** UAT replaces UAF-1 in *Westminster* and subsequent ships; **Builders** Swan Hunter; **Laid down** 18 January 1991; **Launched** 4 February 1992; **Completed** 19 November 1993; **Commissioned** 13 May 1994; *Note:* The first of class to receive SSCS Phase 1 automated weapon system control; subsequent ships received improved versions; first warship to commission in the Pool of London.

Name *Northumberland*; **Pennant number** F238; **Flight deck code** NL; **Builders** Swan Hunter; **Laid down** 4 April 1991; **Launched** 4 April 1992; **Completed** 1994; **Commissioned** September 1994.

Name *Richmond*; **Pennant number** F239; **Flight deck code** RM; **Builders** Swan Hunter; **Laid down** 16 February 1992; **Launched** 6 April 1993; **Completed** November 1994; **Commissioned** December 1994; *Note:* Last warship built for the Royal Navy by Swan Hunter.

Name *Somerset*; **Pennant number** F240; **Flight deck code** n/a; **Builders** Yarrow; **Laid down** 12 October 1992; **Launched** June 1994; **Completed** 1996; **Commissioned** 1996.

Name *Grafton*; **Pennant number** F241; **Flight deck code** n/a; **Builders** Yarrow; **Laid down** 13 May 1993; **Launched** November 1994; **Completed** 1997; **Commissioned** 1997.

Name *Sutherland*; **Pennant number** F242; **Flight deck code** n/a; **Builders** Yarrow; **Laid down** 14 October 1993; **Launched** 1996; **Completed** 1997; **Commissioned** 1997.

Iron Duke *during helicopter sea trials for the new Merlin in the English Channel.* (Westland)

This class of general-purpose frigate was designed to operate independently in the Norwegian Sea, hunting Soviet nuclear-powered submarines trying to break out from the Barents Sea. The Type 23 frigate features an advanced technology towed array sonar and the Merlin HAS 1 anti-submarine helicopter.

Much work was carried out to make the design stealthy in appearance (against optical and electronic systems) and to reduce the risk of detection by submarines. For the latter, electric motors were installed for very quiet running.

With the reduction of threat following the demise of the Soviet Union, the Type 23 has easily adapted to new roles, including providing the West Indies guardship. *Lancaster* was deployed to the Caribbean Sea for much of 1993, where it was involved in anti-drug smuggling operations with the US Coast Guard. The ship's command and control system, stealthy technology, helicopter and advanced sensors provided the USCG with the sensor platform capability they otherwise lack. *Monmouth* was West Indies Guardship in 1995 before transiting the Panama Channel to South-East Asia. The West Indies Guardship (WIG) is a role to which several Type 23s have been allocated until the command and control system has been fully proved. This is why the class has not been operational in the Armilla Patrol nor in the Adriatic Sea off Yugoslavia.

A further three Type 23s will have invitations to tender issued in 1995 and it is possible that the class will have 16 members by 2000. The original plan of 23 warships in the class has apparently been scrapped as unnecessary and too expensive.

Pennant number change *Lancaster* was originally F232 but the Admiralty Board deemed 232 to be unlucky as it is the number of the Royal Navy form for grounding and collisions at sea.

Planned improvements If funds allow, the Type 23s will be retro-fitted with the Type 2057 towed array sonar. One ship is designated as trials ship for the Type 2081 active low frequency variable-depth sonar. There is still speculation that the last seven will have a 7 m section in the hull forward of the bridge to accommodate more Seawolf missiles and to provide for the 30 mm Goalkeeper CIWS.

Operational *Grafton, Iron Duke, Lancaster, Marlborough, Richmond, Westminster* to form Fourth Frigate Squadron (F4) at Portsmouth; *Argyll, Monmouth, Montrose, Norfolk, Northumberland, Somerset* and *Sutherland* to become Sixth Frigate Squadron (F6) at Plymouth.

Type 22 Batch 1

The first Type 22 frigates – *Broadsword, Battleaxe, Brilliant* and *Brazen* – were sold to the Brazilian Navy in November 1994, and delivered from 1995.

Type 22 Batch 2

Class 'Broadsword'

Name *Boxer*; **Pennant number** F92; **Flight deck code** XB; **Standard displacement** 3,500 tons; **Full displacement** 4,800 tons; **Length** 148.1 m overall; **Beam** 14.8 m; **Draught** 6.0 m; **Propulsion** COGOG 2 x Rolls-Royce Olympus TM3B (50,000 hp), 2 x Rolls-Royce Tyne RM1C (9,900 hp) gas turbines, driving two shafts; **Complement** 30 officers and 243 ratings; **Armament** 4 x Exocet anti-ship missile

launchers, 2 x Seawolf GWS 25 Mod 4 (32 missiles), 4 x BMARC 30 mm/75 GCM-A03 gun, 2 x Oerlikon 20 mm GAM-B01, 6 x STWS Mk 2 torpedo tubes, 2 x Plessey Shield, 4 x Sea Gnat CM launchers, DEC laser dazzle sights, 1 x 182 torpedo decoy; **Sensors** 1 x 967/968 air/surface search, 1 x 1007 navigation, 2 x 910 fire control radar, Sea Archer optronics, UAA-2 and 670 electronic warfare systems, Marisat SATCOM; **Sonar** 1 x 2016 bow-mounted active, 1 x 2031Z passive towed array; **Aircraft** 2 x Lynx HAS 3; **Builders** Yarrow; **Laid down** 1 November 1979; **Launched** 17 June 1981; **Completed** 1983; **Commissioned** 14 January 1984.

Name *Beaver*; **Pennant number** F93; **Flight deck code** VB; **Builders** Yarrow; **Laid down** 20 June 1980; **Launched** 8 May 1982; **Completed** 1984; **Commissioned** 18 December 1984.

Name *Brave*; **Pennant number** F94; **Flight deck code** BA; **Length** 146.5 m overall; **Propulsion** Rolls-Royce Spey SM1C replaces SM1A; **Armament** Seawolf GWS 25 Mod 3 and subsequent ships; **Sensor** 2 x 911 with two radar

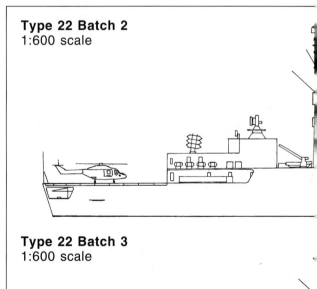

Type 22 Batch 2
1:600 scale

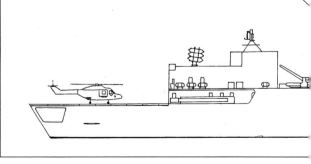

Type 22 Batch 3
1:600 scale

channels, and in subsequent ships, 1 x 967M replaces 967/968; **Aircraft** Lynx can be substituted by Sea King HAS 6 or replaced by Merlin HAS 1; **Builders** Yarrow; **Laid down** 24 May 1982; **Launched** 19 November 1993; **Completed** 1986; **Commissioned** 4 July 1986; *Note:* Conducted Sea King trials and received first operational Spey SM1C in 1990.

Name *London*; **Pennant number** F95; **Flight deck code** LO; **Builders** Yarrow; **Laid down** 7 February 1983; **Launched** 27 October 1984; **Completed** 1987; **Commissioned** 5 June 1987; *Note: London* was originally named *Bloodhound*.

Name *Sheffield*; **Pennant number** F96; **Flight deck code** SD; **Builders** Swan Hunter; **Laid down** 29 March 1984; **Launched** 26 March 1986; **Completed** 1988; **Commissioned** 26 July 1988.

Name *Coventry*; **Pennant number** F98; **Flight deck code** CV; **Builders** Swan Hunter; **Laid down** 29 March 1984; **Launched** 8 April 1986; **Completed** 1988; **Commissioned** 14 October 1988.

The Type 22 frigates were specified as general-purpose warships without guns. The Batch 1 design was found to be too small and lacking a naval gun system for bombardment during the Falklands conflict. The Batch 2 design is bigger (the same length overall as the later Batch 3), but again lacking the gun.

The class was designed to replace the many roles of the 'Leander' class and was first ordered in 1974.

Operational All Batch 2 frigates are members of the First Frigate Squadron (F1).

Type 22 Batch 3

Name *Cornwall*; **Pennant number** F99; **Flight deck code** CW; **Standard displacement** 4,200 tons; **Full displacement** 4,900 tons; **Length** 148.1 m overall; **Beam** 14.8 m; **Draught** 6.4 m; **Propulsion** COGOG, 2 x Rolls-Royce Spey SM1A (29,500 hp), 2 x Rolls-Royce Tyne RM3C (10,680 hp) gas turbines, driving two shafts; **Speed** 30 knots (18 knots on Tynes only); **Range**

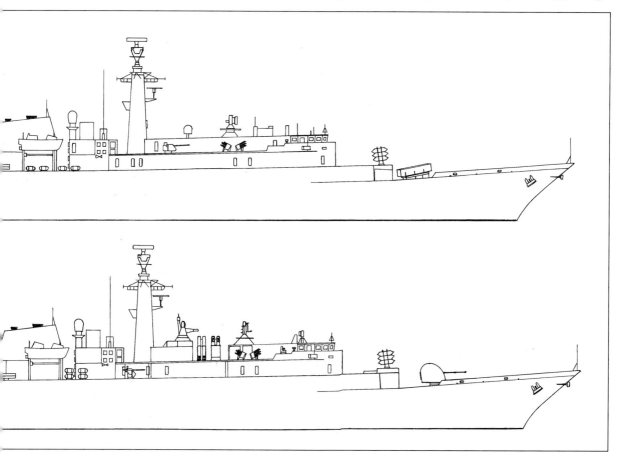

Campbeltown – *operating in the Adriatic, with sister ship* Coventry *and a German tanker.* (Paul Beaver)

4,500 nm at 18 knots (Tynes only); **Complement** 31 officers and 219 ratings; **Armament** 8 x Harpoon Block 1C anti-ship missile launchers, 2 x Seawolf GWS 25 Mod 3 (32 missiles), 1 x 114 mm Mk 8 dual-purpose gun, 1 x 30 mm

Chatham – *a Swan Hunter-built Type 22 Batch 3 frigate.* (Photo Press)

Goalkeeper, 2 x DES 30 mm/75 Mk 1 gun, 6 x STWS Mk 2 torpedo tubes, 4 x Sea Gnat CM launchers, DEC laser dazzle sights, 1 x 182 torpedo decoy; **Sensors** 1 x 967/968 air/surface search, 1 x 1007 navigation, 2 x 911 fire control radar, Sea Archer optronics, UAF-1 Cutlass and 675(2) electronic warfare systems, SCOT 1D SATCOM; **Sonar** 1 x 2016 hull-mounted active (to be replaced by 2050), 1 x 2031 passive towed array; **Aircraft** 2 x Lynx HAS 3 or 1 x Sea King HAS 6 (provision for Merlin); **Builders** Yarrow; **Laid down** 14 December 1983; **Launched** 14 October 1985; **Completed** 1988; **Commissioned** 23 April 1988.

Name *Cumberland*; **Pennant number** F85; **Flight deck code** CL; **Builders** Yarrow; **Laid down** 12 October 1984; **Launched** 21 June 1986; **Completed** 1988; **Commissioned** 10 June 1989; *Note:* Equipped with Sea King.

Name *Campbeltown*; **Pennant number** F86; **Flight deck code** CT; **Builders** Cammell Laird; **Laid down** 4 December 1985; **Launched** 7 October 1987; **Completed** 1989; **Commissioned** 27 May 1989.

Name *Chatham*; **Pennant number** F87; **Flight deck code** CM; **Builders** Swan Hunter; **Laid down** 12 May 1986; **Launched** 20 January 1988; **Completed** 1990; **Commissioned** 4 May 1990. *Note:* Sea King-equipped.

Improvements in the Batch 3 class include the fitting of the 114 mm (4.5 in) dual-purpose gun and a larger flight deck to accommodate the Sea King HAS 6 medium anti-submarine warfare helicopter and the Merlin HAS 1 when the latter enters service.

There are various modifications to the action information system, the electronic warfare suites and the provision of sensors for the various modification states (Mods) of the weapons, especially the Seawolf.

Batch 3 frigates have accommodation for a flag officer and staff.

The Batch 3 propulsion system has been improved to accommodate better performing gas turbine engines.

Operational All Batch 3 Type 23 frigates are members of the Second Frigate Squadron (F2).

MINE WARFARE FORCES
The Royal Navy has developed a world leadership in many aspects of mines countermeasures, but the ending of the Cold War has seen a reduction in the numbers of MCMVs in service.

The backbone of the flotilla of minor war vessels are now the 13 members of the 'Hunt' class and the 'Sandown' class which are still building. The simple but effective 'River' class are being withdrawn from service and sold overseas.

In July 1994, the UK Ministry of Defence announced that a further seven 'Sandown' class minehunters would be ordered in a contract worth £250 million.

Coastal minesweepers/minehunters

Class 'Hunt'

Name *Brecon*; **Pennant number** M29; **Standard displacement** 615 tons; **Full displacement** 750 tons; **Length** 60 m overall; **Beam** 10 m; **Draught** 3.4 m at screws; **Propulsion** 2 x Ruston-Paxman 9-59K Deltic diesels (1,900 hp), 1 x Ruston-Paxman Deltic auxiliary/pulse, driving two shafts, bow thruster; **Speed** 15 knots (diesels), 8 knots (hydraulics); **Range** 1,500 nm at 12 knots; **Complement** 6 officers and 39 ratings; **Armament** 1 x BMARC 30 mm DS 30B, 2 x Oerlikon 20 mm GAM-C01 guns, 2 x 7.62 mm GP machine-guns, 2 x Wallop Barricade Mk III CM launchers, 2 x Irvin Replica decoys, Matila E and Mentor A electronic warfare systems; **Sensors** 1 x 1006 navigation, Inmarsat SATCOM; **Sonar** 1 x 193M hull-mounted minehunting, 1 x Mil Cross Mine Avoidance Sonar, 1 x 2059 for PAP 104/105 operations; **Equipment** 2 x PAP 104/105 remotely controlled vehicles, MS14 magnetic sweep, Scarab mine destruction, MSSA Mk 1 towed acoustic sweep, Oropesa Mk 8 sweep, CAAIS DBA 4 action data automation; **Builders** Vosper Thornycroft; **Laid down** 15 September

Chiddingfold – although state-of-the-art in the 1980s, the 'Hunt' class is about to undergo a major improvement programme to prepare it for the 21st century. (Robin Walker)

Brecon
1:600 scale

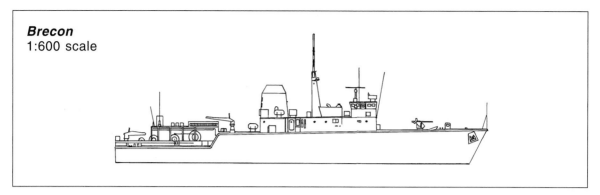

1975; **Launched** 21 June 1978; **Completed** 12 December 1979; **Commissioned** 21 March 1980.

Name *Ledbury*; **Pennant number** M30; **Builder** Vosper Thornycroft; **Laid down** 5 October 1977; **Launched** 5 December 1979; **Completed** 18 March 1981; **Commissioned** 11 June 1981.

Name *Cattistock*; **Pennant number** M31; **Builder** Vosper Thornycroft; **Laid down** 20 June 1979; **Launched** 22 January 1981; **Completed** 5 March 1982; **Commissioned** 16 July 1982.

Name *Cottesmore*; **Pennant number** M32; **Builder** Yarrow; **Laid down** 1980; **Launched** 9 February 1982; **Completed** 1982; **Commissioned** 24 June 1983.

Name *Brocklesby*; **Pennant number** M33; **Builder** Vosper Thornycroft; **Laid down** 1980; **Launched** 12 January 1982; **Completed** 25 October 1982; **Commissioned** 3 February 1983.

Name *Middleton*; **Pennant number** M34; **Builder** Yarrow; **Laid down** 1981; **Launched** 10 May 1982; **Completed** June 1984; **Commissioned** 15 August 1984.

Name *Dulverton*; **Pennant number** M35; **Builder** Vosper Thornycroft; **Laid down** 1981; **Launched** 3 November 1982; **Completed** 5 October 1983; **Commissioned** 3 November 1983.

Name *Bicester*; **Pennant number** M36; **Builder** Vosper Thornycroft; **Laid down** 1984; **Launched** 4 June 1985; **Completed** 14 February 1986; **Commissioned** 20 March 1986.

Name *Chiddingfold*; **Pennant number** M37; **Builder** Vosper Thornycroft; **Laid down** 4 May 1982; **Launched** 6 October 1983; **Completed** 9 July 1984; **Commissioned** 10 August 1984.

Name *Atherstone*; **Pennant number** M38; **Builder** Vosper Thornycroft; **Laid down** 1985; **Launched** 1 March 1986; **Completed** December 1986; **Commissioned** 30 January 1987; *Note: Atherstone* was refitted at Rosyth Royal Dockyard in 1993, the first commercial refit of a 'Hunt' class ship.

Brocklesby – *one of the Vosper Thornycroft-built MCMVs.* (Photo Press)

Name *Hurworth*; **Pennant number** M39; **Builder** Vosper Thornycroft; **Laid down** 21 February 1983; **Launched** 25 September 1984; **Completed** 14 June 1985; **Commissioned** 2 July 1985.

Name *Berkeley*; **Pennant number** M40; **Builder** Vosper Thornycroft; **Laid down** 24 September 1985; **Launched** 3 December 1986; **Completed** 1987; **Commissioned** 14 January 1988.

Name *Quorn*; **Pennant number** M41; **Builder** Vosper Thornycroft; **Laid down** June 1986; **Launched** 1988; **Completed** 1989; **Commissioned** 21 April 1989.

The 'Hunt' class design was originated at Vosper Thornycroft, using glass-reinforced plastic (GRP) construction techniques, which included much of the work being completed undercover in a large building hall. The ships were launched virtually complete. Two were built at Yarrow.

These GRP designs were the first in the world and were the result of work carried out on *Wilton*, a 'Ton' class minesweeper, which was remodelled with GRP.

GRP was used to reduce the magnetic signature of the craft and the initial problems with seaworthiness in a storm were overcome by using increased ballast.

The 'Hunt' class uses advanced sonar techniques to hunt mines and destroy them by placing charges or by conventional sweeping arrangements. The PAP 104 (later replaced by ten PAP 105 RPVs) are used to place charges, although each ship carries a number of specially trained clearance divers for the role.

During the Iran–Iraq war and the Gulf conflict, 'Hunt' class mines countermeasures vessels were deployed to protect friendly shipping in the Islamic Gulf. Tactics were developed to use the ships in conjunction with Lynx helicopters equipped with passive infra-red and other detection systems, to spot mines on or close to the surface.

This class was described as the leading edge of technology in the 1980s and certainly did good work in the waters around the Falkland Islands (Malvinas) as well as in the Islamic Gulf.

Planned improvements The class will be refitted, if funds permit, with a series of upgrades covering a new variable-depth sonar, the Nautis command system and a new remotely controlled vehicle. A new influence sweep system such as AMASS may be added.

Offshore minehunters

Class 'Sandown'

Name *Sandown*; **Pennant number** M101; **Standard displacement** 450 tons; **Full displacement** 484 tons; **Length** 52.5 m overall; **Beam** 10.5 m; **Draught** 2.3 m; **Propulsion** 2 x Paxman Valenta diesels (1,500 hp), driving two shafts with Voith-Schneider propulsion, 2 x bow thruster; **Complement** 5 officers and 29 ratings; **Speed** 13 knots (diesels), 6.5 knots (electrics); **Range** 3,000 nm at 12 knots; **Armament** 1 x DES 30 mm DS 30B, 2 x 7.62 mm GP machine-guns, 2 x Wallop Barricade Mk III CM launchers, 2 x Irvin Replica decoys; **Sensors** 1 x 1007 navigation, Racal Hyperfix, Decca Navigator Mk 21; **Sonar** 1 x 2093 variable-depth sonar; **Equipment** 2 x PAP 104 remotely controlled vehicles, ECA mine disposal system; **Builders** Vosper Thornycroft; **Laid down** 2 February 1987; **Launched** 16 April 1988; **Completed** 1989; **Commissioned** 9 June 1989.

Name *Inverness*; **Pennant number** M102; **Builder** Vosper Thornycroft; **Laid down** 1989; **Launched** 27 February 1990; **Completed** 1990; **Commissioned** 24 January 1991.

Name *Cromer*; **Pennant number** M103; **Builder** Vosper Thornycroft; **Laid down** 1989; **Launched** 6 October 1990; **Completed** 1992; **Commissioned** 7 April 1992.

Name *Walney*; **Pennant number** M104; **Builder** Vosper Thornycroft; **Laid down** 1991; **Launched**

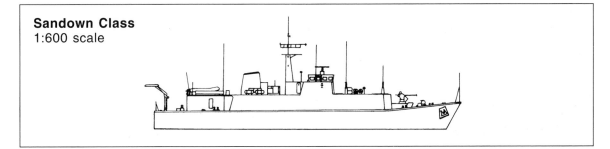

Sandown Class
1:600 scale

Walney – *a minesweeper cum navigation training ship, now attached to the Britannia Royal Naval College, Dartmouth.* (Vosper Thornycroft)

Sandown – *the lead ship of a class destined to become the standard mines countermeasures vessels of the next century.* (Photo Press)

25 November 1991; **Completed** 1992; **Commissioned** 20 February 1993.

Name *Bridport*; **Pennant number** M105; **Builder** Vosper Thornycroft; **Laid down** 1992; **Launched** 20 July 1992; **Completed** 1993; **Commissioned** 6 November 1993.

The 'Sandown' class was designed to be able to hunt and destroy mines in open, exposed and often deep water – more exposed conditions than those the 'Hunt' class would be operating in, yet not quite oceanic conditions.

Again the design is based on a GRP hull, but with a wider beam to improve seakeeping qualities. Again, Vosper Thornycroft have used the production line, all-weather building and construction idea, launching the ships almost complete.

The sonar system is deployed from a well within the hull and the vessels use the Remote Control Mine Disposal System, ECA mine disposal equipment and two PAP 104/105 vehicles.

The first ship was ordered from Vosper Thornycroft in August 1985 and a further four ships were ordered on 23 July 1987. An order for a second batch, in 1990, was deferred in 1991 and tenders were again issued in December 1993 for four, plus an option on three. The order for four was placed with Vosper Thornycroft in 1994 after the 'Front Line First' defence cuts.

The first of seven Batch 2 'Sandown' class MCMVs, *Penzance*, was laid down on 26 September 1995. It will be fitted with the GEC Nautis-M command system.

Operational All 'Sandowns' are members of the Third Mines Countermeasures Squadron (MCM3).

Coastal minesweepers (patrol craft in peacetime)

Class 'River'

Name *Blackwater*; **Pennant number** M2008; **Full displacement** 890 tons; **Length** 47.5 m overall; **Beam** 10.5 m; **Draught** 2.9 m; **Propulsion** 2 x Ruston 6RKC diesels (3,100 hp), driving two shafts; **Complement** 7 officers and 23 ratings; **Armament** 1 x Bofors 40 mm/60 gun, 2 x 7.62 mm GP machine-guns; **Sensors** 2 x TM 1266C navigation; **Sonar** None; **Equipment** EDATS wire sweep; **Builders** Richards; **Laid down** n/a; **Launched** n/a; **Completed** 1985; **Commissioned** 5 July 1985.

Name *Itchen*; **Pennant number** M2009; **Laid down** n/a; **Launched** n/a; **Completed** 1985; **Commissioned** 12 October 1985.

Name *Orwell*; **Pennant number** M2011; **Laid down** 1983; **Launched** n/a; **Completed** 1985; **Commissioned** 27 November 1985.

Name *Spey*; **Pennant number** M2013; **Laid down** 1984; **Launched** n/a; **Completed** 1985; **Commissioned** 4 April 1986.

Name *Arun*; **Pennant number** M2014; **Laid down** 1984; **Launched** n/a; **Completed** 1985; **Commissioned** 29 April 1986.

The 'River' class was ordered from Richards at Lowestoft and Great Yarmouth, Norfolk, in September 1982. The construction is traditional steel and the ships were designed to be operated as deep sea team sweepers, crewed initially by the Royal Naval Reserve.

Operational With the paying off of most of the craft and their subsequent sale to the navy of

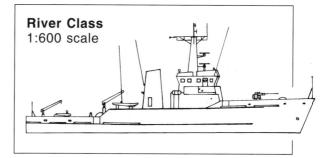

River Class
1:600 scale

Bangladesh, the remaining five craft have been assigned non-MCM roles; *Blackwater*, *Itchen*, *Spey* and *Arun* were assigned to the Northern Ireland Squadron, under Commodore Minor War Vessels. *Orwell* replaced *Wilton*, the last of the 'Ton' class, as the Dartmouth Training Ship in September 1994.

PATROL CRAFT

The Royal Navy operates a variety of patrol craft in the South Atlantic, off Northern Ireland, in Hong Kong and as part of the commitment to fishery protection.

Blackwater alongside at the Clyde Submarine Base. (HMS Neptune)

Squadron	Class	Location
Fishery Protection	'Leeds Castle'	Offshore
	'Island'	Offshore
Hong Kong	'Peacock'	South China Sea
Northern Ireland	'River'	Irish Sea
South Atlantic	'Dumbarton Castle'	Falkland Islands
	Cordella (commercial)*	(Falklands Government)

* Ship taken up from trade for fishery protection.

Ice Patrol Ship

Name *Endurance*; **Pennant number** A171; **Full displacement** 6,500 tons; **Length** 91 m overall; **Beam** 17.9 m; **Draught** 6.5 m; **Propulsion** 2 x Bergen BRM8 diesels (8,160 hp), driving a single shaft, bow and stern thrusters; **Speed** 15 knots; **Range** 6,500 nm at 12 knots; **Complement** 15 officers and 107 ratings, 14 Royal Marine Commandos; **Armament** None in peacetime; **Sensors** 1 x Furuno surface search, 1 x 1006 navigation, Inmarsat SATCOM; **Sonar** None; **Equipment** Special survey craft; **Builders** Ulstein Hatlo (Norway); **Laid down** n/a; **Launched** n/a; **Completed** 1985; **Commissioned** 21 November 1991; **Refits** 1992, 1993, 1994.

'Endurance' is the traditional name of the Royal Navy's Ice Patrol Ship, which is also the guard vessel for the British Antarctic Survey. The ship was leased from its previous owners in 1991 as *Polar Circle* and bought outright in 1992 and commissioned as *Endurance*. The ship's nickname, derived from her red paintwork, is 'Red Plum'.

The ship is painted in the traditional bright red and white markings seen on previous ships of the name. The current *Endurance* is not armed in peacetime and has a standard of accommodation for all the ship's company which is probably the most comfortable in the Royal Navy.

Endurance operates in the South Atlantic during the Antarctic summer and has been built to break ice of 1 m thickness at 3 knots.

Offshore patrol craft

Class 'Castle'

Name *Leeds Castle*; **Pennant number** P258; **Full displacement** 1,427 tons; **Length** 81 m overall; **Beam** 11.5 m; **Draught** 3.6 m; **Propulsion** 2 x Ruston 12RKC diesels (5,640 hp), driving two shaft; **Speed** 19.5 knots; **Range** 10,000 nm at 12 knots; **Complement** 6 officers and 39 ratings, 25 Royal Marine Commandos; **Armament** 1 x DES 30 mm/75 (on Lawrence Scott Mk 1 mounting), can lay mines, 4 x Plessey Shield CM launchers; **Sensors** 1 x 944 surface search, 1 x 1006 navigation, Radamec 2000 optronics, Inmarsat SATCOM; **Sonar** None; **Equipment** 2 x Sea Riders/Pacific 22 boats; **Builders** Hall Russell; **Laid down** n/a; **Launched** 29 October 1980; **Completed** 1981; **Commissioned** 27 October 1981.

Name *Dumbarton Castle*; **Pennant number** P265; **Laid down** 1980; **Launched** 3 June 1981; **Completed** 1982; **Commissioned** 26 March 1982.

The two 'Castle' class offshore patrol vessels were the second such design, the first being the smaller 'Island' class (see below).

The class has the ability to lay mines and has a flight deck capable of operating one Sea King HAS 6/HC 4 or a Lynx HAS 3/AH 7. There are no undercover facilities for the helicopters.

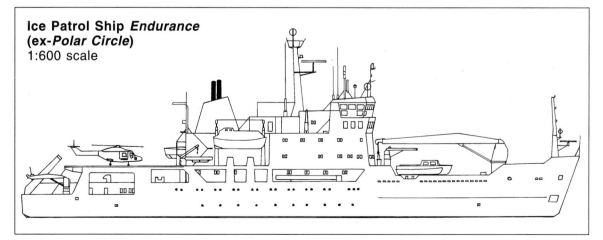

**Ice Patrol Ship *Endurance*
(ex-*Polar Circle*)**
1:600 scale

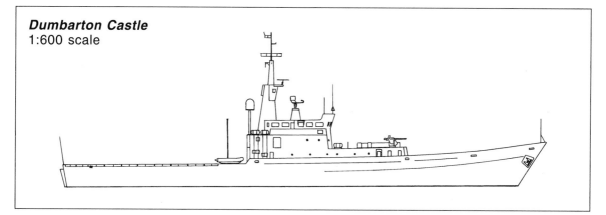

Dumbarton Castle
1:600 scale

Operational *Leeds Castle* is currently a member of the Offshore Division of the Fishery Protection Squadron at Rosyth; *Dumbarton Castle* is deployed to the South Atlantic as the Falklands guardship.

Class 'Island'

Name *Anglesey*; **Pennant number** P277; **Standard displacement** 925 tons; **Full displacement** 1,260 tons; **Length** 59.5 m overall; **Beam** 11 m; **Draught** 4.5 m; **Propulsion** 2 x Ruston 12RKC diesels (5,640 hp), driving a single shaft; **Speed** 16.5 knots; **Range** 7,000 nm at 12 knots; **Complement** 4 officers and 35 ratings; **Armament** 1 x Bofors 40 mm Mk 3, 2 x 7.62 mm GP machine-guns; **Sensors** 1 x 1006 navigation, SATCOM; **Sonar** None; **Equipment** 2 x Sea Riders/Pacific 22 boats; **Builders** Hall Russell; **Laid down** 6 February 1978; **Launched** 18 October 1978; **Completed** 1979; **Commissioned** 1 June 1979.

Name *Alderney*; **Pennant number** P278; **Laid down** 11 June 1978; **Launched** 27 February 1979; **Completed** 1979; **Commissioned** 6 October 1979.

Name *Guernsey*; **Pennant number** P297; **Armament** 1 x DES 30 mm/75 Mk 1 (replaces Bofors); **Laid down** 14 May 1976; **Launched** 17 February 1977; **Completed** 1977; **Commissioned** 28 October 1977.

Name *Shetland*; **Pennant number** P298; **Laid down** 1976; **Launched** 22 October 1976; **Completed** 1977; **Commissioned** 14 July 1977.

Name *Orkney*; **Pennant number** P299; **Laid down** 1976; **Launched** 29 June 1976; **Completed** 1977; **Commissioned** February 1977.

Name *Lindisfarne*; **Pennant number** P300; **Laid down** 1977; **Launched** 1 June 1977; **Completed** 1978; **Commissioned** 3 March 1978.

The first five of the class were ordered from Hall Russell in July 1975 and a further two were ordered in October 1977, despite criticism at the time that the class had insufficient speed to catch and board some types of trawlers.

The class is powered by the Ruston diesel to give good fuel economy on patrols in British coastal and offshore waters. Each ship expects to board and inspect 150 trawlers in a 12-month period and with increasing pressure on British fishing grounds, especially in the Irish Box (centred on the Irish Sea), this is becoming increasingly fraught.

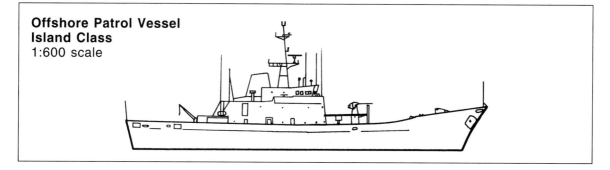

**Offshore Patrol Vessel
Island Class**
1:600 scale

The 'Island' class has the CANE (Computer Assisted Navigation Equipment) automated command and control system fitted to fix the ship's position in the event of an incident which will require further, legal action.

Disposals *Jersey* was paid off and sold in 1993.

Class 'Peacock'

Name *Peacock*; **Pennant number** P239; **Full displacement** 690 tons; **Length** 62.6 m overall; **Beam** 10 m; **Draught** 2.7 m; **Propulsion** 2 x Crossley Pielstick V280 diesels (14,000 hp), driving two shafts, retractable Schottel propeller; **Speed** 28 knots; **Range** 2,500 nm at 17 knots; **Complement** 6 officers and 30 ratings; **Armament** 1 x 76 mm OTO Melara, 4 x 7.62 mm GP machine-guns; **Sensors** 1 x 1006 navigation, SATCOM, Trimble GPS, Sea Archer optronics; **Sonar** None; **Equipment** 1 x Sea Riders, 2 x Watercraft fast pursuit craft; **Builders** Hall Russell; **Laid down** January 1982; **Launched** 1

December 1982; **Completed** June 1983; **Commissioned** 20 July 1984.

Name *Plover*; **Pennant number** P240; **Laid down** 1982; **Launched** 12 April 1983; **Completed** 1983; **Commissioned** 20 July 1984.

Aboard HMS *Plover*

Although the British territory of Hong Kong will be handed back to the mainland Chinese government at midnight on 30 June 1997, there is still an important Royal Naval presence there. Cornerstone to the British presence are the three 'Peacock' class patrol craft of the Hong Kong Squadron. In 1994–95, the Squadron leader was *Plover*, which was specially built for operations in Hong Kong waters.

Plover's main role is the maintenance of the sovereignty and integrity of Hong Kong waters, in close co-operation with the Royal Hong Kong Police and other law enforcement agencies. The 'Peacock' class are also the main long-range

Plover – the Royal Navy maintains at least one of the three 'Peacock' class patrol craft at sea in Hong Kong waters at all times. (Paul Beaver)

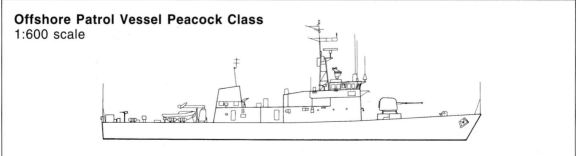

Offshore Patrol Vessel Peacock Class
1:600 scale

On the bridge aboard Plover *– the coxswain is on the wheel (nearest camera), the First Lieutenant is Officer-of-the-Watch, and the Captain (white shirt) is talking to the Navigating Officer.* (Paul Beaver)

search & rescue assets in the Territory.

Plover's appearance shows that she has been designed and built for the role. She and her sister ships have the capability of staying at sea during a typhoon and the class possesses a powerful dual-purpose gun, the 76 mm OTO Melara, which makes them seem like 'real patrol craft'. The machinery spaces are automated and every effort has been made to allow the ship to be run by the smallest possible ship's company.

There is no Operations Room and the ship would be fought from the bridge. In everyday, peacetime operations, the bridge is the focal point of navigation, pilotage and policing operations. The bridge has the display from the Type 1006 navigation radar, used to detect and track suspicious vessels entering or leaving Hong Kong waters. Co-located is the display for the Sea Archer thermal imaging camera – known aboard as the Tic.

The future of these warships after 1997 is uncertain. It is thought that they will be sailed back to the United Kingdom and be put up for sale – unless a buyer can be found in South-East Asian waters.

Name *Starling*; **Pennant number** P241; **Laid down** 1982; **Launched** 7 September 1983; **Completed** 1984; **Commissioned** 7 August 1984.

The class was designed for the Hong Kong role: protecting the Colony's maritime interests, interdicting smugglers and providing long-range search & rescue facilities. The Hong Kong government paid 75 per cent of the original building costs for the five craft which were ordered in June 1981. They replaced the 'Ton' class patrol craft in 1984 and are based at the Stonecutters' naval base in Hong Kong. There is always one of these craft at sea within Hong Kong's territorial waters. The craft are manned by UK and HK Chinese personnel and carry three Royal Marines coxswains for the fast pursuit craft, plus a number of young officers under training.

Disposals *Swallow* and *Swift* were paid off in November 1988 and sold to Ireland; *Peacock*, *Plover* and *Starling* will remain in Hong Kong until 1997 when the Colony reverts to China.

TRAINING AND PATROL CRAFT

University naval training craft

Class 'Archer'

Name *Archer*; **Pennant number** P264; **Full displacement** 49 tons; **Length** 20.8 m overall; **Beam** 5.8 m; **Draught** 1.8 m; **Propulsion** 2 x

Biter – *one of the 'Archer' class coastal training craft.* (Robin Walker)

Rolls-Royce M800T diesels (1,590 hp), driving two shafts; **Speed** 22 knots; **Range** 550 nm at 15 knots; **Complement** 2 officers and 10 ratings; **Armament** 1 x 20 mm Oerlikon (fitted for but not with); **Sensors** 1 x Decca 1216 navigation; **Sonar** None; **Builders** Watercraft; **Laid down** 1985; **Launched** 1985; **Completed** 1985; **Commissioned** August 1985.

Name *Biter*, **Pennant number** P270; **Laid down** 1985; **Launched** 1985; **Completed** 1986; **Commissioned** February 1986.

Name *Smiter*, **Pennant number** P272; **Laid down** 1985; **Launched** 1985; **Completed** 1986; **Commissioned** February 1986.

Name *Pursuer*, **Pennant number** P273; **Laid down** 1985; **Launched** 1985; **Completed** 1986; **Commissioned** February 1988.

Name *Blazer*, **Pennant number** P279; **Laid down** 1985; **Launched** 1985; **Completed** 1985; **Commissioned** February 1988.

Name *Dasher*, **Pennant number** P280; **Laid down** 1985; **Launched** 1985; **Completed** 1985; **Commissioned** May 1988.

Name *Puncher*, **Pennant number** P291; **Laid down** 1985; **Launched** 1985; **Completed** 1985; **Commissioned** July 1988.

Name *Charger*, **Pennant number** P292; **Laid down** 1985; **Launched** 1985; **Completed** 1985; **Commissioned** June 1988.

Former RNXS tenders

Name *Example*; **Pennant number** A153; **Laid down** 1985; **Launched** 1985; **Completed** July 1985; **Commissioned** September 1985.

Name *Explorer*, **Pennant number** A154; **Laid down** 1985; **Launched** 1985; **Completed** 1986; **Commissioned** January 1986.

Name *Express*; **Pennant number** A163; **Laid down** 1986; **Launched** 1986; **Completed** 1986; **Commissioned** May 1988.

Name *Exploit*, **Pennant number** A167; **Laid down** 1986; **Launched** 1986; **Completed** 1986; **Commissioned** August 1988.

Gibraltar guard ships

Name *Ranger*, **Pennant number** P293; **Laid down** 1985; **Launched** 1985; **Completed** 1985; **Commissioned** September 1988.

Name *Trumpeter*; **Pennant number** P294; **Laid down** 1986; **Launched** 1986; **Completed** 1988; **Commissioned** September 1988.

Commercial shipping In 1985, *Northella* was taken up from trade to act as a navigation training craft (it had previously been used as an auxiliary minesweeper in the South Atlantic). The ship was returned to trade in 1994.

SURVEY SHIPS

In the 1960s and 1970s, the Hydrographer to the Navy was not only responsible for the creation and accuracy of naval charts, but increasingly for detailed seabed mapping for nuclear submarines.

When the first Polaris boats came into service, it was increasingly important that the structure, temperature, salinity and other features of the Atlantic and Arctic Oceans were thoroughly mapped and understood. This would allow the boats to operate to the best advantage of cover.

Increasingly in the late 1980s and 1990s, the Admiralty Board has been forced to make cuts in the service provided by the Hydrographer and there is increasing reliance on the private sector for survey data.

The policy now is to commission a new 13,000 tonnes survey ship in 1997 to replace *Hecla*. The new ship, unnamed when ordered in January 1995, is claimed to be the most sophisticated ever built for the Royal Navy. The UK government's policy is to maintain a certain number of survey ships in commission and to charter private sector craft for the use of Naval Parties when required. In 1994, *Proud Seahorse*, a motor fishing vessel, was chartered for Naval Party 1016 and *Marine Explorer* for Naval Party 1008.

Disposals *Roebuck* (A130) has been put up for sale, even though she was only commissioned in October 1986. The two remaining 'Bulldog' class, *Bulldog* (A317) and *Beagle* (A319), are expected to pay off in 1995.

Two 'Hecla' class craft were sold off in 1986 and 1990 and *Herald* (A138) (see below) is often used as a mines countermeasures depot ship for South Atlantic or Gulf deployments. *Hecla* will be paid off when the new survey ship commissions.

New survey ship

Name Unknown; **Full displacement** 13,000 tonnes; **Length** 130 m overall; **Beam** 21 m; **Draught** 8.3 m; **Propulsion** 2 x medium speed diesels, driving a single shaft; **Speed** 17.5 knots; **Complement** 70; **Equipment** Multi-beam echo sounder.

This is the first ocean-going survey ship to be purpose-built for the Royal Navy and it was ordered from BAeSEMA in January 1995. It is designed to operate as efficiently as possible, producing three-dimensional images of an area of 60 sq nm to a depth of 5,000 m. The ship is contracted to cost £40 million and the hull will be built by Appledore with YARD exercising design authority.

Class 'Hecla'

Name *Hecla*; **Pennant number** A133; **Flight deck code** HL; **Full displacement** 2,733 tons; **Length** 79.3 m overall; **Beam** 15 m; **Draught** 4.7 m; **Propulsion** 3 x Paxman diesels (3,600 hp), 1 electric motor, driving a single shaft, bow thruster; **Speed** 14 knots; **Range** 12,000 nm at 11 knots; **Complement** 13 officers and 102

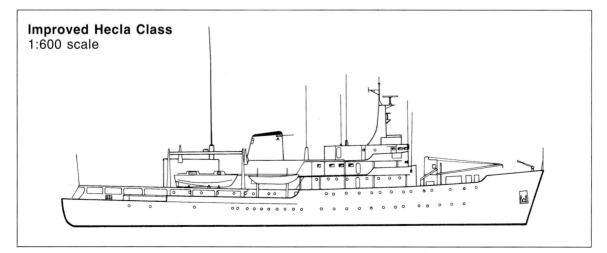

Improved Hecla Class
1:600 scale

Gleaner – *one of the smallest ships in the Royal Navy, used for inshore survey work.* (Robin Walker)

ratings, 6 civilians; **Armament** 2 x 20 mm Oerlikon (fitted for but not with); **Sensors** 1 x 1006 navigation, SATCOM; **Sonar** None; **Aircraft** 1 x Lynx HAS 3; **Equipment** 2 x 9 m survey craft, Hyperfix, Decca Navigator, Gravimeter, Magnometer; **Builders** Yarrow; **Laid down** 6 May 1964; **Launched** 2 December 1964; **Completed** 9 June 1965; **Commissioned** 9 September 1965.

Class Improved 'Hecla'

Name *Herald*; **Pennant number** A138; **Flight deck code** HE; **Full displacement** 2,945 tons; **Length** 79 m overall; **Beam** 15.4 m; **Draught** 4.9 m; **Propulsion** 3 x Paxman diesels (3,600 hp), 1 electric motor, driving a single shaft, bow thruster; **Speed** 14 knots; **Range** 12,000 nm at 11 knots; **Complement** 12 officers and 104 ratings; **Armament** 2 x 20 mm Oerlikon (fitted for but not with); **Sensors** 1 x 1006 navigation, UAR 1 electronic warfare, SATCOM; **Sonar** None; **Aircraft** 1 x Lynx HAS 3; **Equipment** 2 x 9 m survey craft; **Builders** Robb Caledon; **Laid down** 9 November 1972; **Launched** 4 October 1973; **Completed** 31 October 1974; **Commissioned** 22 November 1974; **Refit** 1988 (flight deck).

The 'Hecla' class were the first combined scientific and hydrographic ships in the Royal Navy

and they were built on merchant hulls for greater stability and better seakeeping.

Propulsion by diesel-electric drive, operated from the bridge, allows for delicate positioning during survey operations.

Herald acted as a hospital ship in the Falklands conflict (with *Hecla*) and as the Ice Patrol Ship in the South Atlantic in 1992 and 1993.

Herald is normally operating in the North Norwegian Sea. *Hecla* will pay off in 1997.

Class 'Gleaner'

Name *Gleaner*; **Pennant number** A86; **Full displacement** 22 tons; **Length** 14.8 m overall; **Beam** 4.7 m; **Draught** 1.3 m; **Propulsion** 2 x Rolls-Royce diesels (524 hp), 1 Perkins diesel motor, driving three shafts; **Speed** 14 knots (diesels), 7 knots (motor); **Range** 500 nm at 10 knots; **Complement** 1 officer and 4 ratings; **Armament** None; **Sensors** 1 x navigation; **Sonar** None; **Builders** Emsworth; **Laid down** n/a; **Launched** n/a; **Completed** October 1983; **Commissioned** 5 December 1983.

This craft is a Survey Motor Launch for inshore survey operations, especially around the approaches to Portsmouth Harbour.

CHAPTER FOUR

Naval weapons and sensors

NAVAL GUNNERY

Vickers 114 mm (4.5 in) Mk 8
Medium-calibre multi-purpose naval gun
After the Second World War, the Royal Navy developed the 114 mm (4.5 in) naval gun as the standard-calibre weapon system for frigates and destroyers.

In 1966, Vickers Shipbuilding & Engineering Limited (VSEL) was given a contract to develop a naval gun mounting which was efficient, safe and did not require personnel actually to man the tur-

ret. The first warships destined to receive the system would be the Type 82 destroyers of the 'Bristol' class and the Type 21 frigates of the 'Amazon' class. The Mk 8 mounting was ready in 1968 and used a modified 105 mm British Army artillery gun from the Abbott self-propelled gun. Technically, the weapon is 113 mm bore.

After two urgent export orders, to Iran and Libya, were met, *Bristol* commissioned the first Mk 8 in the Royal Navy in March 1973. It was not until the South Atlantic conflict that the Mk 8 gun proved its worth. It was found that naval gun-

A Vickers 114 mm gun on Campbeltown's fo'c'sle. (Paul Beaver)

fire support still had a major role to play in naval operations in the latter quarter of the 20th century and so the design philosophy which had allowed the Type 22 frigates to be gunless was found to be wanting.

As a direct result of the naval experience in Operation Corporate, the Type 22 Batch 3 frigates were modified to have the Mk 8 mounting fitted. The Mk 8 was also found to be good for dual-purpose operations, engaging and destroying an Argentine aircraft and sinking an Argentine transport.

The Type 23 frigates entering service in the 1990s are all armed with the VSEL Mk 8 quick-reaction short-range air defence and surface target gun, which is claimed to be effective against even small fast attack craft, such as those operating in the Islamic Gulf.

How it works

The Mk 8 mounting has a special ammunition feed system, with the operators situated in the warship's Operations Room. The gun crew consists of a loading supervisor and two loaders. The gun mounting is completely enclosed in a glass-fibre shield which protects it against the environment, blast and shrapnel.

The loading system is hydraulically operated from below the decks; the ammunition comes up into the gun by a hoist and the shell is transferred to the breech by means of a power ram. After the shell is fired, the casing is extracted automatically and ejected through a chute in the front of the mounting.

Traverse 340°; **Elevation** −10° to +55°; **Muzzle velocity** 869 m/sec; **Rate of fire** 25 rounds/min; **Range** 11.9 nm (against ship targets).

BMARC GAM-B01 20 mm mounting
Multi-purpose cannon

For the last 50 years, the British Manufacturing & Research Company (BMARC), now part of British Aerospace Dynamics, has produced naval mountings based on the Swiss Oerlikon designs for the Royal Navy. The Navy has employed a variety of systems in that period, including the very popular 20 mm mountings found on all surface escorts and patrol craft from about 1965 until 1990. Following the increasing threat posed by

Goalkeeper on Illustrious*'s bow – as well as being a powerful gun, the weapon is self-contained with tracking and fire control radar. (Paul Beaver)*

sea-skimming missiles and low-flying strike aircraft, the Royal Navy required a more modern, more advanced and more sophisticated system.

In 1974, to answer the need for such a new design, BMARC began development of the GAM mountings, initially with the Oerlikon KAA gun, designated the GAM-B01. The programme has been very successful, with over 20 navies besides the Royal Navy acquiring the weapon.

Calibre 20 mm; **Traverse** 360°; **Elevation** −15° to +60°; **Crew** 2; **Muzzle velocity** 1050 m/sec; **Rate of fire** 1000 rounds/min; **Range** 1 nm (against ship targets), 1500 m (against aircraft/missiles).

BMARC GCM 30 mm mounting
Anti-aircraft cannon

Development of this system began in the mid-1960s to meet a perceived requirement from the Royal Navy for a new anti-aircraft gun system, probably, it was thought at the time, remotely controlled. During the 1970s the design was further developed into the GCM series.

Most Royal Naval warships are armed with the GCM-A03 version which was developed with Falklands (Malvinas) conflict data, first appearing in 1986. In British service, the weapon system is manned and is fitted to larger surface combat ships, including the 'Invincible' class aircraft carriers.

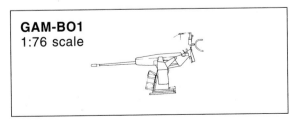

GAM-BO1
1:76 scale

GCM-A03 – a single 30 mm cannon on Norfolk's *starboard side.* (Paul Beaver)

A DES 30 mm on the new DS 30B mount. (Paul Beaver)

Calibre 30 mm; **Traverse** 360°; **Elevation** −13° to +75°; **Crew** 1; **Muzzle velocity** 1080 m/sec; **Rate of fire** 650 rounds/min/barrel; **Range** 1.6 nm (against ship targets), 2,500 m (against aircraft/missiles).

Bofors 40 mmL/60 mounting
Multi-purpose cannon

During the Second World War, the Royal Navy was in desperate need of an effective multi-purpose, dual-role cannon. The 40 mmL/60 naval mounting was derived from the anti-aircraft guns of the British Army. The first system was introduced in 1941 and has been updated steadily ever since. The current system is the Mk 9 but it is fading from service as the older warships are paid off.

Calibre 40 mm; **Traverse** 360°; **Elevation** −5° to +90°; **Crew** 2; **Muzzle velocity** 881 m/sec; **Rate of fire** 60 rounds/min; **Range** 6.5 nm (against ship targets), 4,000 m (against aircraft/missiles).

DES 30 mm mounting
Multi-purpose cannon

A new series of mountings was developed for the Royal Navy by Lawrence Scott and others in the late 1970s and into the 1980s. Initial firing trials took place in 1981 with the Royal Ordnance Rarden 30 mm gun, later replaced by the Oerlikon KCB gun after it was proved that the Rarden was too slow. The new DS 30B mounting was ordered by the Royal Navy to replace all existing 20 mm and 40 mm mountings.

Calibre 30 mm; **Traverse** 360°; **Elevation** −25° to +70°; **Crew** 1; **Muzzle velocity** 1080 m/sec.

Close-in weapon systems

Vulcan Phalanx 20 mm system
The second 'Invincible' class aircraft carrier, *Illustrious*, was the first warship in the Royal Navy to be fitted with the Phalanx close-in weapon system to provide a last-ditch defence against sea-skimming missiles and attack aircraft. This form of defence was found lacking when Argentine aircraft attacked the Fleet in the South Atlantic.

In 1982, as an emergency measure, the UK Ministry of Defence ordered a number of US Navy CIWS Mk 15 systems for aircraft carriers and destroyers, which were viewed as being particularly vulnerable to air attack. The Mk 15 system uses the General Electric Gatling-type gun with a self-contained acquisition and tracking unit. The gun is automatic and moves in computer-controlled 'jerks', and with its outstretched

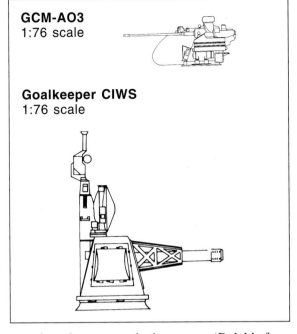

GCM-AO3
1:76 scale

Goalkeeper CIWS
1:76 scale

Phalanx, the powerful 20 mm Vulcan Gatling-type cannon, provides close-in defence for the Type 42. (Paul Beaver)

gun barrels, attracted the name 'Dalek' from naval crews.

Calibre 20 mm; **Traverse** 360°; **Elevation** −35° to +90°; **Crew** 0; **Muzzle velocity** Classified; **Rate of fire** 1,200 rounds/min; **Range** About 1 nm; **Ammunition** Discarding SABOT.

Goalkeeper 30 mm system
In 1984, the Royal Navy selected the combination of the General Electric 30 mm seven-barrelled

Goalkeeper amidships and immediately before Campbeltown's mainmast. (Paul Beaver)

GAU-8/A gun and radar from Holland Signaalapparaten (now part of Thomson-CSF), known as Goalkeeper (incidentally, the Royal Navy's expression for the frigate which protects an aircraft carrier in hostile waters).

On account of its range and destructive power, the system has replaced the majority of the Vulcan Phalanx on the larger warships in the Royal Navy, including the aircraft carriers and the new Type 23 frigates.

Calibre 30 mm; **Traverse** 360°; **Elevation** −25° to +85°; **Crew** 0; **Muzzle velocity** 1021 m/sec; **Rate of fire** 4,200 rounds/min; **Range** More than 1 nm.

GUIDED MISSILES

Sea Dart GWS 30
Area air defence missile system
The Sea Dart is the Royal Navy's longest-range shipborne air defence missile, which also has a limited anti-ship capability. The system is becoming obsolete and will be replaced by the end of the 1990s.

Its development began in the 1950s as a replacement for the first medium-range missile system, the Seaslug. The Admiralty required a lightweight, long-range missile to arm the proposed Type 82 destroyers to escort the new generation of aircraft carriers of the abandoned CVA-01 design. In the event only *Bristol* was ever built. Later, the design was specified for the

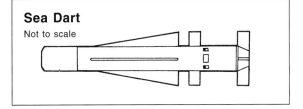

Sea Dart
Not to scale

Type 42 area air defence destroyers and eventually for the 'Invincible' class aircraft carriers.

Initial trials took place in 1965 and the first order was placed in 1967. The system was operational in *Bristol* when she was commissioned in March 1973. The GWS 30 system was to prove extremely successful during the Falklands conflict, destroying seven aircraft definitely and one possible.

Improvements followed the South Atlantic engagements, including the development of a new warhead in 1986, and various modifications were made to the radar and tracking systems.

During the Gulf conflict, a Sea Dart missile launched by the Type 42 destroyer *Gloucester* destroyed an Iraqi Silkworm-type anti-shipping missile which was reportedly aimed at a large warship of the US Navy, possibly an aircraft carrier.

How it works
The target is detected, tracked and acquired by the ship's long-range air/surface search radar, usually Type 1022. Target indication is provided by Type 992Q/R or Type 996 radars. After launch, the missile is tracked by the illuminating Type 909I radar. Data is transmitted to and from the ship's

Close-in defence – Illustrious, immediately after her refit in 1994, showing the Goalkeeper 30 mm Gatling gun (1), the BMARC GAM-BO1 20 mm dual-purpose gun (2) and STWS Mk 2 anti-submarine torpedoes (3). (Paul Beaver)

fire control system for automatic engagement if required. The missile is semi-active, with its own seeker. The explosive power is created by the Royal Ordnance continuous rod warhead and there is a proximity fuze to destroy the aircraft or missile. It is helped to its target by a large booster rocket and is propelled by a Royal Ordnance Chow motor.

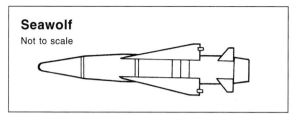

Seawolf
Not to scale

Length 4.36m; **Diameter** 910 mm; **Weight** 550 kg; **Speed** Mach 2 on launch, Mach 3.5 prior to impact; **Range** 21.5 nm (40 km).

Seawolf (GWS 25)
Short-range air defence system
Seawolf is the Royal Navy's standard anti-aircraft and anti-sea-skimming missile defence system. It is fitted in two versions – pedestal-launched and vertical-launched.

Development began in 1964 when a naval staff target was prepared for a quick-reaction, all-weather, point-defence, surface-to-air missile system to replace the Shorts Seacat. The Admiralty had originally specified a system for the anti-aircraft role but the intelligence revelations of an imminent Soviet deployment of SS-N-7 'Starbright' ship-launched anti-ship missiles created a new threat to large warship-type vessels and hence the need for an anti-missile capability. Project definition of Seawolf began in February 1967 when the then British Aircraft Corporation

(now British Aerospace Dynamics) was appointed. GEC-Marconi Radar Systems were responsible for the radar tracker.

Full-scale Seawolf development began in July 1968 with ballistic trials of the missile the following year. Sea trials were undertaken in 1975 in the 'Leander' class frigate *Penelope*. By December 1977, the trials had been completed and the first operational system was available in May 1979 for the new Type 22 Batch 1 frigate *Broadsword*; the Royal Navy designated it GWS 25 Mod 0. It was this version of Seawolf which was credited with the destruction of five Argentine aircraft in the Falklands conflict.

The Seawolf system has been progressively updated as a result of in-service experience, with GWS 25 Mod 3 entering service in April 1988 and GWS 25 Mod 4 available from 1993.

British Aerospace and the Royal Navy successfully demonstrated Seawolf's capabilities to destroy sea-skimming missiles in November 1983 against an Exocet and later against a 114 mm

Seawolf – Campbeltown's after Seawolf is mounted on the hangar roof with the Type 911 tracker a deck above. (Paul Beaver)

naval shell.

Vertical-launch Seawolf (GWS 26)
Fast-reaction short-range air defence system
First considered in 1966 and finally becoming a demonstrator programme in 1968, the VL Seawolf is a remarkable system. The missiles are stored and launched from canisters on the deck of a warship. The advantage is a rapid reaction time and there is no need to move the ship's position nor a launcher to engage a specific threat, thus saving valuable seconds when dealing with a sea-skimming supersonic missile. The missiles can be ripple-launched and actually start to manoeuvre before they reach mast height.

A £130 million production contract was placed with British Aerospace Dynamics and the first production missiles were accepted by the Ministry of Defence in October 1989. Sea trials with GWS Mod 0, in the first Type 23 frigate, *Norfolk*, were completed in July 1990.

It was originally planned that the 'Invincible' class aircraft carriers would be fitted with Seawolf GWS 26 Mod 2, but in July 1991 the project was cancelled following the 'Options for Change' defence review.

How it works
To find its target, the Seawolf missile rides a beam provided by a command system. First the target is detected, tracked and acquired by the Type 967/968 air/surface-search radar, which has two Type 910 or 911 trackers in the GWS 25 version. The trackers send guidance signals to the missile, correcting its flight path as the target's flight path changes. The system is fully automatic when it selects a target, but for safety's sake there is a manual override. The missile has a 14 kg explosive charge, made by Royal Ordnance, with a Thorn EMI fuze. For visual tracking by low-light television, the missile is fitted with flares.

The vertical-launch system, GWS 26, uses the Type 996 radar and the Type 911 Mod 1 tracker.

A major advantage of Seawolf over its predecessors is the ability to store the GWS 25 missile in the ship's magazine in ready-use containers which can be inserted onto the deck-mounted launcher by trolley.

GWS 25: **Length** 2.0 m; **Diameter** 700 mm; **Weight** 82 kg; **Speed** Mach 2.1; **Range** 2.7 nm (5 km).

GWS 26: **Length** 3.3 m; **Diameter** 700 mm; **Weight** 140 kg; **Speed** Mach 2.5; **Range** 3.2 nm (6 km).

Vertical-launch Seawolf blasting away from a Type 23 frigate during trials – note the debris as the hatch cover is blown away. (BAe Dynamics)

Manportable missiles
Increasingly since the Falklands (Malvinas) campaign, the Royal Navy has been augmenting its close-in air defence of warships, auxiliaries and ships taken up from trade (STUFT) with manportable, shoulder-launched air defence missiles.

Initially, the Blowpipe air defence missile was the standard air defence troop weapon with the Royal Marines, who provided the missile operators. Then the Javelin and later the Starburst entered service.

How they work

The Royal Marine aircraft sentry scans the horizon visually or may be alerted by the ship's broadcast system of an air raid. The target is acquired with the missile launcher's monocular sight and the sighting system is switched on, then the guidance transmitter frequency and fuze modes are selected. The safety catch is released and the act of squeezing the trigger firing mechanism initiates the firing mechanism. The missile is ejected from its shoulder-held container by a booster rocket which only burns for 0.2 sec before the sustainer rocket ignites. The aiming unit has a sensor which detects the missile in relation to the line-of-sight, aided by flares which provide both visual and automatic infra-red tracking. The manual visual system gathers the missile to its target.

	Blowpipe	*Javelin*	*Starburst*
Length	1.35 m	1.39 m	1.39 m
Diameter	76 mm	76 mm	76 mm
Wingspan	275 mm	275 mm	275 mm
Speed	Mach 1	Mach 1	Mach 1
Range	700–3500m	300–4500m	300–4500m
Warhead weight	2.2 kg	2.74 kg	2.74 kg
Guidance	CLOS	SACLOS	Laser beam rider

CLOS: Command to line-of-sight
SACLOS: Semi-automatic command to line-of-sight

Anti-ship missiles

Compared to many nations, the Royal Navy was late into the technology of anti-ship missiles and when it did acquire a system, UK industry was unable to deliver, so a French system was procured. Some critics have argued that the UK Ministry of Defence maintained a reliance on medium-range missiles at the expense of medium-range naval gunnery – a problem for the Task Force in the South Atlantic in 1982. In the early 1980s, it was decided to procure the US Navy's Sub-Harpoon system for the 'Trafalgar' class attack submarines, and the surface-launched version was acquired later for the new frigates. In 1994, Secretary of State for Defence, Malcolm Rifkind, announced the acquisition of the Hughes/McDonnell Douglas BGM-109 Tomahawk submarine-launched cruise missile for a land attack role in the 'Trafalgar' and Batch 2 'Trafalgar' submarines.

MM38 Exocet

This French-made, short-range first generation

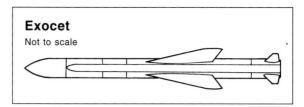

Exocet
Not to scale

anti-ship missile achieved international fame when an air-launched version hit the guided missile destroyer *Sheffield* off the Falkland (Malvinas) Islands in 1992. In fact, the missile's limited capabilities fall far short of the image created of the weapon; nevertheless, the Royal Navy still fits the system to Type 22 frigates.

How it works

Exocet is carried in watertight canister-launchers on the main deck of the frigate. After launch, the winglets unfold and the missile is guided by inertial gyroscopes in conjunction with three accelerometers. The inertial system is directly coupled to a radio altimeter which allows it to fly at sea-skimming, pre-set height to the target. Towards the end of its course, the active radar seeker in the nose is activated to detect and acquire a target – usually the largest object in its range. In this terminal phase, the missile descends to as low as 3 m above sea level to avoid anti-missile defences.

Length 5.21 m; **Diameter** 0.35 m; **Launch weight** 735 kg; **Warhead** 165 kg high explosive; **Propulsion** Solid fuel; **Range** 22 nm.

Harpoon launchers give Campbeltown *an excellent anti-ship capability.* (Paul Beaver)

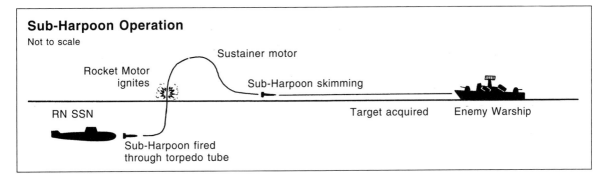

Sub-Harpoon Operation
Not to scale

Sustainer motor

Rocket Motor
ignites

Sub-Harpoon skimming

RN SSN

Target acquired   Enemy Warship

Sub-Harpoon fired
through torpedo tube

RGM-84 Harpoon

This is the new generation of sea-skimming, anti-ship missile which entered service with the Royal Navy in the Type 22 Batch 3 frigates and is also fitted to the Type 23s now entering service. The missile was designed by McDonnell Douglas Missile Systems in the USA.

How it works

Harpoon is powered by a turbofan sustainer engine but is launched by a booster motor which is jettisoned after launch. The missile then descends to a low-level cruise flight pattern which is pre-set into an altimeter. The direction of flight is determined by the launch information given to the missile and it uses an inertial platform of gyroscopes to guide it towards the target area, often over the horizon. At a pre-set point, the missile's active radar homing system switches on to search for and acquire the designated target. Unlike Exocet, Harpoon can discriminate one target echo from another using pre-programmed algorithms. If no target is visible to the radar, the missile begins a pre-set search pattern and if no target is again sighted, the system will self-destruct. If a target is detected, however, the missile pops up to a height of 1.5 to 2 km to dive down on the target at an angle of about 30°. In some versions, the final phase is sea-skimming rather than diving attack.

Length 4.62 m; **Diameter** 0.34 m; **Launch weight** 682 kg; **Warhead** 220 kg high explosive; **Propulsion** Booster/turbofan; **Range** 70 nm.

UGM-84 Sub-Harpoon

Before the surface ship Harpoon was selected and ordered, the Royal Navy had acquired the submarine-launched, version, Sub-Harpoon, for the nuclear-powered submarines of the 'Swiftsure' and 'Trafalgar' classes. This missile is identical to the surface ship version but it is launched underwater. The current standard for the Royal Navy is the UGM-84D-2, which is understood to have sea-skimming terminal phase trajectory.

How it works

The Sub-Harpoon is stored in the weapons compartment of the submarine in a special watertight capsule. It is launched through the torpedo tube, with the fins unfolding before it broaches the surface to ensure that the trajectory is correct for the booster ignition. The capsule is discarded and the missile is boosted away to begin its initial cruise to the target area using the sustained turbofan motor. The missile then activates its radar seeker and if no target is found, it flies a pre-set search pattern.

Length 4.64 m; **Diameter** 0.34 m; **Launch weight** 682 kg; **Warhead** 220 kg high explosive; **Propulsion** Booster/turbofan; **Range** 70 nm.

Strategic weapons

The United Kingdom's independent nuclear deterrent force is provided by the Polaris missiles of the Royal Navy's 'Resolution' class nuclear-powered submarines. The Polaris system is being steadily replaced by the Trident missiles carried by the 'Vanguard' class nuclear-powered submarines.

A-3TK Polaris Chevaline
Submarine-launched ballistic missile

The standard Polaris intermediate-range ballistic missile was designed in the USA by Lockheed Missile & Space Corporation. It entered service with the US Navy in 1971, but the United Kingdom continued to use the system through lack of funds to build newer submarines. The United Kingdom acquired 48 missile bodies and developed its own warhead and penetration system.

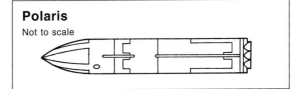

Polaris
Not to scale

The Polaris missile's capabilities were gradually improved in the 1970s and by November 1980, the A-3TK Chevaline upgrade was ready for test firing. Development of Chevaline ended in February 1982 with a series of test launches from *Renown* and *Revenge*. By 1986, the booster motors had also been upgraded and replaced, creating a total package of a multiple re-entry vehicle missile system, with countermeasures-proof warheads, which was still viable as a deterrent into the early 1990s.

British Aerospace was the principal contractor for the Chevaline programme which remained secret until the early 1980s. Polaris remained limited by range and its operational effectiveness began to be in doubt because of the ageing submarine design and the lack of US support facilities for the rockets.

How it works
Polaris missiles are launched from a submerged 'Resolution' class submarine using the Penetration Aid Carrier, a warhead-dispensing system which is capable of manoeuvring in space and uses classified guidance sensors to achieve the correct orbit. The Chevaline Carrier has a number of penetration aids to confuse enemy defences and the warheads are protected against electro-magnetic penetration by anti-ballistic missile systems.

Length 9.55 m; **Diameter** 1.37 m; **Launch weight** 13.6 tonnes; **Warhead** Up to 3 x 200 Kt nuclear warheads; **Propulsion** Two-stage solid-fuel motor; **Range** 2,500 nm; **Accuracy** 900 m.

Trident 2D5
Submarine-launched ballistic nuclear missile
In the late 1970s, it became obvious that the Polaris system would need more than the Chevaline update. After a research period when cruise missiles and air-launched weapons were investigated, it was decided to acquire the rights to the US Navy's Trident system.

Trident 2D5 is the advanced, inter-continental ballistic missile system which is now state-of-the-art with the US Navy. It has an extended range over Polaris and improved warhead capabilities. Although Trident could carry up to eight warheads on each missile, the UK government says it will limit the 'Vanguard' class payload to 96 warheads for the 16 missiles carried. A total of 67 missile bodies have been ordered on contract hire from the US Navy. It is understood that there will be a pooling arrangement by which bodies will be rotated through the US Navy's Atlantic Fleet facilities for servicing. As with the Polaris programme, the warheads for the US Mk 4 re-entry vehicles are the responsibility of the Atomic Research Establishments at Aldermaston and Burghfield.

The UK and the USA are known to be considering a downscaled version of Trident with a single tactical, low-yield nuclear warhead and even a conventional system of either high explosive or electro-magnetic pulse.

How it works
The Trident missile is launched from the submerged 'Vanguard' class submarine by compressed air and chemical explosion; the first stage rocket motor ignites when it broaches the surface. The missile gains orbit and can check its position using global position system, stellar sights and other mid-course guidance developments. Unlike Polaris, Trident is fitted with multiple, independently targeted re-entry vehicles (MIRVs) which have special, classified terminal guidance features.

Length 13.42 m; **Diameter** 2.11 m; **Launch weight** 59.1 tonnes; **Warhead** Up to eight MIRVs, up to 475 Kt yield in each warhead; **Propulsion** Three-stage, solid-fuel motors; **Range** 6,480 nm; **Accuracy** Less than 90 m.

Torpedoes

Spearfish
Heavyweight torpedo
Spearfish is the most advanced and latest heavyweight torpedo to enter service in the Western world. Initially, it is equipping the 'Vanguard' class submarines which carry the Trident missiles, but by 1997 it will be in service with most 'Trafalgar' class attack submarines. By the end of the decade, all British nuclear-powered submarines will have replaced Tigerfish with Spearfish. The torpedo's prime contractor is GEC-Marconi.

Length 7.0 m; **Diameter** 533 cm; **Weight** 1,850 kg; **Warhead** 300 kg high explosive, shaped charge; **Propulsion** Electric/chemical motor; **Range** Up to 30 nm; **Depth** 700 m; **Speed** 70 kt.

Tigerfish
The Mk 24 torpedo was the standard active and passive submarine-launched attack torpedo in the Royal Navy until the Spearfish entered service in 1994. Tigerfish has been fielded in a number of Mod states and the latest Mod 2 standard still equips 'Trafalgar' and 'Swiftsure' class boats. It is wire-guided to its target and has been described by the Royal Navy as 'an underwater guided missile for use against submarines and surface ships'.

Spearfish, the latest underwater weapon, shown aboard Vanguard *prior to her first cruise.* (HMS *Neptune*)

Length 6.46 m; **Diameter** 533 cm; **Weight** 1,550 kg; **Warhead** 134 kg high explosive; **Propulsion** Electric motor; **Range** 22 nm; **Depth** 600 m; **Speed** 35 kt (active mode), 25 kt (passive).

SELF-DEFENCE SYSTEMS

Laser dazzle sight
Electro-optical countermeasure system
The very existence of the laser dazzle sight (LDS) was a well-guarded secret until 1990 when a Royal Navy frigate was photographed in Spain carrying a new electro-optical countermeasure. Some observers had been aware that the system had been deployed to the South Atlantic in 1982 in order to improve the Fleet's air defences, but details were not available from open sources.

The Royal Navy actually released a picture of a frigate carrying the system in 1987, during the height of the tanker war in the Islamic Gulf, but few recognized the bridge wing-mounted system for what it was in reality.

It is understood that the LDS was developed by the Royal Signals and Radar Establishment and the Admiralty Research Establishment in 1981. It was fitted to frigates and destroyers of the Armilla Patrol from 1984; the first recipient was *Glamorgan*, the Type 42 area air defence destroyer.

The UK Ministry of Defence say that the system is neither a gun nor a blinding device, the latter being allegedly illegal under international law. Instead the LDS is said to be 'a laser dazzle device developed as a non-lethal defence against aircraft'. It is clearly a short-range, daylight system for use against low-performance aircraft and fast suicide 'Boghammer'-type boats.

No details have been released about the technical specification of the system. It is however manually operated and it resembles a large camera, about 2 m long with a range of 1.5 nm.

Naval countermeasures launchers

Barricade
Barricade provides warships and auxiliaries with defence against sea-skimming anti-ship missiles launched from aircraft, surface ships or submarines. It is lightweight and easily installed in existing warship or merchant ship designs.

The system deploys rockets with a variety of chaff (specially cut aluminium foil strips to confuse enemy missile homing radar) or flares (to decoy heat-seeking missiles). It is used as part of

Passive defence – a variety of chaff and flare launchers. (Paul Beaver)

a layered defence system for a warship or a group of warships.

A ship would carry six sets of triple launchers on port and starboard weather decks to give all-round coverage of possible attack arcs. The 57 mm rockets fired are: Palisade rockets for short-range

Corvus – firing chaff and flares to defend against sea-skimming missiles. (Paul Beaver)

threats, Stockade rockets for medium-range distraction (by presenting the incoming missile with an alternative target selection), and long-range engagements with chaff (to confuse enemy search radar before a missile has been launched).

Corvus

An older-style countermeasures launcher system which has been in service for several decades, this is also lightweight and provides a quick reaction alert for defence against anti-ship missiles launched from aircraft, ships or shore.

Corvus uses multi-barrelled rocket launchers fitted to the weather deck. The 16 rockets which can be carried ready for use provide defence against three separate missile attacks.

Sea Gnat

Fitted to the Type 23 frigates, Sea Gnat is the latest countermeasures launcher system to be acquired for the Royal Navy. It is a six-barrel fixed launcher system, carried abeam the frigate's forward superstructure. GEC-Marconi designed and built the system.

Shield

This is a fully automatic countermeasures system which is micro-processor controlled to decoy attacking missiles with chaff and flares. The micro-processors allow the right pattern to decoy or confuse a missile to be selected in a matter of milliseconds.

Shield is fully automatic, linked to ship sensors, or it can be triggered manually in emergency for several positions, including the bridge and Operations Room.

Super RBOC

This US system was fitted as an emergency measure to *Invincible* and later *Illustrious* for their tours of duty in the South Atlantic. It is now found on most major surface combat ships which were built or refitted in the 1980s. It has six tubes and is manufactured by Loral Hycor and known in the USN as the Mk 36 countermeasures launcher. It can throw chaff and flares to 2.2 nm.

Anti-submarine countermeasures

Magazine Torpedo Launch System

When the Type 23 frigate was first proposed, it was decided by the Admiralty Board that the warship would be fitted with a new type of anti-submarine torpedo launcher for last-ditch defence. The requirement was for a system which did not require operating from the deck. Ease of loading directly from the ship's magazine was also specified: the system can be reloaded in nine minutes.

The main weapon is the Stingray lightweight torpedo which is also carried by the ship's Lynx, Sea King or Merlin helicopter. The launcher is 324 mm diameter and made of glass-reinforced fibre.

Development began in 1983 and MTLS entered production in 1985, with *Norfolk* undertaking the initial service trials in June 1990. It is integrated with the frigate's Types 2031 and 2050 sonar.

Prairie Masker

An adopted US Navy noise suppression system which masks the ship's noise from submarines listening at long range. It uses basic physics, with the creation of an equal and opposite noise to that of the ship's machinery. It is fitted to the 'Invincible' class aircraft carriers.

Shipborne Torpedo Weapon System

STWS is the early development of the close defence ship-launched anti-submarine torpedo system and was adapted from the US Navy's Mk 32 launcher system. It consists of three torpedo tubes which have to be manually loaded, trained and reloaded. The standard weapon is the Stingray lightweight torpedo, but the Type 46 is also utilized.

STWS Mk 1 was the first Royal Navy version. Manufactured by Plessey in California, it entered service in November 1975 aboard *Cleopatra*, a 'Leander' class frigate. It is now out of service.

STWS Mk 2 was developed in the late 1970s and entered service in 1980 aboard *Andromeda*, also a 'Leander' class frigate. The Type 42 destroyers were also fitted with the system, followed by all the Type 22 frigates.

STWS Mk 3 is a development of the system for Type 42 Batches 1 and 2 destroyers, using the MILS micro-processor facilities and enhanced environmental features. It differs from Mks 1 and 2 in having only two tubes in each launcher.

Type 182

This is the standard surface ship towed submarine decoy system which transmits the signature of the ship which carries it. It is towed in the water at about 1 nm behind the ship.

Type 2071

Most British submarines have been fitted with this system of noise generation and augmentation to decoy acoustic torpedoes.

Bandfish

This is a submarine-launched countermeasures system to counter incoming acoustic homing torpedoes, designated sonar Type 2066.

SSE launchers

Submarines carry a variety of decoys and countermeasure systems, generally classified in detail. They are launched through the torpedo tubes or from special launchers in the hull. Like the chaff and flare dispensers of surface ships, they are designed to decoy enemy weapons, in this case homing torpedoes.

STWS, the Shipborne Torpedo Weapon System – for Type 46 or Stingray torpedoes. (Paul Beaver)

SSE Mk 6 This Submarine Signal Ejector is fitted to the 'Swiftsure' class.

SSE Mk 8 'Trafalgar' class.

SSE Mk 10 'Vanguard' class, to be fitted to 'Trafalgar' Batch 2 on building.

SSDE The Submerged Signal & Decoy Ejector carried in 'Resolution' class and all other Royal Navy submarines; it will be linked to a new Submarine Acoustic Warfare System in the late 1990s.

Talisman

This is a joint US/UK programme to produce a Surface Ship Torpedo Defence system, which in 1995 was still being fought out by two rival industry consortia. It has been designated Type 2070 sonar.

Teluma

A British programme to provide the 'Trafalgar' Batch 2 and earlier submarines on refit with an acoustic warfare system, linked to the Submerged Signal & Decoy Ejector. Details secret.

ACTION INFORMATION SYSTEMS

The speed of action in the modern naval engagement means that computer assistance to the team fighting the warship is vital. Since the early 1960s, the Royal Navy has progressively developed systems which assist with the 'tactical picture' and its compilation.

ADAWS (Action Data Automation Weapon System)

This is one of the oldest command and weapon control systems still in service. It was first developed for the Royal Navy's fixed-wing aircraft carriers in the 1950s, going to sea in 1964. Later it was developed in the 'County' class guided missile destroyers which carried the Seaslug missile. The heart of the system is the Ferranti FM1600 computer.

ADAWS 2 was developed for the single Type 82 escort destroyer, *Bristol*, but when the class was cancelled after her completion, the Admiralty began work on **ADAWS 4** for the area air defence destroyers of the Type 42 destroyers, ordered in 1967. The system entered service aboard *Sheffield* in February 1975 and was subsequently fitted to all Type 42 Batch 1 warships.

Development of a simpler system, **ADAWS 5**, began in 1967 for Ikara-equipped 'Leander' class frigates, using a single Ferranti FM1600 computer. It is no longer in service.

ADAWS 6 was developed to control the Sea Dart missile system of the first 'Invincible' class aircraft carriers, *Invincible* and *Illustrious*. It was developed into **ADAWS 7** for the Type 42 Batch

2 destroyers and with improved facilities for the Type 42 Batch 3, known as **ADAWS 8**.

ADAWS 10 is now fitted in *Ark Royal*.

New-generation weapons like Goalkeeper and the vertical-launch Seawolf have created a major problem for ADAWS. It simply cannot handle the volume of data. To overcome this a phased upgrade, ADIMP (ADAWS Improvement Programme), has been underway since a requirement was issued in 1988. This programme is led by Ferranti (now GEC-Marconi Defence) and will involve new processors and software, upgrade existing displays and fit the captain's Combat Aid System (CAS).

CAAIS (Computer Assisted Action Information System)

This tactical picture compilation system was developed as an Action Information Organization (AIO) for warships of frigate size and above. In 1967, the Admiralty required a smaller, simpler system than the existing ADAWS AIO and the contract was taken on by Ferranti.

The core was the FM1600 family of computers linked to the CA1600 family of display systems, which themselves were derived from commercial Decca (now Racal-Decca) navigation system consoles.

The system is officially described as a tactical picture compilation system for air, surface and sub-surface warfare. It provides automatic tracking of air and surface targets, sonar and electronic warfare processing, can operate a digital data link (such as NATO Link 11), designate targets, and control torpedo and vector attacks by anti-submarine helicopters and fixed-wing aircraft.

CAAIS was first selected for the Type 21 'Amazon' class frigates and known as Outfit DBA. The first production system, **DBA 2**, entered service when *Amazon* was commissioned in May 1974. Outfit DBA was then selected to refit 'Leander' class frigates. The first, Outfit **DBA 1**, entered service with the 'Leander' Batch 2TA frigate *Cleopatra* in November 1975. Later the system was fitted to 'Leander' Batch 2 (Exocet) frigates.

'Leander' Batch 3A frigates received an improved system, Outfit **DBA 5**. This was fitted to *Andromeda* in November 1980 and then selected for the new Type 22 Batch 1 frigates of the 'Broadsword' class, entering service in *Broadsword* in May 1979. It interfaces with the GWS 25 and 2016 sonar.

CAAIS was also selected for *Hermes* in her anti-submarine warfare role from 1977 until she paid off into the Indian Navy a decade later. The system was for the 'Hunt' class of mines countermeasures vessels as Outfit **DBA 4**. It entered service in *Brecon* in March 1980.

CANE (Command & Navigation Equipment)

This is a generic name for a family of tactical data handling systems which have been evolved from computer-based navigation equipment. The initial Royal Navy requirement was for an enhanced navigation system for fast patrol craft, offshore patrol vessels and an experimental hydrofoil. Modern CANE systems are fully distributed command and control systems with stand-alone work stations.

The first CANE entered service, as **DEA-1**, in February 1977 with the 'Island' class offshore patrol craft; the similar **DEA-2** was fitted to *Speedy*, the now-defunct experimental hydrofoil. By 1981, the system had been improved for fitting to the 'Castle' class offshore patrol craft, as **DEA-3**.

A later system has been fitted to the Aviation Training Ship *Argus*, and a mine warfare version, designated **MAINS** (Minehunting Action Information and Navigation System), has been developed.

Special features include the Automatic Chart Table which uses a light spot to indicate own ship and target positions. The system in *Argus* is networked with five consoles.

CACS (Computer-Assisted Command System)

This command system was born out of a UK Ministry of Defence requirement for a cost-effective system for the Type 21 and later Type 22 frigates. The Naval Staff Requirement came out in January 1979 and Ferranti was selected as the first commercial company to receive design authority for a major command and control system for the Royal Navy. In the event, CACS was not fitted to the Type 21, but it was planned to see widespread service:

CACS 1 Type 22 Batch 2 frigates
CACS 2 Type 42 destroyers (replacing ADAWS)
CACS 3 Type 43 destroyers (project cancelled in 1981)
CACS 4 Type 23 frigates
CACS 5 Type 22 Batch 3 frigates

CACS turned out to be a problem, to say the very least. The first system went to sea in *Boxer* in 1982 and began sea trials three years later. These showed that the software was inadequate and led to the abandonment of the programme for the Type 23. Type 22 frigate software processor improvement cost £30 million in 1991 and the whole programme cost the taxpayer in excess of £100 million.

CACS 5, the command system aboard Campbeltown – *manned by the ship's Operations Room staff in white anti-flash protection.* (Paul Beaver)

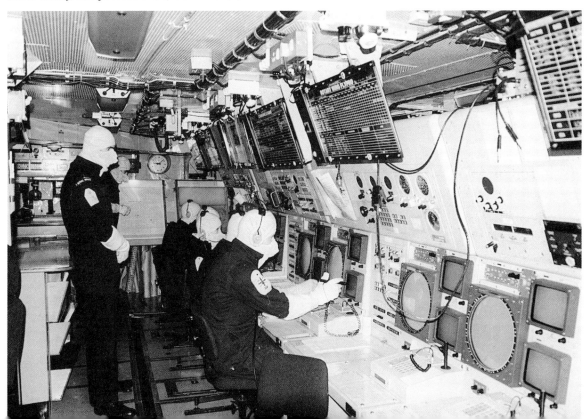

NAUTIS (Naval AUTonomous Information System)

This command and control system began development in 1983, when Plessey Display Systems (later Plessey Naval Systems, now part of GEC-Marconi Defence) began development of an intelligent workstation called Nautic. One module became NAUTIS as a purely tactical picture compilation system. Now it has developed into a command and weapon control system.

The first Royal Navy order, in 1985, was for the new 'Sandown' class of single role minehunters, designated NAUTIS-M by the Ministry of Defence. It went to sea in *Sandown* in June 1989. The assault ship *Fearless* has a NAUTIS-L system with seven consoles installed in the Operations Room.

SSCS (Surface Ship Command System)

Developed for the Type 23 frigates by BAeSEMA after the problems with the CACS system, this is very similar to the SMCS system for the 'Vanguard' class ballistic missile submarines.

Outfit DNA 1 is the interim fit for the Type 23 frigates; **Outfit DNA 2** is the standard fit for the 'Fort Victoria' class of auxiliary replenishment ships.

Submarine command systems

Outfit DCA The first system designed for nuclear-powered submarines which entered service in *Swiftsure* in April 1973. It is now out of service.

Outfit DCB Submarine command and weapon control system for 'Swiftsure' class submarines, with the capability of launching the UGM-84 Sub-Harpoon missile system. The system went to sea in *Superb* in November 1976. It uses two Ferranti FM1600B computers and Coral software language.

Outfit DCG An improved version, linked to the submarine's Action Information Organization computer. It takes navigational, tactical and sensor data from Outfit DCB to analyse. Outfits DCB/DCG are carried by all current 'Resolution', 'Swiftsure' and 'Trafalgar' class nuclear-powered submarines.

SMCS The latest-generation command and weapon control system developed for the 'Vanguard' and 'Trafalgar' Batch 2 submarines entering service or under design study. Studies for SMCS (SubMarine Command System) began in 1983 and the first system went to sea in *Vanguard* a decade later. It is similar to the BAeSEMA SSCS (Surface Ship Command System) for the Type 23 frigates.

Fire control systems

Radamec 2000 series This electro-optic fire control and surveillance system is part of a new generation of systems which began to be sent to sea in the late 1980s. It is used as a surveillance, tracking and fire control aid. It is fitted

Command and Control – the latest generation of command system is fitted in the 'Vanguard' class submarines, linking to the Trident missile-firing system. Shown for the first time. (HMS Neptune)

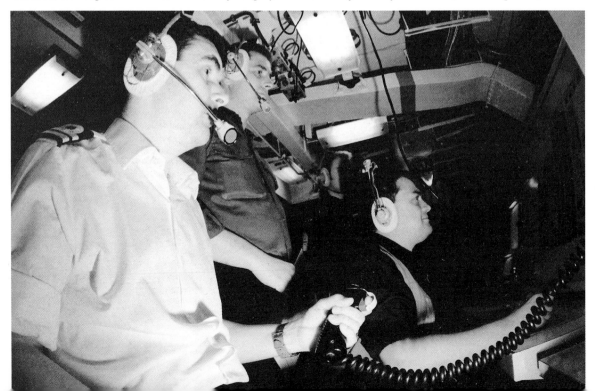

to Type 42 Batches 1 and 3 destroyers, Type 22 Batches 1 and 2 frigates, and the two 'Castle' class offshore patrol vessels.

Sea Archer Mk 1 This electro-optical fire control system was developed as a private venture by Sperry (now British Aerospace). Mk 1A is an enhanced version which provides complete integration of a thermal imaging camera (TIC) sub-system with bridge control by joystick to give an improved surveillance capability. It is used in this role aboard the three Hong Kong Squadron patrol craft of the 'Peacock' class.

Sea Archer 30 Also known as GSA 8 by the Royal Navy, this system is an enhanced version of the 'Peacock' class's fit. Contracts were placed in 1985 by the UK Ministry of Defence for Type 22 Batch 3 frigates; *Cornwall* was the first to be so fitted in 1988. It has been optimized to detect and track air and surface targets for the 114 mm Mk 8 and GCM 30 mm gun mountings on the frigates. It features two directors.

NAVAL RADAR SYSTEMS

Fire control

Type 909 This I/J-band radar provides fire control for the Sea Dart missile system. It is easily identified by the glass-reinforced plastic environment thimble shield. Type 909 Mod 1 entered service in the late 1980s. Ships fitted: 'Invincible' class, Type 42 (all batches).

Type 910 The standard I/Ku-band system for the Seawolf GWS 25 Mod 0 in Type 22 Batch 1 and early Batch 2 frigates. Ships fitted: Type 22 Batch 1, *Boxer*, *Beaver*.

Type 911 Operates in the I/Ku-band and is fitted to provide fire control for the Seawolf air defence missile system. In *Brave*, *London*, *Sheffield* and *Coventry*, the GWS 25 system has a second radar channel instead of a television sensor (known as Mod 3). Ships fitted: Type 22 Batch 2, Type 23 frigates.

Navigation radars

Type 1006 The standard merchant ship/warship I-band radar. Ships fitted: *Invincible*, *Illustrious*, 'Resolution' class, 'Trafalgar' class, Type 22, *Fearless*, *Intrepid*, *Endurance*, 'Peacock' class, 'Castle' class, 'Island' class, 'Hunt' class, 'Hecla' class.

Type 1007 Improved detection and reduced clutter, also operating in the I-band. Ships fitted: *Ark Royal*, 'Trafalgar' class, 'Vanguard' class, Type 23, Type 22 (on refit), 'Sandown' class.

Type 1216 Racal-Decca I-band navigation set for 'Archer' class patrol craft.

TM 1226C I-band system, manufactured by Racal-Decca for small merchant ships and adopted for the 'River' class.

Search radars

Type 967/968 The combined air/surface search system of Type 22 frigates, using the same aeri-

Type 1007 – the standard navigation radar. (Paul Beaver)

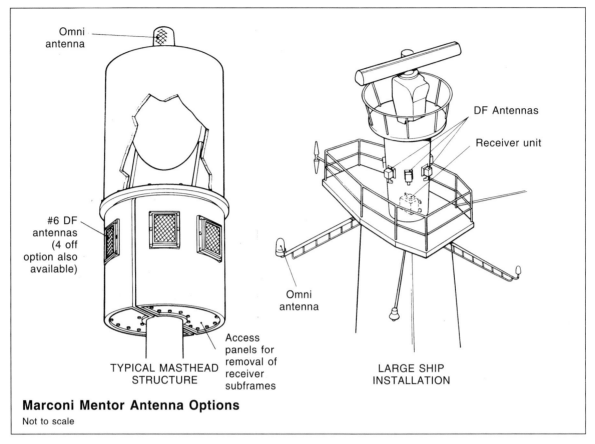

Omni antenna

#6 DF antennas (4 off option also available)

TYPICAL MASTHEAD STRUCTURE

Access panels for removal of receiver subframes

DF Antennas

Receiver unit

Omni antenna

LARGE SHIP INSTALLATION

Marconi Mentor Antenna Options

Not to scale

Type 967/968 – a primary air/surface search radar for Type 22 frigates. (Paul Beaver)

Type 996(1) – the Type 23's 3-D air/surface search radar. (Paul Beaver)

Aircraft carrier radar – the aerials of Illustrious *include Type 1022 (air search), Type 1007 (navigation) and Type 996(2) (surface search).* (Paul Beaver)

al mounting. *Brave* has a special fit of 967M. Operate in D/E-band. Ships fitted: Type 22 (all Batches).

Type 992 E/F-band surface search radar. Ships fitted: *Birmingham*.

Type 992R GEC-Marconi designed E/F-band surface search, being replaced by Type 996. Ships fitted: *Ark Royal*, Type 42 Batch 3.

Type 994 This surface search radar operates in the E/F-band. Ships fitted: *Fearless*, *Intrepid*, 'Castle' class.

Type 996 GEC-Plessey-designed surface search, operating in E/F-band, replaces the Type 992R in aircraft carriers and Type 42s. It is understood that the 'Duke' class have the Mod 1 system fitted at building. Ships fitted: *Invincible*, *Illustrious*, Type 42 (all Batches), Type 23.

Type 1022 GEC-Marconi/Thomson-Signaal D-band air search radar with a range of 145 nm. Ships fitted: 'Invincible' class, Type 42 (all Batches).

Furuno The ice patrol ship *Endurance* is fitted with the commercial E/F-band radar from Japan.

ELECTRONIC WARFARE SYSTEMS

Electronic warfare is a relatively new art and science for the Royal Navy, but it has been shown in the South Atlantic and the Gulf to be absolutely vital. Luckily for the UK Ministry of Defence, there are several highly competent manufacturers in the United Kingdom, including Racal and GEC-Marconi.

There are two basic EW systems: passive surveillance measures (ESM) and electronic countermeasures (ECM).

ESM systems listen to another land station, ship or aircraft's radiated noise, including radar transmissions, to ensure that the ship is fully aware of what is going on around her, but without giving herself away to the enemy or potential enemy.

ECM systems are active, including jammer systems which are used only in cases of detection. They jam enemy transmissions in radio, radar and other wavebands.

Known types carried by British warships are:

Mentor A This is a radar warning receiver, fitted to *Fearless* and *Intrepid*.

Scorpion Advanced ECM system fitted to some Type 23 frigates.

Type 670 An early electronic jammer which is still found in some Type 42 Batch 1 destroyers; initially fitted in Type 42 Batches 2 and 3, Type 22 Batches 1 and 2.

Type 675 Electronic warfare jammer, fitted to 'Invincible' class aircraft carriers and later Type 42 destroyers, Type 23 frigates, Type 22

Batch 3.

DLH In 1994, the UK MoD selected the GEC-Marconi Siren system as the Royal Navy's Outfit DLH offboard jammer and signed a contract worth £80 million for development and initial production. The system is launched into Sea Gnat CM launchers for destroyers, frigates and principal auxiliaries.

UA 11/12 Passive intercept system, fitted to 'Resolution' class.

UAA Passive intercept for *Invincible*, *Ark Royal*, Type 42 (all Batches), Type 22 (all Batches).

UAC Passive intercept for 'Swiftsure' and 'Trafalgar' classes on building.

UAF Passive intercept fitted to *Illustrious* after refit, and probably to *Ark Royal* from 1995; fitted to Type 23 (*Norfolk* to *Montrose*); also known as Cutlass.

UAP Passive intercept system. The UAP Mod 0 is fitted to 'Trafalgar' and later 'Swiftsure' classes on refit and Mod 3 is fitted to 'Vanguard' class on building.

UAT The Thorn EMI-designed system for Type 23 frigates from *Westminster* to *Sutherland*, to be refitted in early ships (*Norfolk* to *Montrose*).

TACTICAL SYSTEMS

Data links
Larger warships, including the aircraft carriers and Type 42 area air defence destroyers, are fitted with data links to talk and pass data directly to each other in clear speech, but secure from eavesdropping. The NATO Link systems available are 11, 12, 14 and 16, which have increasing levels of capability.

Satellite communications
SCOT (Satellite Communications Onboard Terminal) and Inmarsat (International Maritime Satellite) are now common to most warships, especially those on deployment. Satellite communications are unaffected by ionospheric interference and radio station jamming. The aerials are positioned as close to amidships as possible and protected in plastic radome, and they are gyro-stabilized to make reception possible.

NAVAL SONAR SYSTEMS
Sonar is the radar of the sub-surface. It uses sound energy to locate and track objects in the water, including submarines, surface ships and torpedoes. There are two types of sonar: passive (listening) and active (energy/response); and four basic platforms: hull-mounted on surface ships, submarine-mounted, towed arrays or variable-depth systems. Sonars and sonobuoys carried by maritime aircraft are covered separately.

The current sonar systems in service with the Royal Navy are listed below:

Submarine sonars
Type 2001 A long-range, low- to medium-frequency conformal bow-mounted sonar which could operate in passive or active mode. It will be replaced by Type 2074 in remaining hulls. Ships fitted: 'Resolution' (Mod AA) and early 'Swiftsure' (Mod BC) classes.

Type 2007 A low-frequency passive sonar with a 24-hydrophone flank array. Ships fitted: 'Resolution' and 'Swiftsure' classes, plus *Trafalgar*, *Turbulent*, *Tireless*, *Torbay* and *Trenchant*.

Type 2019 Also known as PARIS (passive/active ranging intercept system)

Satellite communications – the SCOT antenna aboard a warship for instant communications. (Paul Beaver)

Towed array – Norfolk's stern shows the scoop in the centre of the sternplate. (Paul Beaver)

which gives a full range of sound analysis. Ships fitted: 'Resolution', 'Trafalgar' and 'Swiftsure' classes.

Type 2020 Low to medium frequency, long-range active/passive sonar with computer assistance. Ships fitted: *Spartan*, *Splendid* and 'Trafalgar' class.

Type 2024 Towed array, clipped onto the submarine externally and linked to Types 2030 (US BQR-22) and 2035 (US BQR-23). After refit, ships will receive 2047 (UK-built narrowband processor). Ships fitted: *Superb*, *Sceptre* and *Splendid*.

Type 2026 Towed array, clipped on, very low fre-

Sonar suite – the multi-functional displays of the Merlin helicopter, showing sonar data. (Westland)

quency type. Ships fitted: *Trafalgar*, *Turbulent*, *Tireless*, *Torbay* and *Trenchant*.

Type 2027 Passive ranging system, linked to Types 2001 and 2020. Ships fitted: *Spartan*, *Splendid*, *Trafalgar*, *Turbulent*, *Tireless*.

Type 2032 Very low frequency bow sonar, which is co-located with Types 2001/2020 system. Ships fitted: 'Resolution', 'Swiftsure' and some 'Trafalgar' classes.

Type 2046 Clip-on towed array system which replaced the Type 2062. Ships fitted: 'Resolution', 'Trafalgar', 'Swiftsure' and 'Trafalgar' classes.

Type 2054 Secret sonar fit for the 'Vanguard' class ballistic missile submarines, linking Types 2043, 2044 and 2045.

Type 2067 Submarine ranging and tracking system, fitted to all submarines in Royal Navy service.

Type 2072 Broadband passive sonar. Ships fitted: *Trafalgar*, *Turbulent* and *Triumph*.

Type 2074 Low-frequency passive/active sonar, which improves and replaces Types 2001/2020. Ships fitted: *Spartan*, *Splendid*, *Trafalgar*, *Turbulent*, *Tireless*.

Type 2076 Integrated sonar suite for new-build 'Trafalgars' and refit programme, called SSN Update II.

Type 2077 High-frequency sonar for passage under ice. Ships fitted: 'Trafalgar' class, *Trafalgar*, *Turbulent*, *Tireless*, *Spartan*, *Splendid*.

Type 2082 Passive/active intercept sonar, designed to replace Type 2019 from 1992 and to be integrated with Type 2076 for the SSN Update I and II programmes. Ships fitted: 'Trafalgar' class.

Surface ship sonars

Type 162M This is the oldest sonar in Royal Navy service, having been developed in 1948 for bottom searches in confined waters. Ships fitted: Type 22 (all batches), Type 23 frigates.

Type 184M This is a medium-range active sonar which is being replaced by Type 2016, but remains fitted to some Type 42 Batch 1 destroyers.

Type 193M Fitted to the 'Hunt' class mine warfare ships, this sonar is used to scan routes and sectors of the sea bed.

Type 2016 Hull-mounted, medium-range, active/passive search and attack sonar which will eventually be replaced by Type 2050. Ships fitted: 'Invincible' class, Type 42 Batches 1 and 2, Type 22 (Batches 1 and 2).

Type 2031 Very low frequency, towed array sonar. Ships fitted: Type 22 Batches 2 and 3 (2031Z) and Type 23.

Type 2050 Medium-range active/passive bow sonar which is being developed for future new builds and refits. Ships fitted: Type 42, Type 23, Type 22 and 'Invincible' class aircraft carriers.

Type 2053 Special side-scan sonar for hydrographic craft.

Type 2059 Sonar with which 'Hunt' class tracks PAP 104/105 vehicles.

Type 2087 A new low-frequency active/passive sonar for future surface ships and refitting to existing hulls. Development date is classified with three consortia seeking an order in 1997.

Type 2093 A variable-depth minehunting sonar developed for the 'Sandown' class, this system will probably be refitted to the 'Hunt' class in the late 1990s.

Type 2094 Proposed hydrographic sonar for new ocean-going survey ship.

Echo-sounders

Type 778 In general service.

Type 780 Hydrographic system, fitted to 'Swiftsure' and 'Trafalgar' class submarines.

Type 788 Specially developed echo-sounder for all Royal Navy submarines; limited noise.

Underwater systems

Type 2008 This is the underwater telephone with trainable arrays on the submarine's fin which is fitted to every Royal Navy submarine.

Type 2009 Underwater recognition system, like an aircraft's IFF (identification, friend or foe).

Type 2010 Underwater teletype receiver/transmitter.

Type 2015 Bathythermograph for water tests.

Type 2019 Spectrum analyser for low-frequency sonar systems, fitted to 'Resolution', 'Trafalgar' and 'Swiftsure' classes.

Type 2039 Bathythermograph for submarines.

Type 2060 New expendable bathythermograph.

Type 2081 Secret environmental sensor to be delivered to the Royal Navy in 1995–96.

Type 2090 Integrated bathymetric information system for submarine operations.

FUTURE NAVAL WEAPONS AND SENSORS

During the next ten years, the Royal Navy will progressively update, improve and replace elements of its war fighting capability. The following list indicates the full scope of these staff targets (ST) – what the navy would like to happen – and staff requirements (SR) – what is funded to happen.

Endorsed staff targets

1999 Bowman – a new combat radio for naval shore patrols and the Royal Marines, to replace the current Clansman.

2001 Seawolf mid-life update – should become a requirement in 1994 but the details remain classified.

2002 Improved Data Link 11 – an improved tactical data link for maritime operations, in line with a NATO requirement to enable warships, naval and maritime aircraft to exchange real time data. Particular emphasis has been given to Electronic Counter-Countermeasures (ECCM) protection.

Endorsed staff requirements

1994

- Sea Dart update – a new fuze will be incorporated by British Aerospace Defence into GWS 30.
- Sea Owl – the Lynx HAS 8 passive identification device has been ordered from GEC Sensors under the brand name Sea Owl. It will enable the Lynx to conduct passive surface search operations.
- Sea Gnat – the infra-red chaff/flare decoy round will enter service under the NATO Sea Gnat programme.
- ADAWS improvement – the CVSs and Type 42 Batches 2 and 3 will have an improved action data automation weapon system from Ferranti, including better computer displays.

1995

- AMRAAM – the Sea Harrier FRS 2 will be armed with the advanced medium-range air-to-air missile (AMRAAM) as part of the Sea Harrier mid-life update. The missiles are being supplied by the US Department of Defense under the Foreign Military Sales agreement.
- Navstar GPS – front-line naval aircraft will be fitted with the global positioning system (GPS), although by mid-1993, a contractor had not been appointed.

Sea Owl – the new passive identification device (PID) for the Fleet Air Arm's Lynx HAS 8 shipborne helicopters. (Westland)

First test firings of the AMRAAM missile – from a Sea Harrier F/A 2 naval fighter equipped with Blue Vixen radar. (GEC-Marconi Avionics)

- Harrier T 8 – the five RN Sea Harrier T 4 trainers will be updated to T 8 standard, to be representative of the Sea Harrier FRS 2.
- Ambulance – the Royal Navy and Royal Marines will receive a new 4 x 4 medium-mobility, four-stretcher ambulance after trials in 1993–94.
- Utility trucks – after trials in 1994, new light- and medium-utility trucks will enter service for a variety of operational roles.
- Ocean survey vessel – *Hecla* is scheduled to be replaced by a ship taken up from trade or a new build.
- Type 2074 – a new bow sonar for the 'Swiftsure' and 'Trafalgar' class SSNs, being built by GEC-Marconi. The submarines will also have a tactical weapon system update by 2000, with GEC (Ferranti)-Thomson and GEC-Marconi in competition. EASAMS-GEC leads a consortium integrating the weapon systems.
- Electronic warfare – Thorn EMI has been awarded the contract to provide intercept and direction-finding equipment for the later Type 23s and the aircraft carriers, under the designation UAT. A further electronic warfare system, for the Type 675 jammer, will enter service in 1996.

1996
- Lynx update – the Lynx HAS 3 will have its

Ferranti Sea Spray Mk 1 radar integrated to the Racal central tactical system.
- Inertial navigation – all warships will be fitted with the GEC-Ferranti Defence NATO ships' inertial navigation system.

1997
- SHF satellite communications – a new system of increased flexibility, super high frequency satellite communications systems. A second phase contract for an in-service date of 1998 has already been awarded to Magnavox.
- Type 23 Surface Ship Command System – the BAeSEMA command system for all Type 23 frigates.

1998
- Merlin helicopter – the first of 44 Merlin helicopters will enter service.
- Merlin simulators – a training and simulation package for the Merlin helicopter is planned, using Loral ASIC as the prime contractor.
- Passive sonobuoys – a new passive search sonobuoy for the Merlin helicopter and a future RAF maritime patrol aircraft. Full development approval is expected in 1994. Project definition is being carried out by Dowty Maritime.

1999
- JTIDS – the RN will receive a secure ECM-

Lynx update – the Racal central tactical system will be integrated with the Seaspray Mk 1 radar in 1996. (RN/HMS *Osprey*)

Bladefold – the first Merlin deck trials aboard Norfolk. *The helicopter is due to enter service in 1998.* (Westland)

resistant line-of-sight communications link for air defence, similar to the US system known as JTIDS.

2000

- Decoy – a new off-board active decoy for all surface warships. The contract was due to be awarded in 1994.
- Torpedo defence – a collaborative programme with the US Navy to develop a system to protect surface ships from torpedo attack. Two competitors are Westinghouse and Martin Marietta.
- Satellite link – enhancement of data link facilities for CVSs, Type 23 frigates and Type 42 Batches 2 and 3. Secure data link will be to NATO Link 16 standard.
- Assault ship replacement – the commissioning of the first of two landing platform dock (LPD)

warships to replace *Fearless* and *Intrepid*. A combat management system will also be required. The Defence Procurement Minister, Roger Freeman, confirmed in January 1995 that there would be two new ships, the first in service by 2001.

2001

- Seawolf Mk 4 – an improved fuze for the Seawolf missile has been ordered from Thorn EMI, probably as part of the Seawolf mid-life update.

2002

- Microwave landing system – naval air stations will have a microwave landing system for day/night adverse weather operations. The contractors will be appointed in 1994.

2005

- Next-generation IFF – procurement of the next-generation identification, friend or foe system for which development is scheduled to begin in 1995.

CHAPTER FIVE

Naval aircraft and air weapons

EMBARKED FIXED-WING AIRCRAFT

British Aerospace Sea Harrier FRS 1

The unique Sea Harrier short take-off and vertical landing (STOVL) fighter aircraft of the Fleet Air Arm is embarked in the 'Invincible' class aircraft carriers of the modern Royal Navy.

The aeroplane's primary role is a fleet air defence fighter, reconnaissance and strike aircraft. It is a single-seat, single-engined combat aircraft, powered by the vectored thrust Rolls-Royce Pegasus 104.

Developed from the Harrier close air support, the main differences from the land-based Harrier are the elimination of magnesium components, a raised cockpit, revised operational avionics, and the multi-mode GEC-Marconi Blue Fox radar with air-to-air intercept and air-to-surface modes in the redesigned nose. This could be folded for stowage aboard ship.

The naval programme, then dubbed P 1184, was announced on 15 May 1975. The first prototype flew on 20 August 1978 and was delivered to the Fleet Air Arm on 18 June 1979. The Naval Intensive Flying Trials Unit, 700A Squadron (A

Sea Harrier FRS 1 – soon to leave service and be upgraded to F/A 2 standard. Note the Sea Eagle and insignia of 801 Naval Air Squadron. (Paul Beaver)

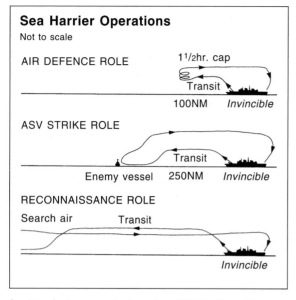

Sea Harrier Operations

Not to scale

AIR DEFENCE ROLE

1¹/₂hr. cap

Transit

100NM   *Invincible*

ASV STRIKE ROLE

Transit

Enemy vessel   250NM   *Invincible*

RECONNAISSANCE ROLE

Search air   Transit

Invincible

for 'Arrier), commissioned at RNAS Yeovilton on 18 September 1979 and after trials were completed became 899 Naval Air Squadron in April 1980. Initial trials were carried out aboard *Hermes* in November 1979.

The Royal Navy ordered three development Sea Harrier airframes, followed by 54 production aircraft from British Aerospace's Military Aircraft Division. The last airframe was completed and delivered in June 1988. The surviving airframes will eventually be converted to Mk 2 standard.

Trials to launch the Sea Harrier from the ski jump, thereby increasing its take-off weight by 1.1 tonnes, as proposed by Lt Cdr D R Taylor RN, took place at sea from 30 October 1980. Subsequently, as a result of successful trials, *Hermes* and all three 'Invincible' class aircraft carriers were fitted with a 7°, later 12/13°, ski-jump ramp from 1989.

Operational The Sea Harrier scored its first operational successes during the Falklands conflict in the South Atlantic, when 29 Sea Harrier FRS 1 aircraft were embarked in *Hermes* and *Invincible*. The aeroplanes flew 2,376 sorties, destroying 22 enemy aircraft in air-to-air combat without loss; four were lost in friendly fire accidents and two to Argentine ground defences. Their main role was to provide air defence for the Task Force, often operating at the extremes of range and weather to intercept incoming Argentine raids on the shipping and troops ashore.

Sea Harriers have again been operational during the UN Protection Force operations in former Yugoslavia, helping to patrol the skies of Bosnia-Herzegovina in Operation Deny Flight. One Sea Harrier FRS 1 from *Ark Royal* was destroyed by a Bosnian-Serb surface-to-air missile near Gorazde

in April 1994 and another, from *Invincible*, was lost on a routine training flight on 15 December 1994.

Typical alarm status includes launch from on-deck alert to 30 nm in under 6 min, and a high-altitude interception radius, with 3 min combat, from a vertical launch is 400 nm.

Deployment Front-line squadrons are 800 Squadron (*Invincible*) and 801 Squadron (*Illustrious*) with eight or nine aircraft each, depending on the role and deployment. In February 1995, 801 began to deploy the Sea Harrier FA 2 improved version aboard *Illustrious*. The training and headquarters unit, 899 Squadron, is permanently based at RNAS Yeovilton, but would form a third operational, embarked squadron in time of war.

Armament There is no built-in armament for the Sea Harrier, but there are four under-wing pylons and a single under-fuselage position for stores (cannon, bombs, rockets and missiles). The inboard wing pylons and the under-fuselage point can carry up to 907 kg (2,000 lb) each, and outboard under-wing pylons up to 295 kg (650 lb) each. Aden 30 mm cannon armament for air combat or ground attack are mounted in place of two under-fuselage fairings. In wartime, the Sea Harrier FRS 1 can fly with an external load of 2,270 kg (5,005 lb) and has flown with 3,620 kg (7,982 lb) during trials. In the ground attack and troop support role, the FRS 1 can carry a variety of free-fall bombs up to 2,270 kg, parachute-retarded bombs up to 2,469 kg (5,444 lb), Lepus illumination flares and 3 kg or 14 kg (6.6 or 31 lb) practice bombs. For air defence, AIM-9L/P Sidewinder missiles are carried on the outboard under-wing pylons. For anti-shipping strike, the FRS 1 can carry two Sea Eagle missiles. Although the Sea Harrier is configured to carry the B 83/WE177E free-fall nuclear bomb/depth charge, the weapon is no longer carried aboard warships of the Royal Navy.

Standard mission equipment The GEC-Marconi Blue Fox multi-mode radar is mounted in the nose, the pilot viewing the data on a TV raster daylight viewing tube which gives flight information as well as radar data. The windscreen has a Smiths electronic HUD (Head Up Display) and a digital weapon-aiming computer. Passive electronic surveillance and warning equipment are housed in the fin and tailcone. The F95 oblique reconnaissance equipment is housed in an optically flat panel in the nose, on the port side. In 1994, the NATO Mk XII IFF was due to be fitted.

Special mission equipment Fuel capacity can be supplemented by two 455-l (100 Imp gal) jettisonable combat tanks, or two 864-l (190 Imp gal) tanks, or two 1,500-l (330 Imp gal) ferry tanks on the inboard wing pylons.

Dimensions

Length (overall)	14.50 m
Length (folded)	12.73 m
Wing span	7.70 m
Height	3.71 m
Wheel track	6.76 m

Weights

Empty	n/a
Operational	6,374 kg (14,055 lb)
Take-off	11,880 kg (26,195 lb)
Landing	n/a

Performance

Max cruise speed	640 knots
Cruise speed	450 knots
Take-off run	305 m (no ski-jump)
Service ceiling	n/a
Endurance	1.5 hours combat air patrol

British Aerospace Sea Harrier FA 2

In January 1985, as a result of the operational experience gained during the South Atlantic conflict, the UK Ministry of Defence issued an improved Sea Harrier mid-life update project definition contract to British Aerospace.

The first Sea Harrier FRS 2 (later redesignated to FA 2) flew on 19 September 1988. There followed, in December 1988, a contract for the conversion of a further 29 FRS 1s to FRS 2 standard. Work began in October 1990 and the first deck landing was carried out on *Ark Royal* on 7 November 1990. The first re-engineered airframe was delivered on 2 April 1993. Trials followed at RNAS Yeovilton and the Aeroplane & Armaments Experimental Establishment at Boscombe Down from June 1993.

The mid-life update includes the provision of a new radar, the GEC-Ferranti Blue Vixen all-weather, look down/shoot down radar, and the ability to carry the beyond-visual-range AIM-120 Advanced Medium-Range Air-to-Air Missile (AMRAAM). The cockpit has been redesigned to include a new head-up display (HUD).

In 1994, the aircraft's designation was changed to FA 2 to reflect its fighter and attack roles, rather than as a reconnaissance/strike fighter. With the development of the Blue Vixen radar and the AIM-120 AMRAAM missile, the Sea Harrier FA 2 is deemed to be the most capable beyond-visual-range interceptor in Europe.

Operational The first Sea Harrier FA 2 fighters deployed to *Illustrious* in February 1995 as part of the UK support for the NATO Operation Deny Flight in the Bosnian air exclusion zone.

British Aerospace and the Fleet Air Arm have developed the FA 2's combat potential from aircraft carriers with a 12° ski-jump to include a combat air patrol of 1.5 hours at a radius of 100 nm from the parent ship. The aircraft would carry four AIM-120 AMRAAMs, or two AMRAAMs and two 30 mm guns, plus two 864-l (190 Imp gal) combat drop tanks. In the battlefield or maritime reconnaissance role, the aircraft is claimed to be able to cover 130,000 sq nm at low level in 1.75 hours for a radius of 525 nm from the air-

A Sea Harrier F/A 2 during first operational deployment in Illustrious. *(RN/Stu Antrobus)*

craft carrier, armed with two 30 mm guns and two 864-l (190 Imp gal) combat drop tanks. For anti-shipping strike with the Sea Eagle, the FA 2 has a high-low-high attack profile of 200 nm. As an interceptor, the FA 2 can engage sub-sonic enemy aircraft at a combat radius of 116 nm from Alert Two (Sea Harrier on deck, manned and ready).

Deployment 899 Squadron, the headquarters unit, was completely re-equipped with the Sea Harrier FA 2 in 1994; the first front-line operational unit was 801 Squadron which embarked in *Illustrious* in February 1995.

Armament As with the FRS 1, there is no built-in armament for the Sea Harrier FA 2, but there are four under-wing pylons and a single under-fuselage position for stores (cannon, bombs, rockets and missiles). The inboard wing pylons and the under-fuselage point can carry up to 907 kg (2,000 lb) each, and outboard under-wing pylons up to 454 kg (1,000 lb) each. Aden 30 mm cannon armament for air combat or ground attack are mounted in place of two under-fuselage fairings. In the close support/attack role, the FA 2 can carry a variety of free-fall bombs up to 2,270 kg (5,005 lb), parachute-retarded bombs up to 2,469 kg (5,444 lb), Lepus illumination flares and 3 kg or 14 kg (6.6 or 31 lb) practice bombs. For air defence, there is provision for four AIM-120 AMRAAM missiles on the two under-fuselage and/or outboard pylons (although AIM-9L/P Sidewinder missiles can be carried). For anti-shipping strike, the FA 2 can carry two Sea Eagle missiles. Although the Sea Harrier is configured to carry the B 83/WE177E free-fall nuclear bomb/depth charge, the weapon is no longer carried aboard warships of the Royal Navy. A further enhancement to the role will be the carriage of ALARM anti-radiation missiles to suppress air defences.

Standard mission equipment The GEC-Marconi Blue Vixen look down/shoot down, all-weather multi-mode radar is mounted in a redesign nose radome with a new Smiths electronic HUD and a digital weapon-aiming computer. Passive electronic surveillance and warning equipment are carried in the fin and tailcone.

Special mission equipment Fuel capacity can be supplemented by two 455-l (100 Imp gal) jettisonable combat tanks, or two 864-l (190 Imp gal) tanks, or two 1,500-l (330 Imp gal) ferry tanks on the inboard wing pylons.

Dimensions

Length (overall)	14.17 m
Length (folded)	13.16 m
Wing span	7.70 m
Height	3.71 m
Wheel track	3.45 m

Weights

Empty	6,374 kg (14,055 lb)
Operational	11,880 kg (26,195 lb)
Take-off	11,880 kg (26,195 lb)

Performance

Max cruise speed	640 knots
Cruise speed	450 knots
Service ceiling	n/a
Endurance	1.5 hours

LAND-BASED AND TRAINING AIRCRAFT

Sea Harrier T 4(N)

In 1982, the Fleet Air Arm received the first of its two-seat trainers for Sea Harrier pilot conversion and refresher training at Yeovilton. The aircraft are operated by 899 Squadron.

Dimensions

Length (overall)	17.00 m
Length (folded)	n/a
Wing span	7.70 m
Height	4.17 m
Wheel track	3.45 m

Weights

Empty	6,693 kg (14,758 lb)
Operational	11,880 kg (26,195 lb)
Take-off	11,880 kg (26,195 lb)
Landing	n/a

Performance

Max cruise speed	625 knots
Cruise speed	480 knots
Service ceiling	15,600 m
Endurance	2 hours

Sea Harrier T 8

In February 1992, the UK MoD ordered five new training Sea Harriers for the Fleet Air Arm. Designated T 8, these aircraft are tandem-seat trainers configured to support the Sea Harrier FA 2 conversion and training programmes but without the radar fitted.

Dimensions

Length (overall)	17.50 m
Length (folded)	n/a
Wing span	7.70 m
Height	4.17 m
Wheel track	3.45 m

Weights

Empty	n/a
Operational	11,880 kg (26,195 lb)

| Take-off | 11,880 kg (26,195 lb) |
| Landing | n/a |

Performance

Max cruise speed	635 knots
Cruise speed	480 knots
Service ceiling	15,600 m
Endurance	2 hours

British Aerospace Jetstream T 2

The Jetstream trainer, developed from the short-haul airliner, is used by the Fleet Air Arm to train observers in navigation skills. The rear cabin has been converted into a classroom for two instructors and three students. The aircraft first entered service in April 1979 and serves with 750 Squadron at Culdrose.

Dimensions

Length (overall)	14.36 m
Length (folded)	n/a
Wing span	15.80 m
Height	5.32 m

Weights

Empty	3,965 kg (8,743 lb)
Operational	5,692 kg (12,551 lb)
Take-off	5,692 kg (12,551 lb)

Performance

Max cruise speed	248 knots
Cruise speed	245 knots
Service ceiling	7,925 m
Endurance	n/a

British Aerospace Jetstream T 3

In 1986, four improved performance versions of the Jetstream were delivered, equipped with Racal 360° radar for observer training prior to the introduction of new radars in the Lynx and Merlin helicopters. However, as a result of defence cuts and the delay in bringing the Merlin into service, three T 3s are now with Yeovilton Station Flight and the fourth is in storage.

Dimensions, **weights** and **performance** details are as for Jetstream T 2.

FRADU at Yeovilton and Culdrose has received a number of BAe Hawk T1 and T1A training aircraft to replace the Hunters for Fleet Requirements and Air Direction duties.

NAVAL SHIPBORNE HELICOPTERS

EH Industries Merlin

Designed and built by Agusta of Italy and Westland of the United Kingdom, the Merlin is the Royal Navy's version of the multi-purpose EH 101 helicopter design. It is almost unique in having a three-engined configuration.

The original design stems from the Westland WG 34 first mooted in 1978 and selected by the Royal Navy to replace the Westland Sea King in late summer 1978. Because of the close similarities between the Italian MMI and UK Royal Navy requirements, a joint venture company was established and the EH 101 programme was given the go-ahead in January 1984.

The Royal Navy version is powered by the Rolls-Royce/Turbomeca RTM 322 turboshaft engine selected in June 1990 and the UK MoD ordered the helicopter into production with a £1.5 billion contract for 44 Merlins on 9 October 1991. The prime contractor is Loral ASIC, an American company with considerable experience, as IBM Federal Systems, in the integration of the US Navy LAMPS III helicopters. Loral ASIC will also provide the Merlin Training System at RNAS Culdrose from June 1998, in readiness for the IFTU to be formed the following year.

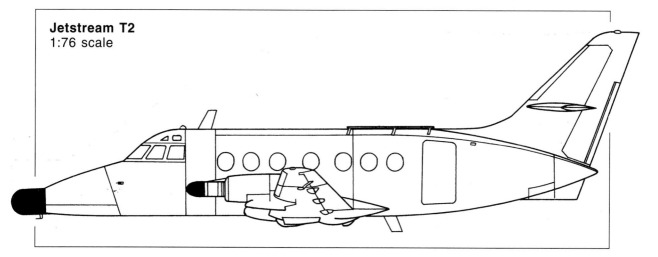

Jetstream T2
1:76 scale

Safe landing – a Merlin HAS 1 during preliminary ship's interface trials aboard Iron Duke. (Westland)

Merlin HAS 1 is the standard Royal Navy version which has been designed to operate from the flight decks of Type 23 frigates rather than immediately replace the Sea King aboard the 'Invincible' class aircraft carriers. The plan is to form an intensive flying trials unit in 1999, although first deliveries are expected in 1996. Primary deck landings were carried out aboard *Norfolk* in 1990, interface trials the following year and *Iron Duke* was the sea acceptance trials ship.

Armament The Royal Navy plans to have Merlin carry up to four lightweight torpedoes of the Stingray type.

Standard mission equipment GEC-Marconi Blue Kestrel has been selected as the Merlin's 360° surface search radar, supported by Racal Orange Reaper electronic surveillance measures. The primary anti-submarine sensor is the Ferranti-Thomson/Sintra FLASH (folding lightweight acoustic system for helicopters) dipping sonar with GEC-Marconi AN/AQS-903 advanced sonobuoy processing equipment with NGL mission recorder and sonobuoy/flare dispenser, and Chelton sonobuoy homers. GEC-Plessey GPS (global positioning system) receiver will also be

fitted to production aircraft. Merlin will have two sonobuoy dispensers and a Fairey Hydraulics external rescue hoist for search & rescue operations.

Dimensions

Main rotor diameter	18.59 m
Main disc area	271.51 sq m
Tail rotor diameter	4.01 m
Length (overall)	22.81 m
Length (folded)	16.00 m
Width (folded)	5.49 m
Height (overall)	6.65 m
Wheel track	n/a

Weights

Empty	7,121 kg (15,702 lb)
Operational	9,298 kg (20,502 lb)
ASW patrol	13,000 kg (28,665 lb)
Take-off	13,500 kg (29,767 lb)

Performance

Max cruise speed	167 knots
Cruise speed	150 knots
Service ceiling	n/a
ASW patrol endurance	n/a

Westland Lynx HAS 3/8

This twin-engined multi-purpose helicopter was developed under the auspices of the Anglo-French Helicopter Agreement of 1968 and the first prototype flew on 21 March 1971. The first production Naval Lynx HAS 2 flew on February 20 1976 but it was not until December 1977 that the first Royal Naval operational unit (702 Squadron) was formed on completion of intensive flight trials.

Lynx HAS 3 is the current shipborne version and it is described as an advanced surface search (radar and electronic surveillance measures), anti-shipping strike (Sea Skua missiles) and anti-submarine warfare (Stingray and Mk 46 torpedoes). Its other duties include spotting for mines coun-termeasures vessels and deploying landing/search parties. In total, 23 new-build Lynx HAS 3 were delivered between March 1982 and April 1985; the remaining 53 HAS 2s were upgraded to HAS 3 standard with Rolls-Royce Gem 41-1 (1,120 shp) turboshaft engines by 1989.

Improvement programme The Lynx has been proposed for a new, 360° surveillance radar, passive thermal-imaging equipment and a complete tactical command system refit. Seven Lynx HAS 3s were delivered in 1987–88. The sub-type is Phase 1 of the funding-dogged HAS 8 conversion programme, which calls for the fitting of GEC-Marconi AD 3400 secure speech radios (blade aerial beneath mid-point of tailboom) and upgraded ESM to 106 airframes in due course. Phase 2 is

Ready to lift – a Lynx HAS 3 on a surface search sortie from Campbeltown. *This machine is modified to Gulf standards but without the additional passive defence systems visible.* (Paul Beaver)

Lynx HAS 3
1:76 scale

Lynx HAS 3CTS which adds the Racal RAMS 4000 central tactical system and a flotation bag each side of the nose. The prototype made its maiden flight on 25 January 1989. Service flight clearance was granted in August 1991.

Lynx HAS 3GM is a specially modified batch of 19 airframes for use by the Armilla Patrol in the Islamic Gulf; they have better cooling and standard passive countermeasures.

Lynx HAS 3SGM is a hybrid with HAS 3S modifications, converted at RNAY Fleetlands from April 1989. Work is apparently continuing on these upgrades.

Lynx HAS 8 is the Fleet Air Arm's latest variant of the Lynx and a steady trickle are being delivered to RNAS Portland with the bulk of the deliveries completed by February 1995. The first deck landing trials were carried out aboard *Montrose* alongside at Devonport in November 1994 and trials continue.

The HAS 8 features GEC-Marconi Sea Owl passive identification system, CAE AN/ASQ-504(V) internal MAD (magnetic anomaly detector), reverse direction tail rotor control, British Experimental Rotorcraft Programme composite main rotor blades besides the HAS 3CTS Racal RAMS 4000 central tactical system. RAMS 4000 considerably eases the pilot and observer's workload by centrally processing sensor data and presents mission information on multi-function CRT display systems. These modifications have taken the helicopter's take-off weight to 5,125 kg (11,300 lb). Phase 3 conversions to HAS 8 standard began in 1992 and the conversion is planned of 45 HAS 3/3S/3CTS to HAS 8 standard; the work will be carried out at Westland and then RNAY Fleetlands.

Lynx HAS 3 helicopters are operated by ship's flights and parented by 815 Naval Air Squadron at RNAS Portland, due to move to RNAS Yeovilton in 1998. Training is carried out by 702 Squadron at RNAS Culdrose with 12 Lynx HAS 3; the squadron is also scheduled to move to RNAS Yeovilton in 1998.

Armament For armed escort and over-water strike missions, all versions can be equipped with two 20 mm cannon mounted externally or pintle-mounted 7.62 mm GPMG inside the cabin. For anti-submarine operations, the Lynx can carry two Mk 44, Mk 46 or Stingray lightweight torpedoes and six marine markers; or two Mk 11 depth bombs. Some Lynx were nuclear capable. In the primary anti-shipping role, the Lynx is armed with up to four British Aerospace Dynamics Sea Skua semi-active missiles which are facilitated by the Seaspray radar.

Standard mission equipment The Lynx HAS 3 series has the GEC-Marconi ARI5979 Seaspray Mk 1 lightweight search and tracking radar, for detecting small surface targets in low visibility/high sea conditions. For search & rescue, with three crew, there is provision for a waterproof floor and a 272 kg (600 lb) capacity clip-on hydraulic winch on the starboard side of the cabin, by the main door.

Special mission equipment Throughout its life, the Lynx has been modified for specific duties with a variety of equipments, including Tracor M-130 chaff/flare dispensers and Ericsson Radar Electronics AN/ALQ-167(V) D-J band missile jamming pods installed from 1987. During the Gulf conflict in 1991, the Fleet Air Arm acquired a number of Loral Challenger infra-red jammers, two fitted above the cockpit. GEC Sandpiper Forward-Looking Infra-Red pods are optional.

Dimensions

Main rotor diameter	12.80 m
Main disc area	128.7 sq m
Tail rotor diameter	2.21 m
Length (overall)	15.16 m
Length (folded)	10.62 m
Width (folded)	2.94 m
Height (overall)	3.48 m
Wheel track	2.78 m

Weights

Empty	2,740 kg (6,041 lb)
Operational	3,343 kg (7,371 lb)

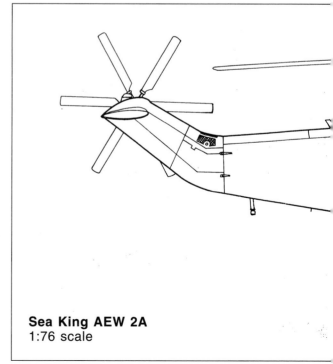

Sea King AEW 2A
1:76 scale

ASW patrol	3,472 kg (7,656 lb)
Take-off	4,876 kg (10,752 lb)

Performance

Max cruise speed	125 knots
Cruise speed	70 knots
Service ceiling	2,575 m
ASW patrol endurance	2.5 hours

Westland Sea King AEW 2A

Following the experiences of the South Atlantic maritime air operations and the lack of timely warning of air attack, the Fleet Air Arm worked with Westland Helicopters to create an airborne early warning version of the Sea King. The helicopter is standard, with Rolls-Royce Gnome turboshaft engines, retaining the thimble radome of the removed radar in the dorsal position.

Ten Sea King HAS 2 airframes were eventually taken in hand and modified to AEW 2 (later AEW 2A) standard with the Thorn EMI Searchwater radar. The first flight deck trials were carried out on 2 August 1982 and acceptance followed quickly to allow the aircraft to be deployed aboard *Illustrious* in the South Atlantic.

After these South Atlantic operational trials, more work was carried out at Boscombe Down and other establishments before 849 Squadron's A Flight took the first three Sea King AEW 2s to sea in *Illustrious* in 1985 for exercise Ocean Safari.

The following April, 849B Flight was formed and embarked in *Ark Royal* and the headquarters flight formed at RNAS Culdrose. A sea-going flight is made up of three Sea Kings and five complete crews. There were eight Sea King AEW 2A operational in January 1996, with 849A Flight embarked in *Invincible* and 849B Flight in *Illustrious*.

The standard crewing is a pilot, observer and systems operator. The observer acts as the safety member in the helicopter's left-hand seat during take-off and recovery.

Operational, the Sea King AEW 2A (known as the Sea King Whiskey in the Fleet Air Arm) flies missions which enable the aircraft carrier's radar horizon to be considerably extended. The helicopter can be used for surface search, having the Racal Orange Crop MIR-2 electronic surveillance measures equipment fitted, and for airborne early warning. Hostile aircraft can be detected at 100 nm (185 km) range and the ship's combat air patrol of Sea Harrier fighters vectored to intercept.

The Searchwater radar's pressurized dome is swung in the vertical position after take-off and swung back to the horizontal for recovery.

Armament None.

Standard mission equipment The primary sensor is the Searchwater radar, assisted by the Cossor Jubilee Guardsman IFF system (identification, friend or foe) and the Racal Orange Crop ESM.

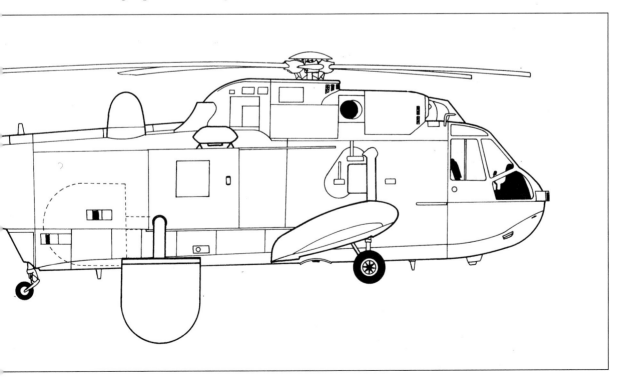

Sea King AEW 2A – providing air direction and airborne early warning to the Fleet. (Paul Beaver)

Dimensions

Main rotor diameter	18.90 m
Main disc area	280.6 sq m
Tail rotor diameter	3.16 m
Length (overall)	22.15 m
Length (folded)	14.40 m
Width (folded)	5.0 m
Height (overall)	5.13 m
Wheel track	3.96 m

Weights

Empty	7,870 kg (17,353 lb)
Operational	9,707 kg (21,404 lb)
Take-off	12,292 kg (27,104 lb)

Performance

Max cruise speed	110 knots
Cruise speed	90 knots
Service ceiling	3,200 m
Patrol endurance	4.25 hours

Westland Sea King AEW 5

In late 1994, it was revealed that two HAS 5 airframes would be converted to carry airborne early warning radar. Further details were awaited at the time of closing for press. AEW 7 is another possible designation.

Westland Sea King HAS 5

Between 1980 and 1987, the Fleet Air Arm took delivery of 86 improved Sea King anti-submarine warfare helicopters, including 30 new-build aircraft from Westland. The first HAS 5 was handed over to the Fleet Air Arm at RNAS Culdrose on 2 October 1980.

The Sea King design originated in the USA but entered service in the Royal Navy in 1969. The helicopter is the shipborne medium-range anti-submarine warfare helicopter of the Royal Navy, being embarked in the 'Invincible' class aircraft carriers and aboard Royal Fleet Auxiliaries.

The helicopter has a secondary onshore, search & rescue (SAR) role; in this role it is known as the Sea King HAR 5 and five such airframes are operated from RNAS Culdrose by 771 Squadron, which is also the training unit for the type.

The HAS 5 helicopter had a new radome for the

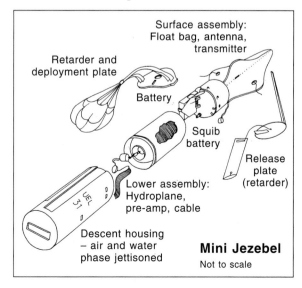

MEL Sea Searcher radar and the internal arrangement of the cabin was redesigned to give more room for the latest generation of anti-submarine warfare equipment. This included the mini-Jezebel sonobuoy dispenser (creating the in-service nickname of Sea King Juliet for the type) and the LAPADS data processing table. The new equipment was needed to cope with the advent of quieter, faster Soviet submarines in the 1980s and for the Sea Kings to be able to operate with Royal Air Force Nimrod and other sonobuoy-equipped long-range maritime patrol aircraft.

In the ASW role, the Sea King carries two pilots, an observer and a sonics operator. In the secondary role when embarked, the Sea King is used for SAR. Both ASW and SAR missions rely on the automatic flight control system which allows the helicopter to hover at pre-set heights above the sea in adverse weather, day or night.

In December 1995, 706 Squadron and one flight of 819 Squadron still operated the Sea King HAS 5, but the Fleet Air Arm had about 25 airframes in strength.

Armament Standard ASW patrol weapons include up to four Mk 44, Mk 46 or Stingray lightweight torpedoes; or Mk 11 depth bombs. The Sea King is equipped to carry nuclear depth charges (these are no longer operational), and pintle-mounted 7.62 mm GPMGs can also be carried.

Standard mission equipment Sea Searcher radar, Racal MIR-2 Orange Crop ESM, Plessey Type 195 (upgraded to Type 2069) dipping sonar, Racal TANS G navigation system, GEC-Marconi LAPADS acoustic processing, CAE AN/AQS-504(V), various sonobuoys. Some aircraft have Ericcson AN/ALQ-167 jammer systems.

Dimensions

Main rotor diameter	18.90 m
Main disc area	280.60 sq m
Tail rotor diameter	3.16 m
Length (overall)	22.15 m
Length (folded)	17.01 m
Width (folded)	5.0 m
Height (overall)	5.13 m
Wheel track	3.96 m

Weights

Empty	7,428 kg (16,379 lb)
Operational	n/a
ASW patrol	n/a
Take-off	9,752 kg (21,503 lb)

Performance

Max cruise speed	112 knots
Cruise speed	100 knots
Service ceiling	3,200 m
ASW patrol endurance	5 hours

Westland Sea King HAS 6

In the mid-1980s, it became apparent that the HAS 5 needed still further sensor improvement and in October 1987, the UK MoD ordered five new-build Sea Kings to HAS 6 standard. These were delivered in 1990 and went to 824 Squadron (later to 819) at RNAS Prestwick for trials and evaluation.

The main recognition feature is the blade aerial on the side of the helicopter, under the starboard nose. The helicopter is also fitted with enhanced sonics and better computing power in the dipping sonar.

Fleet Air Arm squadrons equipped are 810 (from November 1989), 814 (from October 1990), 819 (two flights), 820 (from January 1990) and 824. 826 Squadron disbanded in July 1993 and its role as the parent for the ships' flights for Type 22 and 23 frigates was taken over by 810 Squadron. Trials continue at Boscombe Down. 814 Squadron is embarked in *Invincible* and 820 Squadron in *Illustrious*.

Armament Standard ASW patrol weapons include up to four Mk 44, Mk 46 or Stingray lightweight torpedoes; or Mk 11 depth bombs. The Sea King is equipped to carry nuclear depth charges (these are no longer operational), and pintle-mounted 7.62 mm GPMGs can also be carried.

Standard mission equipment Sea Searcher

Riding shotgun for Vanguard, *this Sea King HAS 6 displays the markings of 819 Squadron from Prestwick.* (HMS *Neptune*)

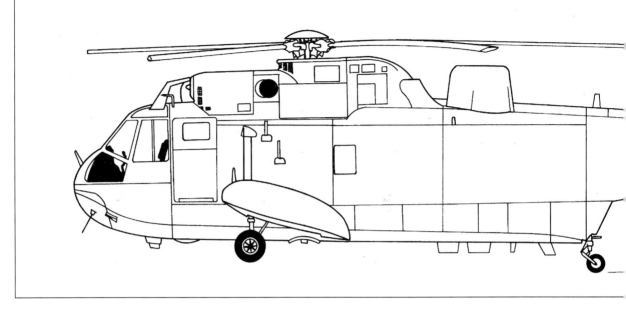

radar, Racal Orange Reaper ESM, GEC-Marconi Type 2069 dipping sonar, Racal RNS 252 navigation system, GEC-Marconi AN/AQS-902G-DS acoustic processing, secure speech, Plessey PTR 446 improved IFF, various sonobuoys. CAE Electronics internal AIMS (advanced integrated magnetic anomaly detection system) ordered in December 1991.

Special mission equipment Some Sea Kings have been fitted with the Ericcson AN/ALQ-167 jammers and the Plessey GPS is due to be fitted in 1997.

Dimensions

Main rotor diameter	18.90 m
Main disc area	280.60 sq m
Tail rotor diameter	3.16 m
Length (overall)	22.15 m
Length (folded)	17.01 m
Width (folded)	5.0 m

Height (overall)	5.13 m
Wheel track	3.96 m

Weights

Empty	7,428 kg (16,379 lb)
Operational	n/a
ASW patrol	n/a
Take-off	9,752 kg (21,503 lb)

Performance

Max cruise speed	112 knots
Cruise speed	100 knots
Service ceiling	3,200 m
ASW patrol endurance	5 hours

NAVAL LAND-BASED HELICOPTERS

Except for the Gazelle training helicopters, all the

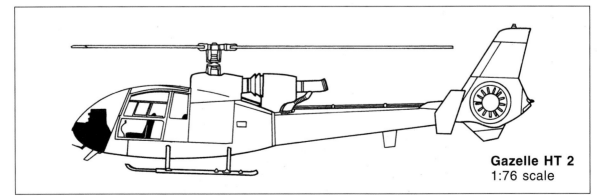

Gazelle HT 2
1:76 scale

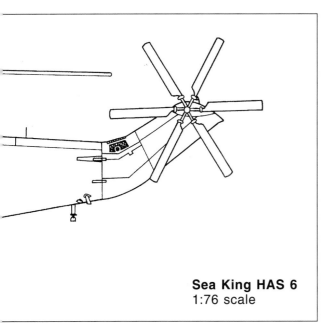

Sea King HAS 6
1:76 scale

Until the 'Options for Change' and 'Front Line First' defence cuts, the Fleet Air Arm's Gazelles also formed the Sharks helicopter display team. Members of the Squadron represented the United Kingdom at the 1994 World Helicopter Championships in Russia, winning third place.

Armament None, but could be configured to carry skid-mounted light machine-guns in a national emergency.

Standard mission equipment The helicopters are configured for training only in peacetime.

Special mission equipment The wartime role is thought to include emergency communications and bomb damage assessment of naval air stations and other installations. It is not known whether a proposal to use the Gazelles for nuclear-biological-chemical (NBC) defence survey has been adopted.

Dimensions

Main rotor diameter	10.50 m
Main disc area	86.59 sq m
Tail rotor diameter	0.37 sq m
Length (overall)	9.53 m
Length (folded)	9.53 m
Width (folded)	2.04 m
Height (overall)	3.18 m

Weights

Empty	980 kg (2,161 lb)
All-up	1,800 kg (3,969 lb)

Performance

Max cruise speed	143 knots
Cruise speed	120 knots
Service ceiling	4,300 m

helicopters in the Fleet Air Arm are capable of being embarked aboard ships of the Royal Navy or Royal Fleet Auxiliary. As a rule, however, the Commando Air Squadrons at RNAS Yeovilton, flying the Sea King HC 4, are land-based, embarking only when required for operations.

Aerospatiale Gazelle HT 2
This is the basic training helicopter of the British Armed Forces in which Fleet Air Arm pilots gain their first rotary-wing experience. The red/white-painted helicopters have been based at Culdrose, Cornwall with 705 Squadron since 1975. The Gazelles are powered by a single Turbomeca Astazou turboshaft engine and maintenance is carried out under contract.

Westland Sea King HC 4
The main support helicopter for 3 Commando Brigade, Royal Marines, the Sea King HC 4 is the

Sea King HC 4 – the standard commando logistic support helicopter which has seen service in the Falklands (Malvinas), Beirut, Kurdistan and Bosnia. (Paul Beaver)

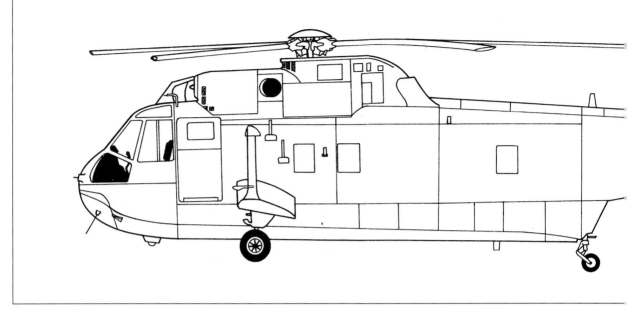

Royal Navy's version of Westland's Commando modification of the US Sikorsky SH-3 design. The Fleet Air Arm acquired the Sea King HC 4s after the Egyptian Navy cancelled an order for anti-submarine Sea Kings from Westland after most of the aircraft had already been built. The careful observer will note the plated-over sonar well in the HC 4's main cabin floor.

Operational During the Falklands (Malvinas) conflict Sea Kings of 845 and 846 Squadrons lifted over 450 tonnes of freight during the first day of the San Carlos landings. The helicopters were later deployed to Beirut to evacuate British and Commonwealth civilians. Although Norway and supporting the Royal Marines in the field is the standard operational role, since 1992, a detachment from 845 Squadron has been deployed in Bosnia-Herzegovina and Croatia in support of the UN Protection Force (UNPROFOR). During this time, the unit has carried out numerous casualty evacuations, carried VIPs and come under sniper fire from all sides. The Sea King HC 4 is flown by the following squadrons: 707 (Commando Training), 772 (Search & Rescue), 845 and 846 (Operational Commando).

Armament The standard weapon fit is a 7.62 mm General Purpose Machine-Gun in the main door on a pintle-mounting.

Standard mission equipment The helicopters are now all fitted for night vision goggle operations with blue/green instrument floodlights. A Fairey Hydraulics rescue hoist is routinely carried, mounting at the main cabin door. A self-defence countermeasures suite is fitted on

deployment, including the AN/APR-39(V) warning receiver. There is combat seating for a maximum of 28 fully equipped Royal Marines and the Sea King HC 4 can carry 3,402 kg (7,501 lb) of freight underslung for a single cargo hook. It carries flotation devices on the undercarriage sponsons at all times.

Special mission equipment Depending on the threat perceived in the operating area, the Sea King HC 4 can be fitted with a variety of add-on self-defence and countermeasure suites. Improved PALL sand filters can also be carried as required, although there is said to be a degrading of performance to the Rolls-Royce Gnome turboshafts in this event.

Dimensions

Main rotor diameter	18.90 m
Main disc area	280.60 sq m
Tail rotor diameter	7.80 sq m
Length (overall)	17.01 m
Length (folded)	17.42 m
Width (folded)	4.98 m
Height (overall)	4.72 m
Track	3.96 m

Weights

Empty	5,700 kg (12,568 lb)
All-up	9,526 kg (21,005 lb)

Performance

Max cruise speed	113 knots
Cruise speed	95 knots
Service ceiling	9,300 m

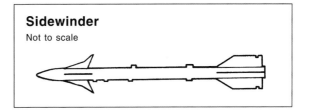

Sidewinder
Not to scale

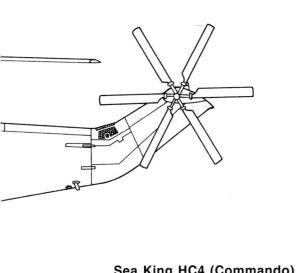

Sea King HC4 (Commando)
1:76 scale

NAVAL AIR WEAPONS

30 mm Aden cannon

The Aden gun was a Second World War development of the Royal Armament Research and Development Establishment at Fort Halstead in conjunction with the Royal Small Arms Factory at Enfield Lock.

The weapon fitted with the Sea Harrier is the fourth generation of Aden cannon, which uses belted ammunition and is mounted in a blister pod under the fuselage of FRS 1 and FA 2. Each Aden has 130 rounds available.

Calibre 30 mm; **Length** 1.64 m (overall), 1.08 m (barrel); **Weight** 87 kg; **Rate of fire** Max 1,400 rounds/min; **Muzzle velocity** 790 m/sec; **Range** Not available.

Aircraft missiles

AIM-9L Sidewinder

Sidewinder is the standard short-range, air-to-air missile in service with the Royal Navy, equipping both marks of Sea Harrier currently embarked in the 'Invincible' class aircraft carriers.

The US-designed AIM-9 missile has been in service around the world for more than 40 years and owes its longevity to the excellent characteristics of the missile body design, coupled with the capability of improving the warhead and seeker

head during its operational life.

The standard variant in the Fleet Air Arm is the third-generation, all-aspect AIM-9L (known as the Nine Lima) which was used operationally in the Falklands (Malvinas) conflict.

Length 2.87 m; **Body diameter** 127 mm; **Wing span** 640 mm; **Launch weight** 87 kg; **Warhead weight** 9.5 kg high explosive; **Fuze** Active laser; **Seeker** All aspect; **Range** 8 km.

AIM-120 AMRAAM

The Sea Harrier FA 2's main armament, it is described as a medium-range (50 km) radar-guided air-to-air missile which comes from GM Hughes in the USA. It has been designed to counter enemy countermeasures and the missile has growth potential which will ensure that it keeps up with technology for at least the next 15 years.

Length 3.65 m; **Body diameter** 178 mm; **Wing span** 530 mm; **Launch weight** 157 kg; **Warhead weight** 22 kg high explosive, directed fragmentation; **Fuze** Active radar; **Seeker** All-aspect.

ALARM

It is likely that the Sea Harrier FA 2 will be configured to carry the ALARM anti-radiation, anti-air defence missile radar missile before the end of the 1990s. It has been designed to attack broadband air defence radars and has the ability to remember the radar's location even if the system has been deactivated during the missile's flight time.

Length 4.3 m; **Body diameter** 224 mm; **Wing span** 720 mm; **Launch weight** 268 kg; **Warhead weight** Classified high explosive; **Fuze** Active laser; **Guidance** Passive radar; **Range** 45 km.

Sea Eagle

This is a British-designed and -developed long-range, radar-guided air-to-surface missile for anti-shipping strike. It equips the Sea Harrier FRS 1 and FA 2 squadrons.

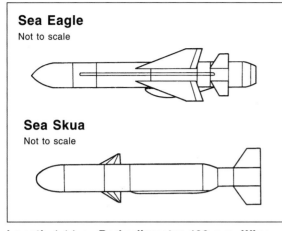

Sea Eagle
Not to scale

Sea Skua
Not to scale

Length 4.14 m; **Body diameter** 400 mm; **Wing span** 1.2 m; **Launch weight** 600 kg; **Warhead weight** 230 kg high explosive, semi-armour piercing; **Fuze** Impact; **Guidance** Inertial and active radar; **Range** 110 km.

Sea Skua

The highly successful medium-range radar-guided anti-shipping missile carried by the Lynx shipborne helicopter which was rushed into service at the end of the Falklands (Malvinas) conflict. During the Gulf conflict, the missile was found to be highly effective against Iraqi patrol boats and about 20 missiles were fired, putting 13 Iraqi or captured Kuwaiti craft out of action.

Length 2.5 m; **Body diameter** 250 mm; **Wing span** 720 mm; **Launch weight** 145 kg; **Warhead weight** 20 kg high explosive, semi-armour piercing; **Fuze** Impact; **Guidance** Semi-active radar; **Range** 18 km.

Sea Eagle – the standard anti-shipping strike weapon of the Sea Harrier fleet. (Paul Beaver)

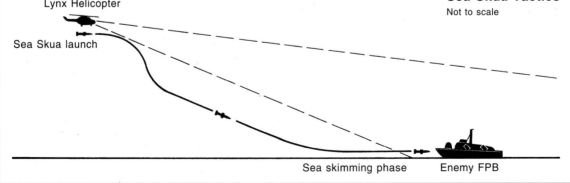

Lynx Helicopter

Sea Skua launch

Sea Skua Tactics
Not to scale

Sea skimming phase   Enemy FPB

Naval aircraft torpedoes and depth charges

Mk 11 depth charge

Now in its Mod 3 state, the Mk 11 depth bomb/charge has been in service for many years. It is carried by all marks of Lynx and Sea King HAS 5 and HAS 6 helicopters for attacking sub-marine targets in shallow water.

Length 1.4 m; **Body diameter** 279 mm; **Weight** 145 kg; **Warhead weight** 80 kg high explosive.

Mk 46 Torpedo

This has been for many years the standard air-launched anti-submarine torpedo for shallow to

Depth charge carried by a Lynx HAS 8. (Westland)

The Mk 46 lightweight ship and aircraft torpedo – now being replaced, it is carried here by a Lynx

Stingray – the latest lightweight torpedo – after release from a Lynx HAS 3 helicopter. (Westland)

intermediate depth action to a range of 11 km. The weapon was used by the Fleet Air Arm in the Falklands (Malvinas) conflict.

Length 2.59 m; **Body diameter** 324 mm; **Weight** 230 kg; **Warhead weight** 44 kg high explosive; **Speed** 45 knots.

Stingray torpedo

This is the latest lightweight torpedo to be developed for the Fleet Air Arm and it is destined to remain in service until 2020, according to latest reports. It is electrically powered and homes to a target submarine by computer-controlled acoustic-linked sonar homing. It entered service in 1991 and is available for Lynx and Sea King helicopters, as well as the various shipborne torpedo weapon systems.

Length 2.6 m; **Body diameter** 234 mm; **Weight** 265 kg; **Warhead weight** 40 kg high explosive; **Speed** 45 knots.

Naval aircraft bombs and rockets

General-purpose bombs Royal Ordnance provides the Sea Harrier fleet with the 227 kg (500 lb) low drag and 454 kg (1,000 lb) general-purpose bomb for ground attack. There are 16 different developed versions of the 454 kg weapon

and the Sea Harrier force can carry the UK Paveway Mk 2 laser-guided version when required.

Cluster bombs These 277 kg weapons can be carried by both marks of Sea Harrier for ground attack, close air support and suppression of enemy air defences.

SNEB rockets The Sea Harrier force is equipped to carry and fire the French-built 68 mm SNEB unguided rocket for the ground attack and close air support roles.

NAVAL AIRCRAFT SENSORS AND EQUIPMENT

Airborne radar

Blue Fox Designed by Ferranti for the Sea Harrier FRS 1, this gives the pilot air search, surface search and air interception capability. It is linked to the aircraft's inertial navigation system and is frequency agile to avoid jamming.

Blue Kestrel The advanced radar for the Merlin helicopter which began flight trials in 1986 and should enter service with the Merlin in about 1998.

Blue Vixen Designed by GEC-Ferranti, this advanced radar has been developed for the Sea Harrier FA 2 to give look down/shoot down capability and good beyond-visual-radar capa-

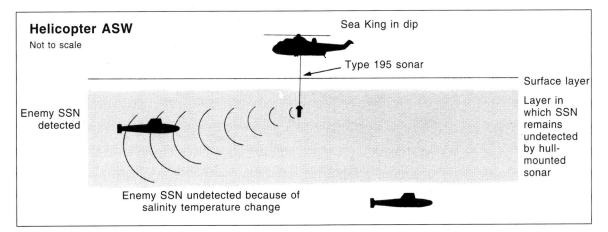

Helicopter ASW

Not to scale

Sea King in dip

Type 195 sonar

Surface layer

Layer in which SSN remains undetected by hull-mounted sonar

Enemy SSN detected

Enemy SSN undetected because of salinity temperature change

bility for the AMRAAM missile system.

Searchwater The airborne early warning radar carried by the Sea King AEW 2A helicopters and developed by Thorn EMI for the detection of low-flying aircraft amd missiles. Also fitted to the Nimrod long-range maritime patrol aircraft. It has advanced processing and classification equipment and is used in conjunction with Jubilee Guardsman IFF and Orange Crop electronic warfare systems.

Sea Searcher The surface radar of the Sea King HAS 5 to give high-definition and over-the-horizon targeting capability. It interfaces with the helicopter's sonar and navigation systems.

Seaspray Mk 1 The original, limited azimuth surface and missile illumination radar for the Sea Skua missile which arms the Lynx HAS 1/2/3 series of shipborne helicopters.

Seaspray Mk 3 The developed 360° radar for the Lynx HAS 8 programme to give better operational capability to the helicopter crews.

Dipping sonar

Type 195M The original Sea King dipping sonar which was fitted to the Sea King HAS 5. The transducer is lowered up to 55 m into the water and it can be used to detect a submarine contact up to 8 nm away. This gives bearing and range data to the sonar operator.

Type 2069 This is the new active dipping sonar for the Sea King HAS 6 which is fitted into the same shape of physical body as the earlier Type 195M.

Type 2095 Said to be the designation which will be used for the new dipping sonar (FLASH) to be carried by the Merlin helicopter.

ROYAL NAVAL AIR SQUADRONS

Squadrons in the Fleet Air Arm are numbered in two series, the 700s for second-line training and trials units, and the 800s for front-line operational squadrons and flights.

702 Squadron The Lynx-equipped small ships training unit at Portland. This unit provides

Dipping sonar – a Sea King HAS 6 bringing its sonar body out of the water on a routine training exercise. (Westland)

operational conversion for pilots and observers.

705 Squadron The basic rotary-wing training squadron, flying the Gazelle HT 2 helicopter at Culdrose. The unit trains and grades helicopter pilots for anti-submarine warfare and commando support duties.

706 Squadron The advanced rotary-wing training squadron for pilots, observers and sonar operators, who have been streamed to fly anti-submarine warfare Sea King (and eventually Merlin) helicopters. Crews graduating to the Sea King AEW 2A fleet are also trained with the unit at Culdrose.

707 Squadron Pilots and aircrewmen who will fly commando support Sea King HC4 helicopters graduate to this unit at Yeovilton. It is also the Fleet Air Arm's centre of excellence for night vision goggle operations. Because of these skills, the unit has been deployed to Northern Ireland to support the security forces from time to time.

750 Squadron The advanced navigation and observer training unit, equipped with the Jetstream turbo-prop trainer.

771 Squadron This unit, based at Culdrose, operates Sea King HAR 5 helicopters for Cornwall and Devon coastal search & rescue duties.

772 Squadron This unit is the search & rescue squadron based at Portland to cover a large area of the Dorset and Devonshire coasts. It is equipped with Sea King HC 4 helicopters.

800 Squadron The squadron converted to Sea Harrier F/A 2 in early 1995 and deployed to the Adriatic in *Invincible* the following July. Its home base is Yeovilton in Somerset.

801 Squadron The first operational Sea Harrier unit to be equipped with the Sea Harrier FA 2, the squadron embarked in *Illustrious* with the aircraft in February 1995. Home base is Yeovilton.

810 Squadron Based at Culdrose, Cornwall, this unit is one of several flying the Sea King HAS 6.

814 Squadron Operational with the Sea King HAS 6 and embarked in *Invincible*. The squadron's home base is Culdrose.

815 Squadron All ships' flights with Lynx helicopters are parented by this unit, based at Portland, Dorset. The unit also carries out trials with new equipment and has been responsible for the changes in the Lynx mission equipment package.

819 Squadron Based at Prestwick, the squadron was expanded in 1993 with the remnants of 826 Squadron and now provides Sea King helicopters for embarkation in Royal Fleet Auxiliaries, Type 22 and Type 23 frigates.

820 Squadron This unit flies Sea King HAS 6 helicopters for anti-submarine duties and is based at Culdrose. Until 1994, it was embarked in *Ark Royal*, but is now *Invincible*'s anti-submarine warfare squadron.

845 Squadron The primary commando air support squadron, equipped with the Sea King HC 4 support helicopter. The unit has a detached flight in Split, Croatia, in support of the United Nations Protection Force (UNPROFOR) and is a centre of excellence for Arctic warfare operations.

846 Squadron The other commando air support

FRADU – the Fan Jet Falcon – in its circa 1990 colours at Yeovilton. (Paul Beaver)

squadron, based at Yeovilton but often deployed to the assault ships or Norway.

847 Squadron In 1995, the former 3 Commando Brigade Air Squadron, Royal Marines, was re-designated as a Royal Naval Air Squadron. It remains based at RNAS Yeovilton.

849 Squadron The world's first helicopter air-borne early warning and control system squadron in 1982. The squadron is divided into three flights equipped with the Sea King AEW 2A: 849A Flight is embarked in *Invincible*; 849B Flight is embarked in *Illustrious*; and 849HQ Flight is based at Culdrose for opera-tional conversion and standards. In the event of war, 849HQ would become 849C and embark in the third aircraft carrier.

899 Squadron The operational conversion and headquarters unit of the Sea Harrier squadrons, based at Yeovilton. Its duties have included bringing the Sea Harrier FA 2 into service and developing the air warfare operational capabili-ties of Sea Harrier pilots. Tactics and doctrine are examined and developed here.

BRNC Flight Aircrew candidates for the Fleet Air Arm are graded for flying duties by the Britannia Royal Naval College Flight, based at Roborough airfield, Plymouth. The Flight was equipped with military-serialled Chipmunk trainers until recently, but grading is now car-ried out in civilian-marked Grob trainers owned by Airwork under contract to the UK Ministry of Defence.

FRADU The Fleet Air Requirements and Direction Unit at Yeovilton is manned and operated by a contractor on behalf of the UK Ministry of Defence. The unit flies civilian-serialled Fan Jet Falcons (FJF). Hunter jets were used to simulate missiles and other fast, sea-skimming targets for warships on work-up until January 1995 when the type was paid off after three decades of service and replaced by Hawks. The FJF corporate jets have been con-figured to carry under-wing pods for electronic warfare and radar training.

CHAPTER SIX

Naval bases and key establishments

AS THE ROYAL Navy has declined in shape and size since the Nott Defence Moratorium in 1981, so the number of bases and establishments has also been reduced. With the ending of the Cold War, the process has been greatly increased in speed and content, resulting not only from the 'Options for Change' and 'Front Line First' cuts, but also from the Conservative Party's political dogma of privatization and competition since 1979.

NAVAL BASES

Devonport

In April 1994, the Naval Base at Plymouth, Devonport, completed a major re-organization to provide a better value-for-money approach to Fleet support operations. Drake, the former Fleet Accommodation Centre, has been enlarged to take over Defiance's Engineering Department and the Fleet Facilities Department. Drake is now a Commodore's command and the whole of the Naval Base is now known as 'HMS *Drake*'. With its proximity to various Royal Marines establishments, Plymouth also has the headquarters of Commodore Amphibious Warfare (COMAW) at Mount Wise.

Faslane

The Clyde Submarine Base, HMS *Neptune*, is home to a squadron of nuclear-powered attack submarines, as well as the United Kingdom's ballistic missile-carrying 'Resolution' and 'Vanguard' class submarines. Faslane has received about £5 billion investment over the last 10 years to make it ready for the 'Vanguard' class submarines, including a new finger-jetty and a covered synchro-lift for work on the new Trident-

carrying submarines. Nearby is the Royal Naval Ordnance Depot of Coulport (on Loch Long) where the Trident ballistic missiles are stored and loaded. In addition, various patrol craft are based at Faslane, which is the headquarters of Commodore Clyde, the local naval commander.

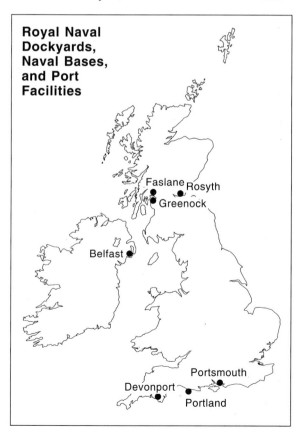

Royal Naval Dockyards, Naval Bases, and Port Facilities

Portland

The naval base facilities are still used for training the ships' companies of British, other European NATO and friendly nations' navies, under the auspices of Flag Officer Sea Training (FOST). Co-located with the naval base is the naval air station, HMS *Osprey*. The naval base is scheduled to close by 1996, with all the facilities moving to Plymouth Devonport. The naval air station will move its operations to Yeovilton in 1998.

Portsmouth

The naval base is home port to the 'Invincible' class aircraft carriers and various destroyer, frigate and mine warfare craft. It is the site of HMS *Victory*'s preservation and is regarded as the home of the Royal Navy. Since 1982, there has been a concentration of the facilities, including the closing of the naval dockyard facilities (which were replaced with the Fleet Maintenance Unit). In 1996, it lost its Flag Officer, becoming the headquarters of Flag Officer Training & Recruitment.

Rosyth

The centre of controversy during the 1994 debate prior to the 'Front Line First' defence cuts, Rosyth has been the Royal Navy's main Scottish mainland naval base for 60 years. It has been the home of the Fishery Protection Squadron, mines countermeasures and frigate squadrons. It was for a time the headquarters of Commodore Minor Warfare Vessels but is now a Forward Operating Base, without a resident squadron. The naval base is a separate entity from the Dockyard.

NAVAL DOCKYARDS

With the rundown of both the surface and submarine fleets, the former Royal Dockyards have been reduced to two – one in England, the other in Scotland. Both are run as commercial concerns by management companies.

The problem for the dockyards has been the move away from steam-driven ships. Modern warships no longer require to have their boilers cleaned every four years and, in fact, the average time between refits is now eight years for surface ships and about ten years in the case of nuclear-powered submarines. For the SSN and SSBN fleet the major work in refit is to replace the nuclear reactor fuel rods and improve sensor systems. For destroyers and escorts, the work is usually on replacing sensors and weapons.

Devonport

Managed by Devonport Maintenance Limited (DML) on behalf of the Secretary of State for Defence, Devonport was once a major shipbuilding centre as well as a major naval base. The

Faslane, the Clyde Submarine Base, from the air. (HMS *Neptune*)

dockyard boasts an impressive three-ship frigate hall for enclosed refit. Under current policies it is scheduled to remain the southern dockyard and will eventually, it is said, be privatized, when DML is expected to be one of the principle bidders. The dockyard will refit 'Vanguard' and 'Trafalgar' class submarines towards the end of the decade.

Rosyth

Said not to have been the Royal Navy's favourite for future ship refits because of the disruption caused by its location (away from the southern-biased geo-centre of the Navy), Rosyth is managed by Thorn-Babcock on behalf of the Secretary of State for Defence. The Rosyth facilities include a synchro-lift for patrol vessels. It has been guaranteed refit work into the next decade.

ORGANIZATION AND MANAGEMENT

Flag Officer Scotland, Northern England & Northern Ireland

FOSNNI's sea areas are now all national waters north of the River Dee (Irish Sea) and River Humber (North Sea). On land, the Command region has been extended to cover Liverpool and Hull; the former becomes a Naval Regional Office (Northern England). The Maritime Headquarters at Pitreavie Castle is retained and it becomes the Naval Regional Office for Scotland and Northern Ireland.

Area Flag Officers

On 1 April 1996, the two South Coast Area Flag Officers, at Portsmouth and Plymouth, hauled down their flags as the modern Royal Navy slimmed down in the wake of Front Line First changes.

Now the United Kingdom has Flag Officer Scotland, Northern England & Northern Ireland (FOSNNI) at Faslane, Plymouth is the headquarters of Flag Officer Sea Training (FOST) and Portsmouth houses Flag Officer Training & Recruitment (FOTR).

Flag Officer Sea Training

Based at Plymouth and responsible for basic operational sea training, including the Channel Exercise Areas. The appointment is Rear Admiral (NATO two-star) level.

Flag Officer Training & Recruiting

This new appointment assumes all responsibility for the Reserves, cadet and university training units. The appointment is Rear Admiral (NATO two-star) level.

Naval Base Commanders

Portsmouth and Plymouth Naval Base Commanders report to the Chief of Fleet Support of all Naval Base activity and to the Second Sea Lord for all personnel matters. Control of the sea areas around the shores of Britain now rests with Commander-in-Chief Fleet. The appointment is Commodore (NATO one-star) level.

Naval regions

In April 1994, there was a major re-organization of the Area Flag Officers' responsibilities and the Naval Regional Boundaries consequentially changed as well. There are now four regions, which the UK MoD says are organized on a 'business basis'. Amongst the regional tasks will be ships' visits and representational tasks.

Following the merger of the duties of the Commander-in-Chief Naval Home Command (CINCNAVHOME) and the Second Sea Lord,

FOTR has taken over regional management of the Royal Naval Reserve, the naval cadets and the University Royal Naval Units.

Naval Regional Office	Land Area
Bristol (Flying Fox)	Wales & Western England
Liverpool	Northern England
London (President)	Eastern England
Pitreavie	Scotland & Northern Ireland

NAVAL AIR STATIONS AND YARDS

Culdrose

Positioned near Helston in Cornwall, Culdrose is home to the Fleet Air Arm's Sea King anti-submarine warfare and airborne early warning squadrons. It is also the main training base.

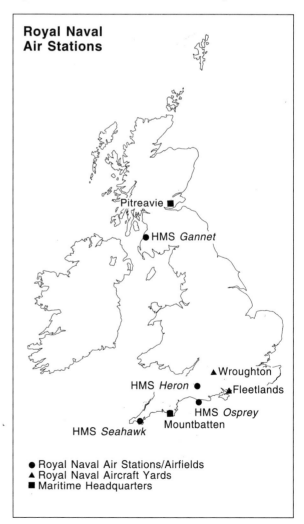

Royal Naval Air Stations

● Royal Naval Air Stations/Airfields
▲ Royal Naval Aircraft Yards
■ Maritime Headquarters

Fleetlands
The all-service helicopter repair yard which was for many years a Royal Naval Aircraft Yard specializing in the maintenance and overhaul of fixed-wing and helicopters. It is located near Portsmouth and Gosport.

Lee-on-Solent
The former naval air station was for many years the Fleet Air Arm's ground training establishment. It is scheduled to close in 1995.

Portland
The helicopter facilities at Portland's HMS *Osprey* are due to close by 1998, when all training flying moves to RAF Shawbury and operational flying will move to Yeovilton. At present, Portland is the home of the small ships' flights equipped with the Lynx helicopter. There is also a resident SAR unit with Sea King HC 4 helicopters.

Prestwick
In December 1993, the Royal Naval Air Station at Prestwick (Gannet) was granted the status of full naval air station. It is the most northerly of the Fleet Air Arm's bases and owes much of its existence to the need to provide anti-submarine warfare helicopter support to the Clyde Submarine Base.

Recent developments to Prestwick include new hangars, accommodation for sailors and a sick bay. In 1993, it was decided to disband 826 Squadron (at RNAS Culdrose) and move the unit's infrastructure to Prestwick for amalgamation with the resident 819 Squadron.

Yeovilton
Established just prior to the Second World War, Yeovilton is the home of the Royal Navy's Sea Harrier force, commando support helicopters, 847 (Royal Marines) Squadron and the Naval Aircraft Servicing Unit. Other lodger units include the Fleet Air Arm Museum and the Fighter Direction School. Besides the Sea Harrier and Sea King HC 4 operational squadrons, the Fan Jet Falcons of FRADU operate from this Somerset air station.

NAVAL ESTABLISHMENTS

Cambridge
The Royal Navy's Gunnery School is on a headland overlooking the approaches to Plymouth Harbour.

Centurion
This is the administration, pay and drafting centre of the Royal Navy, near Gosport.

Collingwood
Weapons engineering and associated skills are taught to Royal Naval ratings at this school near Portsmouth.

Dolphin
The Royal Navy's submarine class at Gosport

Ready for inspection – 'Dolphin', the Submarine Service, prepares to welcome the first Russian submarine to visit Britain. (Paul Beaver)

which was a base for conventional submarines until the paying off of the Type 2400s in 1994. The school and training facilities remain but Flag Officer Submarines moved his headquarters to Northwood in the late 1970s.

Drake
This is the name now given to the Royal Navy's presence at Plymouth. It was formerly the accommodation unit in Devonport.

Dryad
The Royal Navy's School of Maritime Operations is situated at Southwick, near Fareham in Hampshire. It provides warfare training for naval officers and ratings from elementary to the most advanced levels. There are six faculties: operations, above-water warfare, underwater warfare, communications, navigation, and training support. Maritime trade training is carried out at Vernon in Portsmouth.

Excellent
After almost ten years when the name was dormant, the Royal Naval establishment at Whale Island is again named *Excellent*. It now houses the Royal Naval School of Leadership & Management, the *Phoenix* NBCD School, the Royal Naval Regulating School and has several lodger units, including the Headquarters Royal Marines and *King Alfred*.

Haslar
Under 'Front Line First', the current naval hospital will become a tri-Service establishment with satellites at Aldershot, Catterick, Plymouth and one other site to be decided.

Nelson
The administration and accommodation facilities at Portsmouth, closely associated with *Victory*, Admiral Nelson's flagship. Now the headquarters of Flag Officer Surface Flotilla (FOSF).

Northwood
The United Kingdom's joint services command centre and, as Warrior, the headquarters of the Commander-in-Chief Fleet (CINCFLEET) and Flag Officer Submarines (FOSM). Northwood is also a NATO headquarters and is situated north-west of London.

Raleigh
This stone frigate is the Royal Naval Supply School near Plymouth.

Royal Naval Reserve Centre
As part of the Admiralty's plan to integrate the Royal Naval Reserve (RNR) more closely with the Royal Navy, a new RNR Centre was commissioned at Whale Island in June 1994. *King Alfred* will train RNR personnel in the Operations, Logistics, Medical and Public Affairs branches.

Raleigh, the newly refurbished training centre at Torpoint – demonstrating the modern Royal Navy's commitment to training. (RN)

Hong Kong – Tamar, the naval base, moved from Hong Kong Island to Stonecutters' in 1994. It will remain the Royal Navy's last Far East base until 1997. (Paul Beaver)

The Britannia Royal Naval College remains at Dartmouth in South Devon despite defence cuts. (RN)

The Naval Staff College at Greenwich – when it moves to Camberley it will end more than 200 years of direct relationship between Greenwich and the Royal Navy. (Spearhead Exhibitions)

Sultan
This is the marine engineering training school near Gosport.

Overseas establishments

Gibraltar
HMS *Rooke* remains the Royal Navy's administration and accommodation centre at Gibraltar, where there is still a major NATO-orientated communications organization.

Hong Kong
HMS *Tamar* moved from Victoria in 1994 and has taken up residence on Stonecutters', on the other side of the harbour. Here the three remaining patrol craft of the Hong Kong Squadron will remain until June 1997. The facilities have been reduced by about 60 per cent of their size and extent a decade ago, although there is still accommodation/quarters at Victoria (necessitating a regular ferry service to Stonecutters'). The posting of

Captain-in-Charge Hong Kong has been abolished and replaced by Senior Naval Officer Hong Kong, still a Captain RN's appointment.

Naval colleges

Dartmouth
The Britannia Royal Naval College is the naval academy of the Royal Navy to which all potential officers go for training. Situated on the River Dart in Devon, the College is now operator of a training ship, *Waveney*.

Greenwich
Until 1996, this is the Royal Naval Staff College. It is housed in the historical precincts adjacent to the Queen's House and the National Maritime Museum. Under the 'Front Line First' plans, the staff college will move to co-locate with the British Army and Royal Air Force at Camberley, Surrey.

CHAPTER SEVEN

Support services

ROYAL FLEET AUXILIARY SERVICE

The Royal Fleet Auxiliary Service (RFA) is a civilian-manned, UK Ministry of Defence-owned and operated fleet of support ships for the Royal Navy.

Its main task is to resupply warships at sea, providing them with fuel, food, ammunition and other stores whilst the warships are serving away from a shore base. In addition, some ships provide aviation support to the Fleet, others provide logistical support to the Royal Marines, and yet others secure transport for the British Army.

History and origins

The RFA can trace its history back to the days of Elizabethan exploration, when ships known as 'pinks' accompanied fleets. This service was developed during the Napoleonic Wars and following the development of oil-burning warships became increasingly important.

The Royal Fleet Auxiliary Service was first constituted in 1905, when it began its service supporting the Royal Navy with coal and dry stores. When the Fleet started to burn oil instead of coal, around the beginning of the First World War, the RFA bought its first oil tanker.

During the Second World War, the RFA served in every theatre of war, including the Pacific and the Arctic convoys. It has remained civilian-manned since its inception, flying the Blue Ensign (defaced by a gold anchor) and having right of entry to foreign ports.

The tanker and logistic fleets have expanded into new roles since the war and today the task includes giving support to Commonwealth and NATO navies as well as the RN. By 1957, the year after Suez, the RFA had reached a peak in terms of number of hulls, the list including a number of tugs and allied craft now under the control of the Royal Maritime Auxiliary Service (RMAS).

Since 1945, the RFA has been supporting the Fleet in every sea area. It provided invaluable support during the Falklands campaign (1982) and the Gulf conflict (1991).

Today, because most RFAs carry defensive weapons, diplomatic clearance (as for a warship) is normally sought before entry is made.

Modern management

The Royal Fleet Auxiliary Service (RFA) is managed by the Director of Supplies and Transport (Ships & Fuel). DST (SF) is one of five Directorates which make up the Royal Navy Supply and Transport Service (RNSTS), which is headed by the Director General Supplies & Transport (Navy). DGST (N) reports to the Chief of Fleet Support, who has a seat on the Admiralty Board.

In the 1990s, the Royal Fleet Auxiliary Service employs about 2,500 officers and ratings drawn from the British merchant navy, and is one of the largest employers in British shipping.

UK personnel serve under National Maritime Board conditions, supplemented by special RFA clauses on security and actions in the event of war. Personnel usually follow traditional merchant seamen training but a considerable overlay of naval skills training is employed to ensure that officers and ratings can fulfil their wartime tasks.

Many of the current Royal Fleet Auxiliaries carry naval parties aboard to perform key tasks, such as helicopter maintenance. In the event of war, a Royal Navy officer would be appointed to oversee command of the RFA, whose own captain would still be responsible for the RFA's safety and smooth operation.

The opportunity to work with the RFA is open to all UK merchant seamen, who can transfer from their own merchant companies, or to cadets who can enlist from school or college. The work is unusual and interesting; deck officers in particular are expected to fulfil demanding roles such as becoming a Helicopter Controller (HC) or a Flight Deck Officer (FDO).

Deck Officers These officers carry out navigational, tactical and bridge watchkeeping duties on RFAs. Their life differs considerably from life in a regular merchant company: how many officers are allowed to beach a ship deliberately? LSL officers (LSL officers are those with extra training who man the 'Sir Lancelot' class Landing Ship Logistics – most of whom experienced South Atlantic waters in 1982) have to as part of their job! Deck officers are responsible for the cargo in all ships (except in stores support vessels, when they are responsible for the freight only during RAS – replenishment at sea).

Engineer Officers These men control the propulsion and auxiliary systems aboard RFAs, whether they are motor ships with modern diesels, like the 'Rover' class vessels, or steam turbines like those found on ships of the 'Ol' class. Most ships have automatic machinery control and in the main the engines are more powerful than those found in other merchant ships of the same tonnage.

Radio Officers RFAs, because of the naval connection, have highly complex radio equipment for communications both naval and private. Training is frequently carried out at *Collingwood*. Most ships carry extensive electronic test and maintenance gear.

Electrical Officers These are a sub-specialization of the Engineering Department aboard RFAs and are responsible for the maintenance of modern sophisticated electrical machinery.

Pursers These men manage the catering and the pay/accounting functions in the ships of the RFA. Pursers act as medical officers in the absence of a surgeon in the ship's company.

Ships' surgeons All RFAs carry medical personnel and most of the large ones have a surgeon who looks after the ship's company and can on occasions be called upon to perform emergency surgery when an RFA goes to the assistance of a ship in trouble. RFA surgeons work closely with their RN counterparts both ashore and afloat.

Seaman grades are also specialist in nature,

Ranking structure
Officers

Deck branch	Engineer branch	Electrical branch	Purser	Radio	Surgeon
Commodore	Commodore	No equivalent	–	–	–
Master	Chief Engineer	–	–	–	–
Chief Master	Second Engineer	–	–	–	Ship's surgeon
First Off.	–	Senior Elect. Off.	Senior Purser	Senior RO	–
Second Off.	Third Engineer	First Elect. Off.	Purser	First RO	–
Uncertificated SO	Uncertificated Third Engineer	–	–	–	–
Third Off.	Fourth Engineer	Second Elect. Off.	Assist. Purser	Second RO Junior RO	–
	Uncert. Fourth Engineer Junior Engineer	Junior Elect. Off.	–	–	–

Ratings
(Note: RFA Carpenters rank above all other craftsmen including CPO Deck and this position does not 'go through the ranks'.)

Deck Dept	Engineer Dept	Catering	Catering
CPO Deck	CPO	–	Chief Cook
PO Deck	PO Motorman	PO Steward	Ship's Cook
Quartermaster	–	–	–
Seaman IA	Motorman IA	Catering Storekeeper	Second Cook and Baker
Seaman IB	Motorman I	–	–
Seaman II	Motorman II	Steward	Assistant Cook
Junior Seaman	–	–	Junior Catering Rating (JCR)

dealing with the Deck, Engine Room, Catering and Communications Departments. There is a rating uniform but it is not used in practice; enforcement is difficult because of the unionization of the RFA. Many ratings find the standard RN working rig a useful 'uniform', however, when working the ship.

The Service

The most important service provided by the RFA is underway replenishment at sea – RAS – which can transfer either solids, RAS (S), or liquids, RAS (L). This involves precise seamanship as fuel, water, food, ammunition and stores are transferred at sea whilst both vessels are underway. During RAS (L), the two vessels (or more if a group RAS is taking place) are linked by a flexible hose for the transfer of FFO (furnace fuel oil), DIESO or AVCAT (aviation gasoline). The ships maintain a steady course but can manoeuvre if required – in this technique the RN/RFA leads the world.

RAS (S) is carried out by means of jackstay rigs. Today, the weather is not the problem it used to be and the methods and rigs used are constantly being uprated. The increasing use of helicopters, either borne by an RFA vessel or by another ship, has meant that a technique called vertrep (vertical replenishment) has been refined for the transfer of bulky items and of items moving to and from several sources when it is not possible to come alongside. On RFAs, helicopter landing pads are served by special lifts and loads are assembled on the flight deck using rope slings and nets. Weight limits are important and it is interesting to reflect that the flight decks of most RFAs are about 60 ft (18 m) above sea level, higher than is the case on the average aircraft carrier at 50 ft (15 m) above sea level. For anti-submarine warfare helicopter operations, Royal Navy personnel are carried but this does not alter the ships' unique position of being classified as government ships on non-commercial business.

The supplying ship usually maintains a steady course – the role of 'guide' – while the recipient takes 'station' on her, whether for astern or abeam replenishment, the former only being available for liquids when the transfer is 'floated' aft. Lines are put across using the old self-loading rifle, fitted with a special attachment; various wires to show position are sent across in addition to the fuel lines.

The ships

In late 1993, there were 24 Royal Fleet Auxiliaries in commission: 11 Fleet and Support Tankers; six Dry Cargo Fleet Replenishment Ships, five Landing Ships (Logistics), an Aviation Training Ship and a Forward Repair Ship.

A new class of two Auxiliary Oilers Replenishment (AOR), *Fort Victoria* and *Fort George*, has since entered service.

All Royal Fleet Auxiliaries are built and maintained to Lloyds of London and UK Department of Transport standards, with the addition of naval equipment, including search radar, satellite communications systems, air defence missiles and guns. The larger RFAs have helicopters detached from the Fleet Air Arm, including the Sea King HAS 6, and could operate Sea Harrier combat aircraft in an emergency.

Fleet replenishment ships (AOR)

Class 'Fort Victoria'

Name *Fort Victoria*; **Displacement** 32,300 tons (full load); **Length** 203 m overall; **Beam** 30 m; **Draught** 10 m; **Propulsion** 2 x Crossley SEMT-Pielstick diesels (23,904 hp); 2 x shafts; **Speed** 20 knots; **Complement** 126 RFA, 32 RN, 122 aircrew; **Armament** 2 x 20 mm (possible Goalkeeper); **Sensors** 1 x 966 navigational and helicopter control radar; **Aircraft** 5 x Sea King/Merlin (3 in hangar); **Builders** Harland & Wolff; **Ordered** May 1986; **Launched** 1990; **Commissioned** 1994.

In 1978, the Royal Fleet Auxiliary Service developed the concept of a one-stop ship capable of delivering the large variety of stores required by the Royal Navy from one ship. In 1981, a Staff Target was generated and feasibility studies were carried out by the Ministries of Defence and Industry; in 1983, the project became a Staff Requirement and approval was given in 1984. In May 1986, an order was placed with Harland & Wolff after competitive tendering. The ship was four years late entering service.

The AOR is the first modern RFA with a comprehensive weapons fit, including the Seawolf point defence missile system and early warning provided by the Type 996 radar on the foremast. Decoys include the Sea Gnat CM launcher and the Type 182 towed decoy. Command and control operations will be undertaken by a system modelled on the Type 23 frigate's system.

Harland & Wolff (Belfast) was the prime contractor; they worked with Yarrow Shipbuilders Combat System Engineering Centre at Yarrow, the ship weapon system authority, which designed, procured and integrated the Royal Navy manned weapon defence system. Specialist design advice was also provided by BAeSEMA.

Fort Victoria is the most sophisticated replenishment vessel in Europe and the builders, as prime contractors, received the first 'whole ship' contract to be awarded by the Ministry of Defence.

Name *Fort George*; **Displacement** 32,300 tons (full load); **Length** 203 m overall; **Beam** 30 m; **Draught** 10 m; **Propulsion** 2 x Crossley SEMT-Pielstick diesels (23,900 bhp), 2 x shafts; **Speed** 18 knots; **Complement** 126 RFA, 32 RN, 122 aircrew; **Armament** 2 x 20mm (possible Goalkeeper); **Sensors** 1 x 966 navigational and helicopter control radar; **Aircraft** 5 x Sea King/Merlin (3 in hangar); **Builders** Harland & Wolff; **Laid down** 9 March 1989; **Launched** 1 March 1991; **Commissioned** 16 July 1993.

Large fleet tankers

Class 'Ol'

Name *Olwen* (ex-*Olympus*); **Pennant number**

Fort George – one of the new breed of one-stop auxiliaries. (Photo Press)

A122; **Flight deck code** OW; **Standard displacement** 9,360 tons; **Full displacement** 36,000 tons; **Length** 197.5 m overall; **Beam** 25.6 m; **Draught** 11.1 m; **Propulsion** 2 x steam turbines (26,500 shp); **Range** 10,000 nm at 16 knots; **Speed** 20 knots; **Complement** 108 officers and ratings (plus aircrew); **Armament** 2 x Oerlikon 20 mm, guns; **Sensors** Surface search and navigation; **Aircraft** 2 x Sea King HAS 6; **Small craft** 8 x ship's boats; **Builders** Hawthorn Leslie; **Commissioned** 21 June 1965.

The 'Ol' class were the largest and fastest ships in the RFA when first commissioned; *Olwen* and *Olmeda* were originally named *Olympus* and *Oleander* respectively when built in 1965 but, due to confusion with *Olympus* and *Leander*, they were subsequently renamed in 1967. Aircraft hangerage is split into two: three helicopters are stored on the port side and one on the starboard. These ships provide training billets for naval helicopters as well as homes for detached helicopters used in the vertrep role. Each vessel can carry 24,260 tons of oil.

Name *Olna*; **Pennant number** A123; **Flight deck code** ON; **Complement** 27 officers and 62 ratings; **Aircraft** 2 Sea King HAS 6; **Vehicles** May be stored in hangars; **Builders** Hawthorn Leslie; **Commissioned** 1 April 1966; **Other details** As for *Olwen*.

Small fleet tankers

Class 'Rover'

Name *Grey Rover*; **Pennant number** A269; **Flight deck code** GY; **Standard displacement** 4,700 tons; **Full displacement** 11,522 tons; **Length** 140.6 m overall; **Beam** 19.2 m; **Draught** 7.3 m; **Propulsion** 2 x diesels; **Range** 15,000 nm at 15 knots; **Speed** 19 knots; **Complement** 49 officers and ratings; **Armament** 2 x Oerlikon 20 mm, guns; **Sensors** Decca Navigator, SATNAV; **Aircraft** Helicopter-capable up to Sea King size; **Small craft** 3 x ship's boats; **Vehicles** None; **Builders** Swan Hunter; **Commissioned** 10 April 1970.

The 'Rover' class are the small fleet tankers which are used to replenish frigates on deployment and which cost between £3 million and £7 million to build. The original engines have had to be replaced on several occasions but they have a comfortable pitch propeller and a bow thruster for berthing. The two Pielstick diesel engines develop 15,300 bhp. They can be recognized by the large funnel which occasionally bears a badge, such as

Olwen *is due for replacement but still giving sterling service.* (Photo Press)

the 'Children Warning' road sign of the FOST tanker at Portland on sea training duties.

The ships were specially designed to meet the needs of the RFA and are capable of supplying 6,600 tons each of the usual liquids: furnace fuel oil, diesel, aviation spirit, lubricating oil, fresh water and some limited dry cargo which can be handled via vertrep from the flight deck; there is no hangar.

Name *Gold Rover*; **Pennant number** A271; **Flight deck code** GV; **Complement** 16 officers and 38 ratings; **Commissioned** 24 March 1974; **Other details** As for *Grey Rover*.

Name *Black Rover*; **Pennant number** A273; **Flight deck code** BV; **Complement** 16 officers and 38 ratings; **Commissioned** 23 August 1974; **Other details** As for *Grey Rover*.

Support tankers

Class 'Leaf'

Name *Brambleleaf (ex-Hudson Cavalier)*; **Pennant number** A81; **Displacement** 37,747 tons (full load); **Length** 170.7 m overall; **Beam** 25.9 m; **Draught** 11 m; **Propulsion** 2 x diesels; **Range** 15,000 nm at 12 knots; **Speed** 15.5 knots; **Complement** 60 officers and ratings; **Armament** 2 x Oerlikon 20 mm, guns; **Sensors** Navigational radar only; **Small craft** 4 x ship's boats; **Builders** Cammell Laird; **Launched** 22 January 1976; **Completed** September 1979; **Commissioned** 6 May 1980.

These vessels are usually chartered to the Ministry of Defence for the transportation of FFO, DIESO and AV fuel in bulk between oil terminals and MoD (N) storage facilities such as Gosport. They are also used for consolidating Fleet tankers and for replenishment at sea in a limited capacity. On chartering, the vessels have been refitted with RAS gear for the transfer of liquids, mail, personnel and light loads. They have limited helicopter facilities.

Bayleaf and *Brambleleaf* took part in the 1982 Falklands operation, in support of the Task Force.

Name *Bayleaf (ex-Hudson Progress)*; **Pennant number** A109; **Launched** 27 October 1981; **Completed** May 1982; **Other details** As for *Brambleleaf*, but note chartered to UK MoD.

Name *Oakleaf (ex-Oktania)*; **Pennant number** A111; **Displacement** 50,000 tons (full load); **Length** 173 m; **Beam** 32 m; **Draught** 11 m; **Propulsion** 1 x Burmeister & Wain oil engine (12,000 bhp), 1 x shaft; **Range** 15,000 nm at 12 knots; **Speed** 14 knots; **Complement** 36 officers and ratings; **Armament** Guns; **Sensors** Navigational radar; **Builders** Uddevalla (Sweden); **Completed** 1985; **Purchased** 1986.

Name *Orangeleaf (ex-Balder London)*; **Full displacement** 33,751 tons; **Accepted** 26 March 1984; **Commissioned** 2 May 1984.

Fleet replenishment ships

Class 'Fort Grange'

Name *Fort Grange*; **Pennant number** A385;
Flight deck code FG; **Standard displacement**
8,300 tons; **Full displacement** 23,384 tons;
Length 184 m overall; **Beam** 24 m; **Draught**
9 m; **Propulsion** 1 x diesel (23,200 hp); **Range**
10,000 nm at 20 knots; **Speed** 22 knots;
Complement 127 RFA, 45 RN, 36 RNSTS
(civilians); **Armament** 2 x 20 m Oerlikon GAM-
B01, guns; **Sensors** Navigation radar only;
Aircraft 4 x Sea King; **Small craft** 8 x ship's
boats; **Vehicles** Logistic and stacking; **Builders**
Scott-Lithgow; **Laid down** 9 November 1973;
Launched 9 December 1976; **Completed**
November 1978; **Commissioned** 6 April 1978.

Fort Grange and *Fort Austin* are designed to
replenish RN warships with naval armaments and
victualling (including refrigerated) stores underway. Stores are palletized for greater efficiency in
handling. Accommodation standards are high,
with individual cabins for officers and senior POs.

Both ships saw service in the South Atlantic
and *Fort Grange* was the centre of unwanted
attention from an Argentine C-130 Hercules
whilst still an estimated 1,000 nm (1,852 km)
from San Carlos. Luckily, the aircraft did not
attack the unarmed ship; the latter was carrying a
flight of 824 Squadron Sea Kings at the time. *Fort
Austin* served as an ammunition ship during the
San Carlos landings and was also attacked.

Name *Fort Austin*; **Pennant number** A386;
Flight deck code FA; **Standard displacement**
8,300 tons; **Full displacement** 22,890 tons;
Length 184 m overall; **Beam** 24 m; **Draught**
14.9 m; **Propulsion** 1 x diesel (23,200 hp);
Range 10,000 nm at 20 knots; **Speed** 22 knots;
Complement 127 RFA, 45 RN, 36 RNSTS
(civilians); **Armament** 2 x 20 mm Oerlikon GAM-
B01, guns; **Sensors** Navigation radar only;
Aircraft 4 x Sea King; **Small craft** 8 x ship's
boats; **Vehicles** Logistic and stacking; **Builders**
Scott-Lithgow; **Laid down** 9 December 1975;
Launched 8 March 1978; **Completed** January
1979; **Commissioned** 11 May 1979.

Class 'Regent'

Name *Resource*; **Pennant number** A480; **Flight
deck code** RS; **Full displacement** 22,890 tons;
Length 195.1 m; **Beam** 23.5 m; **Draught** 8.7 m;
Propulsion 2 x Foster-Wheeler boilers; 2 x AEI
turbines (20,000 shp); **Range** 12,000 nm at 18
knots; **Speed** 20 knots; **Complement** 134 RFA,
37 RNSTS; **Armament** Fitted for 2 x 20 mm

Oerlikon, 2 x 7.62 mm MGs; **Sensors**
Navigational radar, SCOT; **Aircraft** Flight deck
fitted; **Small craft** 8 x ship's boats, 1 x supply
craft; **Vehicles** Logistic and stacking; **Builders**
Scotts, Greenock; **Commissioned** 16 May 1967;
Refits Several, including 1980–81.

The two fleet replenishment ships of the 'Regent'
class were ordered on 24 January 1963 to operate
in support of the Fleet, particularly the larger
units such as aircraft carriers. *Resource*, the
remaining ship, carries ammunition, explosives,
food and naval stores, including aircraft spares.
Replenishment is carried out at sea using jackstay
rigs or ships' helicopters.

Aviation training ship

Class 'Argus'

Name *Argus* (ex-*Contender Bezant*); **Pennant
number** A135; **Flight deck code** AS;
Displacement 26,420 tons (full load); **Length**
175 m overall; **Beam** 30.4 m; **Draught** 8.2 m;
Propulsion Twin Pielstick 18PC 2.5V engines
(11,700 bhp each); **Range** 20,000 nm at 19
knots; **Speed** 18 knots; **Complement** 23 officers
and 56 men (RFA), 3 officers and 35 ratings
(RN), 42 officers and 95 ratings (Squadron
Training Detachment); **Armament** Guns;
Sensors Navigational and helicopter control;
Aircraft 6 x Sea King (12 x Sea King in
transport); **Conversion** By Harland & Wolff;
Commissioned 1981 and February 1987.

Purchased to replace the ageing helicopter support
ship, *Engandine*, the former ro-ro container cargo
vessel, *Contender Bezant* was converted at Belfast
to a Royal Navy specification. The greatest visible structural change was the addition of a seven-
tier deckhouse which extends the existing
accommodation to cope with a maximum complement of 254 men.

For flying operations, a five-spot flight deck has
been sectionally manufactured to totally enclose
the large hangar deck (larger than that of an aircraft carrier), which is capable of accommodating
the ship's complement of six Sea King helicopters
(both ASW and AEW capable) and up to 12 Sea
Harriers under transportation. Two flight deck lifts
have been installed. The mooring deck has been
extended to form a continuous platform.

For damage control, additional watertight bulk-
heads have been fitted and three special doors
have been fitted to the hangar level deck. There is
vehicular access to the hangar deck via the former
ro-ro door aft (the forward door has been sealed).

Replenishment at sea is possible using a crane

rig for RAS (L) of diesel cargo; the ship can carry 4,436 cu m of the fuel, a capability which greatly enhances its flexibility. Accommodation is of a high standard, with many of the Royal Navy officers and senior ratings having their own single cabins, some with shared toilet facilities. All RFA personnel have single cabins.

Argus is powered by two Pielstick engines and the machinery has been arranged to operate to Lloyds Unmanned Machinery space notation, controlled at all times from the bridge with emergency or maintenance local control. There is an automatic power management system for electrical systems associated with flight deck operations and emergency systems.

Argus was based at Portland until 1996.

Forward repair ship

Class 'Stena'

Name *Diligence* (ex-*Stena Inspector*); **Pennant number** A132; **Flight deck code** DL; **Gross displacement** 6,550 tons; **Full displacement** 10,765 tons; **Length** 112 m overall; **Beam** 20.5 m; **Draught** 6.8 m; **Propulsion** 5 x Nohab-Polar diesels and 4 x electric motors, 1 x shaft (6,000 shp), bow thrusters (3,000 hp), azimuth thrusters (3,000 hp); **Range** 5,000 nm at 12 knots; **Speed** 12 knots; **Complement** 41 officers and ratings (RFA), 80 officers and ratings (RN), accommodation for 202 (some temporary); **Armament** 4 x 20 mm Oerlikon Mk 9, Shield decoy launchers; **Aircraft** Flight deck only; **Builders** Gresundsvaret AB (Sweden); **Completed** 1981; **Chartered** (for Falklands STUFT) 25 May 1982; **Purchased** October 1983; **Accepted** 12 March 1984.

This multi-purpose vessel was designed for operations in the commercial sector of the North Sea but was converted to a naval role acting in the support of warships operating around the Falkland Islands by Clyde Dock Engineering. Submarine accommodation, workshops, cranes, naval communications and other equipment was added during the conversion. The ship has a dynamic positioning system and special anchors. The flight deck is stressed for all helicopter operations up to Chinook size.

Landing ships logistics

Class 'Sir Lancelot'

Name *Sir Bedivere*; **Pennant number** L3004; **Flight deck code** BV; **Light displacement** 3,270

Argus – taken up from trade and deployed around the world, the ship's last overseas operations were in the Adriatic. (Munters)

tons; **Full displacement** 5,674 tons; **Length** 125.6 m overall; **Beam** 18.2 m; **Draught** 4 m (beaching ability); **Propulsion** 2 x Mirrlees diesels (9,400 bhp); **Range** 8,000 nm at 15 knots; **Speed** 17 knots; **Complement** 65 officers and ratings; war load of 340 troops; **Armament** 2 x Oerlikon 20 mm, guns; **Sensors** Navigational radar only; **Aircraft** Accommodation for Gazelle AH 1 or Lynx AH 1/7; **Small craft** 4 x ship's boats, 2 x Gemini; **Vehicles** All types of military vehicle may be carried; **Builders** Hawthorn Leslie; **Laid down** October 1965; **Launched** 20 July 1966; **Completed** 1967; **Commissioned** 18 May 1967.

Name *Sir Geraint*; **Pennant number** L3027;

Sir Bedivere, *the first of the 'Round Table' class, seen here at Gibraltar.* (Photo Press)

Flight deck code GR; **Light displacement** 3,270 tons; **Full displacement** 5,674 tons; **Length** 125.6 m overall; **Beam** 18.2 m; **Draught** 4 m (beaching ability); **Propulsion** 2 x Mirrlees diesels (9,400 bhp); **Range** 8,000 nm at 15 knots; **Speed** 17 knots; **Complement** 65 officers and ratings; war load of 340 troops; **Armament** 2 x Oerlikon 20 mm, guns; **Sensors** Navigational radar only; **Aircraft** Accommodation for Gazelle AH 1 or Lynx AH 1/7; **Small craft** 4 x ship's boats; **Vehicles** All types of military vehicle may be carried; **Builders** Fairfield; **Laid down** June 1965; **Launched** 26 January 1967; **Completed** 1967; **Commissioned** 12 July 1967.

Name *Sir Percivale*; **Pennant number** L3027; **Flight deck code** PV; **Builders** Hawthorn Leslie; **Laid down** April 1966; **Launched** 4 October 1967; **Completed** 1968; **Commissioned** 23 March 1968; **Other details** As for *Sir Geraint*.

Name *Sir Tristram*; **Pennant number** L3036; **Flight deck code** TM; **Full displacement** 5,800 tons; **Length** 134.4 m overall; **Small craft** 4 x ship's boats; **Laid down** February 1966; **Launched** 12 December 1966; **Completed** 1967; **Commissioned** 14 September 1967; **Other details** Rebuilt and lengthened in 1985.

These ships, known as landing ship logistics (LSLs), were originally ordered by the Ministry of Transport for use by the Army but in 1970–71 management and manning was taken over by the RFA. The 'Sir Lancelot' class (all vessels of the class are named for knights of the Round Table) are designed as multi-purpose troop and heavy vehicle carriers and are employed in peacetime on regular voyages from their home in Marchwood, near Southampton, to Antwerpen and Northern Ireland. They are fitted for roll-on-roll-off traffic with bow and stern doors and can undertake vehicle maintenance; helicopters can be operated during day or night from the ships' decks and there is a helicopter deck on the stern. Mexeflotes can be used as pontoons for ferrying troops and vehicles ashore or the craft can beach in the traditional landing craft mode.

LSLs have a unique and vital role anywhere in the world, including east of Suez, where *Sir Lancelot* played an essential part in the East Pakistan flood relief operations of 1970. In wartime, it is not clear what the exact role of the class would be, whether supporting the Army in the Central Front or the Royal Marines and amphibious forces in Norway or the Atlantic islands; the Chiefs of Staff will have to decide the priority.

Sir Galahad – *the replacement for the LSL sunk in the Falklands.* (Photo Press)

All six LSLs were heavily involved in the Falkland Islands conflict of 1982, in which *Sir Tristram* was badly damaged and *Sir Galahad* was sunk (in June). A replacement ship was ordered from Swan Hunter in September 1984.

Name *Sir Galahad*; **Pennant number** L3505; **Light displacement** 3,080 tons; **Full displacement** 8,585 tons; **Length** 140.5 m overall; **Beam** 19.5 m; **Draught** 4.3 m; **Propulsion** 2 x Mirrlees Blackstone diesels, 2 x shafts (13,320 hp); **Range** 13,000 nm at 15 knots; **Speed** 18 knots; **Complement** 49 (17 officers), 343 troops; **Armament** 2 x 20 mm Oerlikon GAM-BO3, 2 x 12.7 mm Mgs; **Aircraft** 1 x Sea King HC 4; **Builders** Swan Hunter.

Ship designations

The Royal Fleet Auxiliary, in common with other NATO-associated organizations, uses abbreviations to describe ships and their role: **AEFS** Fleet Replenishment Ship; **AOF (L)** Large Fleet Tanker; **AOF (S)** Small Fleet Tanker; **LSL** Landing Ship Logistics.

ROYAL MARITIME AUXILIARY SERVICE

In October 1976, the Port Auxiliary Service combined with the Royal Maritime Auxiliary Service (RMAS) to form the organization which now comprises the major part of the Marine Services organization that exists to support the Royal Navy.

The service comprises some 500 hulls, of which approximately 300 are self-propelled. It provides a versatile, flexible and cost-effective service, which includes the use of harbour tugs and pilots to assist ships of the Fleet when berthing and unberthing, delivering fuel, water and victualling stores with purpose-built vessels and craft to ships in harbour and at anchor, transporting ammunition, ferrying personnel to and from ships, and providing specially designed vessels for other tasks such as mooring and salvage, torpedo recovery, underwater research and development and degaussing.

These support operations are carried out mainly in UK waters and at Gibraltar, but some RMAS vessels have been deployed as far afield as Icelandic waters and the South Atlantic.

RMAS vessels are easily recognized by their buff-coloured superstructure and black hulls and by their ensign, which is blue and defaced on the fly by a yellow anchor over two yellow wavy lines.

The service is administered nationally from its Bath headquarters by the Director of Marine Services (Naval); local control of vessels is in the hands of the Captains of the Port or Resident Naval Officer at the vessels' base ports.

RMAS vessels and craft are manned totally by civilians (civil servants). For suitably recommended deck ratings the opportunity exists to attend nautical colleges, where they can prepare for examinations and, if successful, rise to officer status. Engineering officers are recruited from former apprentices, mainly from the Royal

Dockyards. Unless already qualified they also must attend college to obtain the relevant qualifications. Deck and engineering officers may also be recruited directly from external sources provided they have the required UK Department of Transport (DOT) qualification appropriate to the relevant grade.

Ocean tugs

Ocean tugs and large naval base tugs are employed in the towing of vessels from one naval port to another and when HM ships at the end of

Rollicker *guides* Illustrious *into Plymouth Devonport to start her refit in 1991.* (Richard Lappas/Photo Press)

their working life are moved to commercial ports for disposal.

The planning of coastal tows is conducted by the Operations Staff at the Marine Services headquarters, in conjunction with Royal Naval and civilian authorities; the tow is then undertaken by the nominated tugs under the operational control of the appropriate Sea Area Commander.

The tugs are also available for ocean rescue and to give assistance to disabled and stricken vessels.

Class 'Roysterer'

Name *Roysterer*; **Pennant number** A361; **Displacement** 1,630 tons (full load); **Length** 54 m; **Beam** 12.3 m; **Draught** 6.4 m; **Propulsion** 2 x Mirrlees diesels (4,500 bhp); **Range** 12,500 nm at 12 knots; **Speed** 15 knots; **Complement** 28 (10 RN officers and ratings in salvage party); **Armament** None; **Builders** Holmes; **Completed** 26 April 1972.

Name *Robust*; **Pennant number** A366; **Builders** Holmes; **Completed** February 1973.

Name *Rollicker*; **Pennant number** A502; **Builders** Holmes; **Completed** 6 April 1974.

Particularly well suited for ocean salvage, towing and rescue duties, these powerful craft cost about £2 million each. Their bollard pull is 50 tons and they can work in harbours as easily as other large tugs. In fact, they are the largest and certainly the most powerful such vessels to operate with the RMAS or the Royal Navy. In addition to their normal merchant crew, they can accommodate a ten-man RN salvage crew and a large number of survivors for short periods.

Harbour tugs

When berthing and unberthing in Dockyard ports and bases, larger warships and RFAs require assistance. This is undertaken by the combined efforts of the RMAS Pilots, locally based RMAS tugs and shore-based riggers.

The tugs are positioned by Pilots to assist vessels when making tight turns and other manoeuvres. Onshore, the riggers stand by to take lines, position the vessel and provide bows and gangways for safe access.

Class Improved 'Girl'

Name *Edith*; **Pennant number** A177; **Standard displacement** 138 tons; **Length** 18.6 m; **Beam** 5 m; **Draught** 2.2 m; **Propulsion** 1 x diesel (495 hp); **Range** Unknown; **Speed** 10 knots;

Complement 6; **Builders** Dunston; **Completed** 5 June 1969.

Lighter than the 'Girl' class, the modified ships are more similar to the 'Dog' class in appearance, having twin uptakes on the after end of the small deckhouse.

Name *Daphne*; **Pennant number** A165; **Builders** Dunston; **Completed** 19 December 1968.

Class 'Adept' (TUTT)

Name *Adept*; **Pennant number** A224; **Displacement** 450 tons; **Length** 38.8 m overall; **Beam** 9.4 m; **Draught** 3.4 m; **Propulsion** 2 x Ruston diesels (3,000 hp); **Range** Unknown; **Speed** 12 knots; **Complement** 10 officers and ratings; **Armament** None; **Builders** Dunston; **Laid down** 23 July 1979; **Launched** 27 August 1980; **Completed** 20 October 1980.

Name *Bustler*; **Pennant number** A225; **Builders** Dunston; **Launched** 20 February 1981; **Completed** 14 April 1981.

Name *Capable*; **Pennant number** A226; **Builders** Dunston; **Launched** 2 July 1981; **Completed** 11 September 1981.

Name *Careful*; **Pennant number** A227; **Builders** Dunston; **Launched** 12 January 1982; **Completed** 5 March 1982.

The latest tugs (or twin units tractor) to enter service, the 'Adept' class are dual coastal or harbour towing craft with a bollard pull of 27.5 tons. Their appearance is characterized by a large bridge and swat uptakes of twin design. They utilize two Voith-Schneider propulsion units, thus enabling equal thrust in any direction.

Class Improved 'Adept' (TUTT)

Five new TUTTs entered service in 1985–86, to supplement the existing harbour tugs. The craft have minor design changes to the bridge layout and improved fire-fighting capability as a result of the experience gained from the first few years of 'Adept' class service. They were ordered on 8 February 1984.

Name *Forceful*; **Pennant number** A221; **Builders** Dunston; **Completed** 18 March 1985.

Name *Nimble*; **Pennant number** A222; **Builders** Dunston; **Completed** 25 June 1985.

Name *Powerful*; **Pennant number** A223;

Powerful *alongside at Portsmouth.* (Paul Beaver)

Builders Dunston; **Completed** 8 August 1985.

Name *Faithful*; **Pennant number** A228; **Builders** Dunston; **Completed** 13 December 1985.

Name *Dexterous*; **Pennant number** A231; **Builders** Dunston; **Completed** 23 April 1985.

Class 'Dog'

Name See below; **Pennant number** See below; **Full displacement** 248 tons; **Length** 28.7 m; **Beam** 7.5; **Draught** 3.7 m; **Propulsion** 2 x Lister-Blackstone diesels (1,320 bhp); **Range** 2,236 nm at 10 knots; **Speed** 10 knots; **Complement** 7 officers and ratings; **Armament** None; **Builders** See below; **Completed** See below.

Name *Cairn*; **Pennant number** A126; **Builders** Doig; **Completed** 1965.

Name *Dalmatian*; **Pennant number** A129; **Builders** Doig; **Completed** 1965.

Name *Deerhound*; **Pennant number** A155; **Builders** Appledore; **Completed** 1965.

Name *Elkhound*; **Pennant number** A162; **Builders** Appledore; **Completed** 1966.

Name *Labrador*; **Pennant number** A168; **Builders** Appledore; **Completed** 1966.

Name *Husky*; **Pennant number** A178; **Builders** Appledore; **Completed** 1966.

Name *Mastiff*; **Pennant number** A180; **Builders** Appledore; **Completed** 1967.

Name *Saluki*; **Pennant number** A182; **Builders** Appledore; **Completed** 1969.

Sheepdog – *standing by a frigate off Portland.* (Paul Beaver)

Name *Setter*; **Pennant number** A189; **Builders** Appledore; **Completed** 1969.

Name *Sealyham*; **Pennant number** A197; **Builders** Appledore; **Completed** 1967.

Name *Spaniel*; **Pennant number** A201; **Builders** Appledore; **Completed** 1967.

Name *Sheepdog*; **Pennant number** A250; **Builders** Appledore; **Completed** 1970.

Name *Foxhound* (ex-*Boxer*); **Pennant number** A326; **Builders** Dunston; **Completed** 1964.

Name *Basset* (ex-*Beagle*); **Pennant number** A327; **Builders** Dunston; **Completed** 1963.

Name *Collie*; **Pennant number** A328; **Builders** Rowhedge; **Completed** 1964.

Name *Corgi*; **Pennant number** A330; **Builders** Rowhedge; **Completed** 1964.

These craft are classified as medium berthing tugs and are found in the dockyards and ports around the UK where naval vessels operate. In addition, *Sealyham* is stationed at Gibraltar. The craft have a bollard pull of 17.5 tons, which means that two are usually used for frigates and heavier vessels. It should be noted that *Foxhound* was renamed in October 1977 so that *Boxer* could be released for the Type 22 frigate.

Water tractors

A water tractor is defined as a vessel having the point of application of the tow positioned aft of the propeller units, while a conventional screw tug has this point forward of the propeller.

Class 'Triton'

Name See below; **Pennant number** See below; **Standard displacement** 107.5 tons; **Length** 17.6 m; **Beam** 5.5 m; **Draught** 2.4 m; **Propulsion** 1 x diesel (330 bhp); **Range** Unknown; **Speed** 7.5 knots; **Complement** 4; **Armament** None; **Builders** Dunston; **Completed** 1972–73.

These are small water tractors although, like the 'Felicity' class, they are fitted with twin screws. They can be identified by a small funnel adjoining the bridge structure. The last one was delivered to the RMAS in August 1974.

Name	Pennant number	Completed
Irene	A181	15 June 1972
Isabel	A183	17 August 1972

Joan	A190	15 September 1972
Joyce	A193	11 October 1972
Kathleen	A166	16 November 1972
Kitty	A170	15 December 1972
Lesley	A172	29 March 1973
Lilah	A174	10 May 1973
Mary	A175	25 May 1973
Myrtle	A199	25 May 1973
Nancy	A202	31 August 1973
Norah	A205	19 December 1973

Single unit tractor tugs (SUTT)

Class 'Felicity'

Name *Felicity*; **Pennant number** A112; **Standard displacement** 80 tons; **Full displacement** 144 tons; **Length** 21.5 m; **Beam** 6.4 m; **Draught** 3 m; **Propulsion** 1 x Mirrlees-Blackstone diesel (615 bhp); **Range** Unknown; **Speed** 10 knots; **Complement** 4; **Armament** None; **Builders** Dunston; **Completed** 1968.

Name *Frances*; **Pennant number** A147; **Displacement** 89 tons; **Builders** Dunston; **Completed** 19 May 1980.

Name *Florence*; **Pennant number** A149; **Builders** Dunston; **Completed** 8 August 1980.

Name *Genevieve*; **Pennant number** A150;

Builders Dunston; **Completed** 29 October 1980.

Name *Fiona*; **Builders** Hancock; **Completed** 1973.

Name *Georgina*; **Builders** Hancock; **Completed** 1973.

Name *Gwendoline*; **Builders** Hancock; **Completed** 1974.

Name *Helen*; **Builders** Hancock; **Completed** 1974.

These medium water tractors are used at the UK's three main naval bases to move warships and other craft in harbour. They are characterized by their large funnel set clear and aft of the bridge. By means of the Voith-Schneider propeller, these (and the 'Triton' class) are able to use full power in any direction.

Fleet tenders

Class 'Loyal'

Name *Loyal Helper*; **Pennant number** A157; **Displacement** 143 tons; **Length** 24.1 m; **Beam** 6.4 m; **Draught** 2 m; **Propulsion** 1 x Lister-Blackstone diesel (320 hp); **Range** Unknown; **Speed** 10.5 knots; **Complement** 1 officer and 5

The harbour tug Fiona. (Paul Beaver)

ratings; **Armament** None; **Completed** 10 February 1978.

Name *Supporter* (ex-*Loyal Supporter*); **Pennant number** A158.

Name *Loyal Watcher*; **Pennant number** A159.

Name *Loyal Volunteer*; **Pennant number** A160.

Name *Loyal Mediator*; **Pennant number** A161; **Completed** 1978.

Name *Loyal Moderator*; **Pennant number** A220; **Completed** 1978.

Name *Loyal Chancellor*; **Pennant number** A1770; **Completed** 1978.

Name *Loyal Proctor*; **Pennant number** A1771; **Completed** 1978.

Class 'Manly'

Name *Melton*; **Pennant number** A83; **Displacement** 143 tons (full load); **Length** 24.4 m; **Beam** 6.4 m; **Draught** 2 m; **Propulsion** 1 x Lister-Blackstone EsR4 MCR diesel (320 hp); **Range** Unknown; **Speed** 10 knots; **Complement** 1 officer and 5 ratings; **Builders** Dunston; **Completed** By early 1993.

Name *Menai*; **Pennant number** A84; **Other details** As for *Melton*.

Name *Meon*; **Pennant number** A87; **Other details** As for *Melton*.

Name *Milford*; **Pennant number** A91; **Other details** As for *Melton*.

Name *Messina*; **Pennant number** A107; **Other details** As for *Melton*.

Auxiliary training vessels

Class 'Aberdovey'

Name *Aberdovey*; **Pennant number** Y10; **Displacement** 117.5 tons; **Length** 24 m; **Beam** 5.5 m; **Draught** 1.7 m; **Propulsion** 1 x Lister-Blackstone diesel (320 hp); **Range** 700 nm at 10 knots; **Speed** 10.5 knots; **Complement** 3 officers and ratings; **Armament** None; **Builders** Pimblott; **Completed** 1963; *Note:* Transferred for Sea Cadet training.

Name *Abinger*; **Pennant number** Y11; **Builders**

Pimblott; **Completed** 1964. Transferred for Royal Naval Reserve training.

Name *Alnmouth*; **Pennant number** Y13; **Builders** Pimblott; **Completed** 1966.

Name *Appleby*; **Pennant number** A383.

Name *Beddgelert*; **Pennant number** A100.

Occasionally called the 'Cartmel' class, this class was the first postwar design of Fleet tenders. The vessels have accommodation for 200 standing passengers, 25 tons of cargo and/or two standard heavyweight torpedoes. Like all Fleet tenders, these vessels are capable of short coastal voyages and have a single screw.

Class 'Clovelly'

Name *Clovelly*; **Pennant number** A389; **Displacement** 143 tons (full load); **Length** 24.4 m; **Beam** 6.4 m; **Draught** 2 m; **Propulsion** 1 x Lister-Blackstone diesel (320 bhp); **Range** 600 nm at 10 knots; **Speed** 10.3 knots; **Complement** 4 officers and ratings; **Armament** None; **Builders** Pimblott; **Completed** 1972.

Name *Ettrick*; **Pennant number** A274; **Builders** Cook; **Completed** 1972. Transferred to Royal Navy at *Gibraltar*.

Name *Elsing*; **Pennant number** A277; **Builders** Cook; **Completed** 1971. Transferred to Royal Navy at *Gibraltar*.

Name *Epworth*; **Pennant number** A355; **Builders** Cook; **Completed** 1972.

Name *Elkstone*; **Pennant number** A353; **Builders** Cook; **Completed** 1971.

Name *Felsted*; **Pennant number** A348; **Builders** Dunston; **Completed** 1972.

Name *Holmwood*; **Pennant number** A1772; **Builders** Dunston; **Completed** 1973.

Name *Horning*; **Pennant number** A1773; **Builders** Dunston; **Completed** 1973.

Name *Cricklade*; **Pennant number** A381; **Builders** Holmes; **Completed** 1971.

Name *Cromarty*; **Pennant number** A488; **Builders** Lewis; **Completed** 1972.

Name *Dornoch*; **Pennant number** A490; **Builders** Lewis; **Completed** 1972.

Name *Fintry*; **Pennant number** A394; **Builders** Lewis; **Completed** 1972.

Name *Fulbeck*; **Pennant number** A365; **Builders** Holmes; **Completed** 1972.

Name *Grasmere*; **Pennant number** A402; **Builders** Lewis; **Completed** 1972.

Name *Hambledon*; **Pennant number** A1769; **Builders** Dunston; **Completed** 1973.

Name *Harlech*; **Pennant number** A1768; **Builders** Dunston; **Completed** 1973.

Name *Headcorn*; **Pennant number** A1766; **Builders** Dunston; **Completed** 1973.

Name *Hever*; **Pennant number** A1767; **Builders** Dunston; **Completed** 1973.

Name *Lamlash*; **Pennant number** A208; **Builders** Dunston; **Completed** 1974.

Name *Lechlade*; **Pennant number** A211; **Builders** Dunston; **Completed** 1974.

Name *Llandovery*; **Pennant number** A207; **Builders** Dunston; **Completed** 1974.

Name *Lydford*; **Pennant number** A251.

Name *Sultan Venturer*; **Pennant number** A254; **Other details** Manned by Royal Naval personnel.

These vessels were a general improvement over those of the 'Aberdovey' class and have been designed to fulfil a range of tasks including passenger tenders, passenger/cargo tenders and/or training tenders.

Class 'Insect'

Name *Bee*; **Pennant number** A216; **Displacement** 475 tons (full load); **Length** 34.1 m; **Beam** 8.5 m; **Draught** 3.4 m; **Propulsion** 1 x Lister-Blackstone diesel (660 bhp); **Range** 3,000 nm at 10 knots; **Speed** 11.3 knots; **Complement** 7 officers and ratings; **Armament** None; **Builders** Holmes; **Completed** 1970.

Name *Cockchafer*; **Pennant number** A230; **Completed** 1971.

Name *Gnat*; **Pennant number** A239; **Completed** 1972.

Name *Ladybird*; **Pennant number** A253; **Completed** 1973.

Name *Scarab*; **Pennant number** A272; **Completed** 1973.

These craft are capable of coastal or even short sea voyages and for this role *Cockchafer* has been fitted with two cargo handling cranes, whilst *Gnat* and *Ladybird* are deployed as ammunition carriers at Faslane and Devonport. Based at Pembroke Dock, *Scarab* is used for mooring duties and for this role she was fitted with a 3-ton crane which is capable of dealing with 10-ton loads over the bows.

Diving tenders

Class 'Clovelly' (Type X)

Name *Ilchester*; **Pennant number** A308; **Displacement** 143 tons; **Length** 24.1 m; **Beam** 6.4 m; **Draught** 2 m; **Propulsion** 2 x Gray Marine diesels (450 hp); **Range** Unknown; **Speed** 12 knots; **Complement** 6 officers and ratings; **Armament** None; **Builders** Gregson; **Completed** 1974; *Note:* RMAS-manned with naval divers.

Name *Instow*; **Pennant number** A309; RMAS-manned with naval divers.

Name *Ironbridge*; **Pennant number** A310; Transferred to the Royal Navy at *Neptune*.

Name *Ixworth*; **Pennant number** A318; Transferred to the Royal Navy at *Vernon*.

All are of the same 'Clovelly' class as the Fleet tenders of the same name. These craft have recently been reallocated and only the *Ilchester* and the *Instow* are strictly under RMAS control. Nevertheless, for ease of reference, the craft are described as one class.

Degaussing vessels

Class 'Magnet'

Name *Magnet*; **Pennant number** A114; **Displacement** 955 tons (full load); **Length** 54.8 m; **Beam** 11.4 m; **Draught** 3 m; **Propulsion** 2 x Mirrlees-Blackstone diesels (1,650 hp); **Range** 1,750 nm at 12 knots; **Speed** 14 knots; **Complement** 15; **Armament** None; **Builders** Cleland; **Launched** 12 July 1979; **Completed** 1980.

Name *Lodestone*; **Pennant number** A115; **Builders** Cleland; **Launched** 20 November 1979; **Completed** 1981.

Epworth, *a fleet tender.* (Robin Walker)

When it was established that the 'Ham' class conversions were coming to the end of their useful lives, the RN commissioned a study into replacements which resulted in these two vessels from Cleland S.B. Co. Ltd of Wallsend.

Water carriers

Class 'Water'

Name *Watercourse*; **Pennant number** Y30; **Gross displacement** 285 tons; **Length** 40.1 m; **Beam** 7.5 m; **Draught** 2.4 m; **Propulsion** 1 x Lister-Blackstone diesel (660 bhp); **Range** Unknown; **Speed** 11 knots; **Complement** 8 officers and ratings; **Armament** None; **Builders** Drypool; **Launched** 1973; **Completed** 1974.

Name *Waterfowl*; **Pennant number** Y31; **Builders** Drypool; **Launched** 1972; **Completed** 1974.

Name *Waterfall*; **Pennant number** Y17; **Builders** Drypool; **Launched** 1966; **Completed** 1967.

Name *Waterspout*; **Pennant number** Y19;

Builders Drypool; **Launched** 1966; **Completed** 1967.

Name *Waterman*; **Pennant number** A146; **Builders** Dunstan; **Launched** 1977; **Completed** 1979.

These craft are designed for transporting supplies of fresh water to warships and other vessels in naval bases and anchorages. *Waterfall* has its deckhouse extended forward and *Waterfall* and *Waterman* have another deckhouse towards amidships. The latter, built by Dunston at Hessle, and *Waterfowl* have a dry stores carrying capability. They were ordered to replace wartime construction of the 'Spa' and 'Fresh' classes.

Moorage and salvage vessels (MSV)

The Marine Services Mooring Section covers a wide variety of activities, including the tri-Service responsibility for the laying, maintaining and removing of all UK MoD-owned moorings, bombing targets and navigation marks.

In recent years, the craft in this section have been rationalized and the 'Kin' class paid off for disposal or other duties; they have been replaced by three 'Sal' class craft. *Kinbrace* was placed in operational war reserve in December 1986 and *Kinloss* has been converted for a role as a shock trials barge.

Class 'Wild Duck'

Name *Goosander*; **Pennant number** A164; **Standard displacement** 692 tons; **Full displacement** 1,648 tons; **Length** 60.2 m; **Beam** 12.2 m; **Draught** 4.2 m; **Propulsion** 1 x Paxman diesel (750 hp); **Range** 3,000 nm at 10 knots; **Speed** 10 knots; **Complement** 23 officers and ratings; **Armament** None; **Builders** Robb; **Completed** 10 September 1973.

Name *Pochard*; **Pennant number** A165; **Builders** Robb; **Completed** 11 December 1973; **Other details** As for *Goosander*.

The later 'Wild Ducks' are larger than the earlier 'Wild Duck' craft and have a different appearance, obvious even to the casual observer.

Class 'Sal'

Name *Salmoor*; **Pennant number** A185; **Full displacement** 2,225 tons; **Length** 77 m; **Beam** 14.9 m; **Draught** 3.8 m; **Propulsion** 2 x Ruston 8RKCM diesels (4,000 hp); **Auxiliary propulsion** 1 x White Gill vectored thrust; **Range** 5,000 nm; **Speed** 15 knots; **Complement** 4 officers and 13 ratings; **Armament** None; **Builders** Hall Russell; **Completed** September 1985.

Name *Salmaster*; **Pennant number** A186; **Completed** 9 April 1986; **Other details** As for *Salmoor*.

Name *Salmaid*; **Pennant number** A187; **Completed** October 1986; **Other details** As for *Salmoor*.

Class 'Moorhen'

Name *Moorhen*; **Pennant number** Y32; **Full displacement** 530 tons; **Length** 32.3 m; **Beam** 11.5 m; **Draught** 2 m; **Propulsion** 2 x Cummins KT19-M diesels (730 hp); **Range** Unknown; **Speed** 8 knots; **Complement** 2 officers and 8 ratings; **Armament** None; **Builders** McTay; **Commissioned** April 1989.

Name *Moorfowl*; **Pennant number** Y33; **Commissioned** May 1989; **Other details** As for *Moorhen*.

Name *Cameron*; **Pennant number** A72; **Builders** Dunston; **Commissioned** September 1991; **Other details** As for *Moorhen*.

The 'Moorhen' class of vessels are actually classified as powered mooring lighters.

Coastal tankers

Class 'Oil'

Name See below; **Pennant number** See below; **Standard displacement** 280 tons; **Full displacement** 530 tons; **Length** 42.5 m; **Beam** 9 m; **Draught** 2.5 m; **Propulsion** 1 x Lister-Blackstone diesel (405 bhp); **Range** Unknown; **Speed** 9 knots; **Complement** 8 officers and ratings; **Armament** None; **Builders** Appledore; **Launched** See below; **Completed** 1969.

Name *Oilpress*; **Pennant number** Y21; **Launched** June 1968.

Name *Oilwell*; **Pennant number** Y23; **Launched** January 1969.

Name *Oilbird*; **Pennant number** Y25; **Launched** November 1968.

Name *Oilman*; **Pennant number** Y26; **Launched** February 1969.

Ordered in 1967 to provide rapid and cost-effective transmission of oil products between coastal installations, these vessels are now operated as bunkering craft at major naval bases.

Underwater research vessel

Class 'Newton'

Name *Newton*; **Pennant number** A367; **Standard displacement** 3,140 tons; **Full displacement** 4,652 tons; **Length** 98.6 m; **Beam** 16 m; **Draught** 5.7 m; **Propulsion** 3 x Mirrlees-Blackstone diesels (4,350 hp), 1 x GEC motor (2,040 hp), bow thruster; **Range** 5,000 nm at 14 knots; **Speed** 14 knots; **Complement** 64, including 12 MoD scientists; **Armament** None; **Builders** Scott Lithgow; **Launched** 25 June 1975; **Completed** 17 June 1976.

Class 'Auricula'

Name *Auricula*; **Pennant number** A285; **Standard displacement** 940 tons; **Full displacement** 1,118 tons; **Length** 52 m; **Beam** 11 m; **Draught** 3.6 m; **Propulsion** 2 x Mirrlees-

Blackstone diesels (1,300 bhp), bow thruster; **Range** Unknown; **Speed** 12 knots; **Complement** 7 officers and 15 ratings, plus 10 trials party; **Armament** None; **Builders** Ferguson; **Launched** 22 November 1979; **Completed** 1980.

Research ship

Class 'Colonel Templer'

Name *Colonel Templer*; **Pennant number** None; **Displacement** 1,300 tons (full load); **Length** 56.5 m; **Beam** 11 m; **Draught** 5.6 m; **Propulsion** 1 x Mirrlees KSSMR7 diesel, bow thruster; **Range** Unknown; **Speed** 12.5 knots; **Complement** 12 officers and ratings, 12 scientists; **Armament** None; **Builders** Hall Russell; **Commissioned** 1966.

Torpedo recovery vessels

Class 'Tornado'

Name *Tornado*; **Pennant number** A140; **Displacement** 698 tons (full load); **Length** 47 m; **Beam** 9.6 m; **Draught** 3.4 m; **Propulsion** 2 x Mirrlees-Blackstone diesels (2,200 hp); **Range** 3,000 nm at 14 knots; **Speed** 14 knots; **Complement** 14 officers and ratings; **Armament** None (10 torpedoes stored on deck); **Builders**

Hall Russell; **Launched** 24 May 1979; **Completed** November 1979.

Name *Torch*; **Pennant number** A141; **Builders** Hall Russell; **Launched** 7 August 1979; **Completed** February 1980; **Other details** As for *Tornado*.

Name *Tormentor*; **Pennant number** A142; **Builders** Hall Russell; **Launched** 6 November 1979; **Completed** May 1980; **Other details** As for *Tornado*.

Name *Toreador*; **Pennant number** A143; **Builders** Hall Russell; **Launched** February 1980; **Completed** July 1980; **Other details** As for *Tornado*.

These craft are operated by the RMAS for the recovery of exercise and trials torpedoes.

Class 'Torrent'

Name *Torrent*; **Pennant number** A127; **Gross displacement** 550 tons; **Length** 49.4 m; **Beam** 9.5 m; **Draught** 3.5 m; **Propulsion** 2 x Paxman diesels (700 hp); **Range** Unknown; **Speed** 10 knots; **Complement** 18 officers and ratings; **Armament** None (can store 32 torpedoes); **Builders** Cleland; **Completed** 10 September 1971.

Tormentor, the torpedo recovery vessel, towing a target after exercise in the English Channel. (Robin Walker)

Armament carriers

Class 'Throsk'

Name *Kinterbury*; **Pennant number** A378;
Displacement 2,207 tons (full load); **Length** 70.5
m; **Beam** 11.9 m; **Draught** 4.6 m; **Propulsion**
2 x Mirrlees-Blackstone diesels (3,000 hp);
Range 4,000 nm at 11 knots; **Speed** 14.5 knots;
Complement 8 officers and 16 ratings;
Armament None; **Builders** Cleland; **Completed**
November 1980.

Name *Arrochar* (ex-*St George*); **Pennant number**
A382; **Builders** Cleland; **Completed** July 1981;
Other details As for *Kinterbury*.

These craft are used to provide a supply of naval
armaments around the United Kingdom for naval
establishments. They are relatively modern and
specially designed for the task.

Range support vessels

Class 'Warden'

Name *Warden*; **Pennant number** A368;
Displacement 900 tons (full load); **Length** 48.6
m; **Beam** 10.95 m; **Draught** 2.5 m; **Propulsion**
2 x Ruston 8RKC diesels (4,000 hp); **Range**
Unknown; **Speed** 15 knots; **Complement** 4
officers and 7 ratings; **Armament** None;
Builders Richards; **Completed** November
1989.

Name *Falconet* (ex-*Alfred Herring VC*); **Pennant
number** Y02; **Displacement** 70 tons (full load);
Length 23.7 m; **Beam** 5.5 m; **Draught** 1.5 m;
Propulsion 2 x Paxman 8 CM diesels (2,000 hp);
Range Unknown; **Speed** 20 knots; **Complement**
Unknown; **Armament** None; **Builders** James &
Stone; **Commissioned** 1978.

Name *Petard* (ex-*Michael Murphy VC*); **Pennant
number** Y01; **Commissioned** 1983; **Other
details** As for *Falconet*.

Name *RSC 7713* (ex-*Samuel Morley VC*);
Displacement 20.2 tons (full load); **Length** 14.7
m; **Beam** 3.5 m; **Draught** 1.3 m; **Range** 300 nm
at 20 knots; **Speed** 22 knots; **Complement** 3;
Armament None.

Name *RSC 7821* (ex-*Joseph Hughes GC*).

Name *RSC 8125* (ex-*Sir Paul Travers*).

Name *RSC 8126* (ex-*Sir Cecil Smith*).

Name *RSC 8487* (ex-*Geoffrey Rackman GC*).

Name *RSC 8489* (ex-*Sir Evan Gibb*).

Name *RSC 7820* (ex-*Richard Masters VC*).

Name *RSC 7822* (ex-*James Dalton VC*).

Name *RSC 8128* (ex-*Sir Reginald Kerr*).

Name *RSC 8129* (ex-*Sir Humfrey Gale*).

Name *RSC 8488* (ex-*Walter Cleal GC*).

The above vessels are range safety craft of the
'Honours' and 'Sirs' classes, all of which were
completed in the 1982–86 period. Powered either
by two Rolls-Royce C8M 410 or Volvo Penta
TAMD-122A diesels of 820 hp, the craft were
built by Fairey Marine, A.R.P. Whitstable and
Halmatic.

Towed array tenders

Class Not known

Name None recorded; **Length** 20.1 m; **Beam** 6
m; **Draught** 2.4 m; **Propulsion** 2 x Perkins
diesels (400 hp); **Speed** 12 knots; **Complement**
8 officers and ratings.

Three towed array tenders are manned by Royal
Naval personnel and operated at Faslane and
Devonport.

Submarine berthing tugs

Class 'Impulse'

Name *Impulse*; **Pennant number** A344;
Displacement 530 tons (full load); **Length** 32.5
m; **Beam** 10.4 m; **Draught** 3.5 m; **Propulsion**
2 x W.H. Allen 8S12 diesels (3,400 hp), Azimuth
thrusters, bow thruster; **Range** Unknown; **Speed**
12 knots; **Complement** 6 officers and ratings;
Builders Dunston; **Launched** 10 December
1992; **Completed** 11 March 1993.

Name *Impetus*; **Pennant number** A345;
Launched 9 February 1993; **Completed** 28 May
1993; **Other details** As for *Impulse*.

These specialist tugs were designed, developed
and built to support the 'Vanguard' class ballistic
missile submarines at the Clyde Submarine Base,
Faslane.

Impulse and her sister ship Impetus *were specially designed and built to handle the 'Vanguard' class ballistic missile submarines.* (Paul Beaver)

Submarine tender

Class 'Adamant'

Name *Adamant*; **Pennant number** A232;
Displacement Unknown; **Length** 30.8 m; **Beam**
7.8 m; **Draught** 1.1 m; **Propulsion** 2 x Cummins
KTA-19M2 diesels (970 hp), 2 x waterjets; **Range**
250 nm at 22 knots; **Speed** 23 knots;
Complement 5 officers and ratings, room for 36
passengers; **Builders** FBM; **Commissioned** 18
January 1993.

Target vessels

Class 'Goole'

Name *Bullseye*; **Gross displacement** 273 tons;
Length 35.9 m; **Beam** 7.7 m; **Draught** 3.7 m;
Propulsion 1 x Mirrlees diesel (700 hp); **Range**
Unknown; **Speed** 12 knots; **Complement** 2 (only
on passage); **Builders** Goole; **Completed**
Unknown.

Three target vessels, named *Bullseye*, *Magpie* and
Targe, were built by Goole Shipbuilding Co. in
1961–62. They are based at Portland.

Harbour launches

There are still numerous types of craft moving
about the ports of the UK but the policy is to
replace them (when they become life-expired) by
a few standard type hulls. This is already in train
with the introduction of the 11-m harbour launch,

both as a launch and as a diving boat. The 52.5-ft
'New Zealand' class harbour launch (*not* from
New Zealand) has proved a popular craft and
three of them are in service in the Falkland
Islands.

Class 'Catamaran'

Name *8837*; **Displacement** 21 tons (full load);
Length 15.8 m; **Beam** 5.5 m; **Draught** 1.5 m;
Propulsion 2 x Mermaid Turbo 4 diesels (280 hp);
Range 400 nm at 10 knots; **Speed** 13 knots;
Complement 2; **Builders** FBM Marine;
Completed Unknown.

RMAS craft deployment

Clyde
*Roysterer, Waterfall, Goosander, Salmoor,
Tornado, Torreador, Adamant.*

Devonport
Robust, Corgi (reserve), *Salmaid, Moorfowl.*

Portsmouth
Rollicker, Bustler, Powerful, Aberdovey, Pochard
(reserve), *Moorhen, Loyal Mediator.*

Plymouth
Careful, Forceful, Faithful, Magnet (reserve),
*Newton, Tormentor, Loyal Watcher, Loyal
Chancellor.*

Portland
Adept, Lydford, Auricula (laid up), *Torch,*

Bullseye, Magpie, Targe.

Rosyth
Nimble, Dexterous, Salmaster, Loyal Helper.

Pembroke Dock
Warden, Loyal Moderator.

Outer Hebrides
Falconet.

South Wales
Petard.

Greenock
Lodestone.

Kyle
Cairn, Colie, Torrent.

Belfast
Supporter.

Scotland
Loyal Proctor, Loyal Volunteer.

Gibraltar
Edith, Capable, Sealyham, Ettrick (RN-manned),
Elsing (RN-manned).

Grimsby
Abinger.

Liverpool
Alnmouth.

Belfast
Beddgelert.

Bristol
Appleby.

Falmouth
Clovelly, Headcorn, Hever.

CHAPTER EIGHT

The Royal Marines and their weapons

'IF EVER THE hour of real danger should come to England, they will be found the country's sheet anchor.' *Admiral Lord St Vincent, 1802*

The history of the Corps dates from 1664 and the Duke of York's Regiment, later called the Lord High Admiral's Regiment, when soldiers first fought at sea in an organized manner after being specially raised. The present Corps' true roots can be traced to 1755, though, when former soldiers from Maritime Regiments were brought under Admiralty control. Since then, the Royal Marines have given sterling service to the nation, NATO, Commonwealth and the United Nations. In April 1993, the Corps came directly under the command of Commander-in-Chief Fleet.

Following the 1979–81 defence cuts, one Commando (equivalent of a British Army infantry battalion) was disbanded. Since then there have been few cuts in the front-line, operational strength of the Corps, reflecting its operational capabilities.

The Corps has the following roles: **amphibious warfare**, including special operations and raiding, with the added capability of rapid deployment and self-sufficiency in an infantry role; **warship detachments**, when special units are deployed to warships, such as those operating in the Adriatic or Islamic Gulf; **offshore protection** – a special quick reaction force to protect the United Kingdom's offshore installations and to operate in the nautical anti-terrorist role; the **Band Service**, to provide music for the Royal Navy as well as the Corps in peacetime, and medical assistants and stretcher bearers in conflict.

Royal Marine establishments
The headquarters of the Commandant General

Royal Marines (CGRM) is at a new headquarters of Commando Forces on Whale Island at Portsmouth, but the major concentration of facilities has been in the West Country, where there have traditionally been establishments at

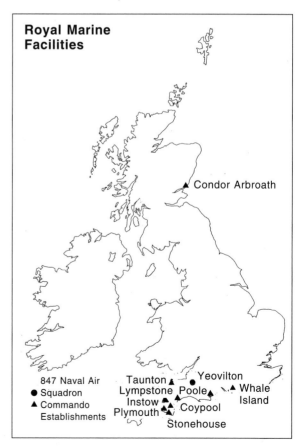

Royal Marine Facilities

Condor Arbroath

847 Naval Air
● Squadron
▲ Commando
Establishments

Taunton
Lympstone
Instow
Plymouth
Stonehouse
Poole
Coypool
Yeovilton
Whale Island

Plymouth (Citadel, Seaton, Coypool, Bickleigh and Stonehouse) and at Lympstone, near Exeter, where the Royal Marines have the Commando Training Centre (CTCRM).

As a result of the 'Options for Change' and 'Front Line First' defence cuts, there has been a series of changes in West Country basing arrangements. The former airfield at Chivenor will now be the home of the Commando Logistics Regiment, because it gives undercover storage for the Regiment's vehicles. In February 1995, it seemed that 42 Commando would also join the move to Chivenor, leaving the commando artillery unit, landing craft operations and signals at Plymouth.

Originally planned to close in 1995, it seems that the training establishment at Poole will remain in being, mainly because it became impossible to find a secure home for the Special Boat Service. If this happens, Poole will also remain the training centre for landing and other waterborne craft, not at Plymouth.

In Kent, Deal, the former headquarters for the Band Service, will close as British military bands are centralized.

Training and Reserves are administered from Portsmouth; the Corps Museum is located nearby.

In Scotland, the only Royal Marines establishment is found in Arbroath and is known as Condor Base, the name of the former Naval Air Station.

Operationally, 40 Commando Royal Marines (40 Cdo RM) is based at Norton Manor Camp, Taunton; 42 Commando Royal Marines (42 Cdo RM) at Bickleigh Barracks, near Plymouth (moving to Chivenor); and 45 Commando Group (45 Cdo Gp) is based near Arbroath. Headquarters 3 Commando Brigade (HQ 3 Bde RM), along with

About to storm an objective – Royal Marines on exercise in the Outer Hebrides. (Paul Beaver)

the Brigade Patrol Troop, part of the Mountain and Arctic Warfare Cadre, are based at Stonehouse Barracks in Plymouth.

Aviation support to the brigade, performed by

Amphibious operations in the Outer Hebrides – it is winter, and a task force with 45 Commando Group

the Commando Brigade Air Squadron Royal Marines (now 847 Squadron), has a permanent base at the Royal Naval Air Station Yeovilton.

Commando Forces (Cdo Forces) broadly comprise: HQ 3 Commando Brigade; 40 Commando; 42 Commando; 45 Commando Group; 3 Commando Brigade Air Squadron; 3 Commando Brigade HQ & Signals Squadron; 539 Assault Squadron; Air Defence Troop; and Commando Logistics Regiment. To complement these forces are several Army units: 29 Commando Regiment, Royal Artillery; 59 Independent Commando Squadron, Royal Engineers; and 131 Independent Commando Squadron, Royal Engineers (Volunteers).

The Commando Logistics Regiment is manned by a joint force of Royal Navy, British Army and Royal Marines personnel and thus is unique in the United Kingdom order of battle. It provides workshop, ordnance, transport and medical back-up. The Royal Navy also provides air lift support in the form of 845 and 846 Squadrons, equipped with Sea King HC 4 helicopters.

Commando units Two of the three Commando units are primarily tasked with Mountain and Arctic Warfare (M&AW) and a third Commando unit has a role in Temperate Climate Operations. All Commando units are trained and ready to operate in other areas, including those outside NATO boundaries, including UN peacekeeping.

Mountain and Arctic Warfare is the popularly acclaimed role of the Royal Marines and today there are two Commando units trained in this role, together with HQ 3 Cdo Bde RM, 847 Squadron and supporting elements. In addition, the RM is ably supported in Norway by elements of the Royal Netherlands Marine Corps (RNLMC), known as 1 Amphibious Combat Group (1 ACG) and Whiskey Company, the latter being an independent unit slightly larger than a regular rifle company. Each year during January–March, the force trains in Northern Norway, around Bardufoss; the exercises which are held usually test the reinforcement, deployment and contingency planning of NATO and/or Anglo-Norwegian arrangements. The modern Royal Marine Commando is equipped to work at temperatures down to –30° C using contemporary over-snow vehicles and techniques.

In peacetime, operational control of the majority of units in Commando Forces (Cdo Forces) is delegated to the Command of 3 Cdo Bde RM. In war or even time of tension, 3 Cdo Bde would comprise all available Commandos, plus 1 ACG and associated logistics and combat support. Such are the number of options available to NATO commanders that the Royal Marines has to be

Organization of 3 Commando Brigade

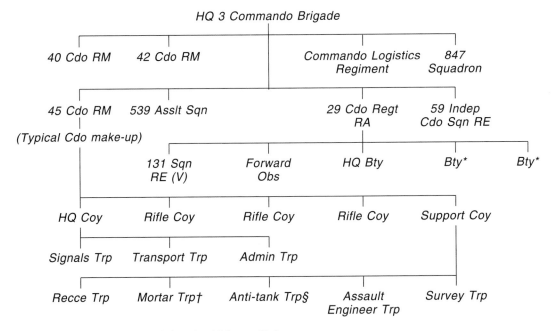

* Each Battery is complemented for six 105 mm light guns.
† The Mortar Troop is complemented for nine 81 mm mortars.
§ The Anti-Tank Troop is complemented for a dozen Milan.

ready for almost any contingency. It is important, says the Corps, that the Royal Marines is not seen as only a specialist Arctic warfare element: it is a Corps with the greatest flexibility in the UK order of battle.

The Northern Flank area remains the Corps' most important training and deployment area, despite the end of the Cold War.

Royal Marine Commandos have been regularly deployed to Northern Ireland for peacekeeping duties as part of the British Army's roulement for infantry battalions.

Each Commando is variously roistered to the British Army Spearhead battalion and can see service as and when requested; in October 1994, for example, 45 Commando was flown to Kuwait when it appeared that Saddam Hussein would again invade the tiny state.

During the Spearhead period, operational control passes to the British Army's Headquarters United Kingdom Land Forces (HQ UKLF) at Wilton. United Nations peacekeeping tours in Cyprus and elsewhere have also been undertaken by individual Companies or whole Commandos in the normal course of their service life.

British operations carried out in the South Atlantic to recover the Falkland (Malvinas) Islands and South Georgia provided the Royal Marines with active service in conditions which, although harsh, they were trained to fight in. Almost every facet of the Commando system was used in the campaign and the Commander Land Forces Falkland Islands (CLFFI) was reportedly pleased with the performance of 3 Cdo Bde RM. It was typical of the 'Out of Area' operations for which these troops are especially suited.

ORGANIZATION

The Royal Marines is organized along British Army lines but has a curious blend of naval traditions and functions. It is commanded by a Lieutenant General who is known as Commandant General Royal Marines (CGRM); he does not have a place on the normal Admiralty Board, but is tasked with advising the Board on all Amphibious and RM matters as a Type commander.

The Corps is split into two parts: the Commando Forces and Training, Reserve and Special Forces. The Headquarters of Commando Forces is at Plymouth and this element is commanded by a Major General whose headquarters is at Mount Wise. He has responsibility for the planning and landing parts of all amphibious operations, whilst the Royal Navy's Commodore Amphibious Warfare (COMAW) is responsible for putting the forces in the right place, on time.

Based at Whale Island, HQ Training, Reserve and Special Forces are also commanded by a Major General. The five major Royal Marine establishments are the responsibility of MGRM TSRF, who is also tasked with the training of individuals, specialists, tradesmen, musicians and commanders.

Organization of a typical Commando

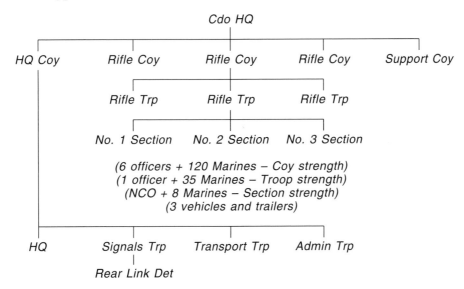

(12 officers and 170 Marines)
(21 vehicles and trailers, including water carriers and radio trucks)

COMMANDO FORCES

The landing force element of the United Kingdom Amphibious Force, which is declared to NATO and would be assigned to SACLANT in time of global war, is the Royal Marines Commando Forces. It is envisaged that the Forces would be deployed to Northern European Command (NEC) which encompasses Norway, Denmark and North Germany. There, they will protect the transatlantic resupply routes in time of war or tension. Commando Forces has an important role to play in NATO thinking at this time.

It is not possible for Cdo Forces to acquire all the necessary expertise that is required from within the Corps so numerous elements of the RN and of the British Army act in supporting roles. Nevertheless, all those from other services are expected to undergo the rigorous All Arms Commando Course at CTCRM, Lympstone; all personnel, once they have passed this course, are entitled to wear the coveted green beret and work alongside the Royal Marines.

Comacchio Group

There are a number of key establishments whose installations require safeguarding by a Royal Marines detachment. Comacchio Company's 160-strong teams are responsible for guarding the 'Vanguard' class nuclear-powered ballistic missile-carrying submarines, the Coulport Trident missile depot and the nuclear weapons convoys on British roads.

M Squadron

Described as a shadow organization, somewhere between the Special Boat Service and the former Mountain & Arctic Warfare Cadre, M Squadron is a specialist unit of less than 50 Royal Marine Commandos. It is understood to work in conjunction with the Special Boat Service and the British Army's Special Air Service (SAS) regiment.

Special Boat Service

This special operations unit is the United Kingdom's amphibious special forces unit and is based at Royal Marines Poole. It is said to be capable of undertaking any operation at sea or up to a limited distance inland, perhaps 12 km. The SBS and the British Army's Special Air Service regiment have run a joint selection course at Hereford and the Brecon Beacons in Wales. It has such an important operational role that elements are always available to NATO or national commanders for special operations.

The main role of the SBS is to provide the Royal Marines with amphibious reconnaissance and intelligence about the enemy and the men assigned to the SBS are therefore specialists in many trades, including photography and explosives. They also have a 'direct action' role but today are probably better known for their anti-terrorist capability; a particular forte is assumed to be the relief of hijacked ships and port installations.

Beach assault – modern means include the Griffon hovercraft and the Rigid Raider (left). (Paul Beaver)

All ranks are classified as swimmer-canoeists and are trained in parachuting and the use of small craft. They would travel to the target area in any vessel and/or aircraft which would seem appropriate to the task and have been known to be dropped from helicopters beyond the target's horizon or to canoe out of a partially submerged landing craft.

The paying off of the Royal Navy's conventional submarines in 1994 is seen as a retrograde step in the deployment of special forces, although it is understood that trials with nuclear-powered submarines have been carried out. There is a reserve SBS unit.

539 Assault Squadron
539 Assault Squadron formed in April 1984 to provide Brigade landing craft support, especially in the Northern Flank area. The Squadron operates a variety of craft including landing craft and rigid raiders; it is commanded by a senior Royal Marines Major. Based at Turnchapel, in Plymouth, the Squadron now includes a variety of new amphibious craft; the new RIBs (Rubber Inflatable Boats) and hovercraft were brought into service in 1994.

Commando Training Centre
Situated at Lympstone, near Exeter, the Commando Training Centre undertakes a recruit selection programme which is one of the toughest in the world. There are two officer selection courses every year and a variable number of recruit courses. Also at Lympstone is the Sniper School, where the Royal Marines train all the British forces in sniping.

Embarked detachments
Whilst all ships of the Royal Navy and Royal Fleet Auxiliary have the emergency capability to embark amphibious troops, there are a certain but declining number of warships which carry a Royal Marines detachment on a regular basis. This is usually a force of one Sergeant, a Corporal and eight Marines; the original system of an officer and 20 men was terminated in 1978. Currently, the following classes of ships on deployment to key flashpoints or operational areas are specially equipped for such detachments: Type 22 and Type 23 frigates, 'Peacock' class patrol craft (three Marines to drive the fast pursuit craft). In addition, there is a detachment aboard the ice patrol ship *Endurance*.

Selection for the embarked detachments is via the regular sea roster, although volunteers are welcomed. Training is carried out at Poole, where the course is split into two weeks at Poole to cover the administrative side, including medicals, four weeks at *Raleigh*, where Royal Marines complete the standard eight weeks' Junior Seaman course in four weeks, followed by a further two weeks at Poole revising weapons drill, learning signal procedures and using the ranges. There is then a ceremonial pass-out before the warship's Captain or Commander. This completes Pre-Embarkation Training (PET), but several courses a year will continue Royal Marine training (PJT) before they join the warship at HMS *Cambridge*, where they are taught aspects of naval gunnery. In the days of the Royal Marine gun turret detachments, this was an important part of the sea service routine, but today the detachment is expected to fulfil different roles, including providing the shore security party and manning the ship's small craft; they will still provide members for the turret crew if required.

Perhaps one of the likeliest operations to be carried out by the Royal Marines detachment is disaster relief in, say, the West Indies, although it is possible that the detachment would be landed at the request of a friendly power to preserve law and order until reinforcements such as the 'Spearhead' battalion from the United Kingdom arrived.

Equipment used is the standard Royal Marine Commando section issue of 5.56 mm SA 80, a 7.62 mm general-purpose machine-gun (GPMG) and anti-tank weapons.

Commando Brigade Air Squadron
Equipped with Westland Gazelle AH 1 light observation helicopters and the Westland Lynx AH 7 anti-tank and utility helicopter, this unit is closely associated with the Army Air Corps at Middle Wallop but is independently based at RNAS Yeovilton as 847 Squadron. The squadron is organized into four flights; each flight is named after an important battle in which the Royal Marines were involved.

In wartime the squadron would operate with 3 Commando Brigade in the Northern Flank area and thus much of the flying training reflects Mountain & Arctic Warfare duties. A flight may be deployed to Northern Ireland as and when required. Various procedures have been adopted for amphibious and embarked operations and aircrews are trained to fly from all amphibious ships, including landing ships. Special modifications have been incorporated into the aircraft to assist their flying environments, including inflation bags and radio altimeters to assist in landing and hovering above snow-covered areas.

The aircraft would be camouflaged white rather than their existing green/black paint scheme if operating in wartime above the Norwegian snow. In peacetime, this emulsion-type covering causes maintenance problems and so is not used.

The majority of aircrew are senior non-commis-

Air squadron – the Commando Brigade has its own organic aviation support of TOW-equipped Lynx and observation Gazelle (foreground) helicopters. (Paul Beaver)

sioned officers and young officers who fly as part of their normal tours; there are no career aviators.

Air Defence Troop

Based on the equivalent units within the British Army's Royal Artillery, the Troop is armed with Javelin/Starburst manportable, surface-to-air missiles. It is attached to HQ 3 Cdo Bde for point defence of Brigade HQ, a strongpoint, bridge or other tactically important location. It is commanded by a senior Lieutenant and consists of about 36 men. Training is carried out at Larkhill.

The Royal Marines and naval helicopters

The concept of using naval helicopters for transporting elements of an RM force ashore, or within an operational area, goes back to the days of the Suez landings and to the later operations on the Malayan Peninsula and in Borneo. Today, the Naval Air Commando Squadrons and the Corps work as a tightly knit community.

To provide Commando air support, especially in terms of logistical supply and troop movement, the Fleet Air Arm provides two front units, both equipped with the Sea King HC 4 helicopter. In addition, the Commando Training Squadron, also equipped with the Sea King, can be called into front-line service in wartime.

The helicopter is a vital tool above the fluid and flexible modern battlefield, when men and equipment have to be moved rapidly across coun-

try. Where there are limited surface transport routes their importance is especially pronounced. In Norway, for example, the roads could be blocked because of weather conditions or through enemy action; the helicopters would then be used to move troops quickly and efficiently.

The Sea King provides a rapid means of moving equipment from ship to ship, it being able to lift 3.4 tonnes (7,500 lb) underslung for short transits or 2.7 tonnes (6,000 lb) on longer sorties. These loads could include the 1-tonne Land Rover and trailer, or the 105 mm light gun and ammunition. Internally, 25 fully armed and equipped mountain troops can be carried over a distance of 65 nm (120 km).

Future equipment for the Sea King includes self-defence warning systems and, possibly, self-defence missiles. The helicopters can be equipped with passive night vision goggles and self-defence, electronic warfare systems, for peace-keeping operations and to enable them to work in forward areas.

Landing Craft Training Unit

The specialist amphibious ships of the Royal Navy carry landing craft which are manned exclusively by the Royal Marines of the Landing Craft Company. The whole branch is controlled from RM Poole. The company is commanded by a Major. The LCTU is responsible for the training of crews for LCVPs (Landing Craft Vehicle and Personnel) and LCUs (Landing Craft Utility). It was still based at Poole in February 1995.

Assault Squadrons

The Landing Craft Assault Squadrons are attached to *Fearless* (4 Assault Squadron) and *Intrepid* (6 Assault Squadron); a third unattached squadron is available. These warships carry LCVPs at davits and each have four craft of this type. The 12-tonne craft are crewed by a Corporal and two Marines. In addition, the LPDs are equipped to carry four LCUs in the dock-type compartment beneath their flight decks and they operate in and out of this when the ship is 'flooded down'.

In the light of experience in Norway, all LCVPs and LCUs are now 'arcticized' for operations in adverse weather north of the Arctic Circle. Covers, heaters and specialist navigational equipment have been provided for this role.

Royal Marines who specialize in landing craft are at the lowest level qualified to cox rigid raiders and Gemini, whilst at the highest level is the Officer In Charge Landing Craft aboard an LPD. Corporals usually provide the cox'ns for LCVPs and LCUs. This use of smaller craft enables the provision of a nautical element to M Squadron and Comacchio Company units, operate in Northern Ireland, with the SBS and in Hong Kong waters. In addition to military tasks, Royal Marine landing craft and other small boats are always ready to provide assistance to the civil powers for disaster relief and casualty evacuation. In line with Britain's policies on assistance for foreign nations, the Company provides men on secondment to the small boats' section of the Royal Brunei Malay Regiment.

THE MARINES AND NORTHERN IRELAND

The Corps has been deployed in the Province since 1969, spending four-month emergency tours there in rotation with British Army units. Royal Marine Commandos have also carried out duties as part of the Resident Battalion. Sea-going intelligence officers with regular naval patrols are often Royal Marines whose primary duty is to assist in the prevention of arms smuggling and the prevention of terrorism in coastal and inshore waters.

THE MARINES AND LOGISTICS

Every Commando unit deployed, even in peacetime, requires the support of specialist logistic personnel, and the Corps has the Commando Logistic Regiment to fulfil this role. This support is based on a fixed time back-up which is available to each Commando, the Brigade air squadron and the Anglo-Dutch amphibious force. In addition, logistic support is supplied to Royal Fleet Auxiliaries with amphibious roles, and the new helicopter carrier (LPH). During and following an assault it is important to maintain administrative and distribution functions at peak efficiency. Supplies can either be ferried ashore from auxiliaries or impressed merchant vessels, or host national assistance may be given. The latter will mainly be concentrated on combat support and medical back-up.

AMPHIBIOUS OPERATIONS

Until replaced in the next decade, the United Kingdom's amphibious lift capability will be provided by one assault ship, *Fearless* (her sister ship *Intrepid* will never put to sea again). In addition, there are four available landing ships assistance from the LSLs.

The Commodore Amphibious Warfare

Hovercraft supplement but are unlikely completely to replace landing craft. (Photo Press)

(COMAW) functions as the naval amphibious group commander (CATF) for brigade-scale amphibious operations. SACLANT will actually assign the use of amphibious warships in a war situation.

The naval role on the Northern Flank still exists, even though the idea of an assault against enemy forces is no longer part of NATO doctrine. The new *modus operandi* is for the amphibious troops to land on a friendly coast without the use of ports and/or airfields. In time of tension the UKNL Force, mainly operating with an assault ship, helicopters and landing craft, would sail before a political decision to mount an amphibious operation had been taken. They would then be positioned over the horizon, as yet uncommitted. All these operations would be undertaken with the assistance of Britain's allies, especially Norway, Denmark, Canada and the United States.

An 'Invincible' class aircraft carrier acting in the secondary role of helicopter carrier is likely until *Ocean* is commissioned in 1997/98. This could be for 'quick dash' operational reinforcement or initial deployments to Norway or some other troublespot. The assault ships are designed to operate as the Joint Headquarters of an Amphibious Group but also provide a troop lift and amphibious docking capability and a platform for support helicopters. The Royal Fleet Auxiliary mans five landing ships, which could be made available to support amphibious operations with the use of their clamshell doors and multi-purpose Mexeflote pontoons.

In 1994, the Royal Marines reintroduced the hovercraft to regular service as a troop prime mover, to replace and supplement landing craft. The Griffon hovercraft were acquired for £1 million and were first deployed on Exercise Royal Dawn in the Outer Hebrides in February 1994.

Amphibious Trials and Training Unit
Based at Instow, this unit, known as ATTURM, is responsible for research and development, as well as trials into the technical aspects of amphibious operations; much of this work is necessarily classified. One function which is important is the waterproofing of vehicles and associated equipment and the recovery of these in the beach landing environment; this work is pioneered at Instow.

Amphibious Beach Unit
Both *Fearless* and *Intrepid* carry an ABU with a Captain RM in command who will be transferred ashore to co-ordinate the landing operations. Their role is vital and capability has been strengthened by attaching an ABU to 539 Assault Sqn RM.

ROYAL MARINES RESERVE
The RMR is a Commando-trained volunteer force which in times of war or tension – or 'mobilization' – is ready and able to join the regular Corps, either in the form of specialist sub-units or as individual reinforcements. Under the terms of the Royal Marines Act 1947, two units of reserves were formed at Glasgow and London under the aegis of the Royal Marines Forces Volunteer Reserve (RMFVR). In 1963, the RMR was formed from the sure foundations of the RMFVR, which title had lost some of its message with the disbandment of National Service.

Today there are five units and ten detachments with some 70 officers and 1,100 other ranks. The units and detachments are:

RMR City of London Portsmouth Detachment; Chatham Detachment.
RMR Scotland Dundee Detachment; Greenock Detachment; Arbroath Detachment.
RMR Bristol Cardiff Detachment; Poole Detachment; Lympstone Detachment; Plymouth Detachment.
RMR Merseyside Liverpool Detachment.
RMR Tyne No Detachments.

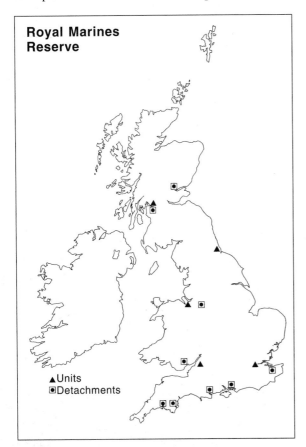

Royal Marines Reserve

▲ Units
◧ Detachments

The RMR has a good, close relationship with neighbouring RNR units, and in several cases they share common establishments. In addition, the RNR has always provided medical assistance and back-up for the RMR and several Reserve Medical Assistants have won the coveted green beret and the right to wear the exclusive 'Royal Naval Commando (R)' shoulder flash.

Those recruited come from all walks of life, from Chartered Surveyor to butcher, but the applicant must be physically fit and mentally alert. He must also be dedicated to his part-time vocation because he must attend a 15-day continuous training period each year, a weekly training night and about one weekend in three. Most employers realize the benefit to the nation, themselves and society in general – but not all have any real idea of how dedicated and professional the RMR really is in a modern warfare context.

Every recruit must undergo about two years' training in order to complete the tough Commando course (at CTCRM Lympstone) and it is after this period that final selection for officer training (a further two years) takes place. Once trained, the Marine Reservist joins Commando Company and is able to train as a specialist in one of many fields, including Mountain & Arctic Warfare. Initial service lasts four years, with re-engagement until 50 years of age.

4 Special Boat Section, the RMR's connection with the SBS, is a long and useful one. 4 SBS(R) acts in support of the regular squadron and trains highly skilled frogmen and parachutists who can approach their objective by parachute, submarine, canoe or by swimming under water, in order to carry out their mission.

608 Tactical Air Control Party is attached to RMR Bristol and is a four-man team led by a subaltern, which provides air liaison to land forces and an aircraft control facility in forward areas. In 1979 this team deployed to Belize with a Regular Army battalion on a Regular Arms Plot Tour. This was the first time that a Reserve or TA unit had done this, and 608 TACP carried out a further tour in 1981.

The RMR offers the opportunity for civilians to undertake arduous training in parachuting, skiing and cliff climbing which would otherwise not be possible in their normal occupations. In addition, they can specialize as Assault Engineers, Signallers, PT Instructors, Cooks or in supporting weapons (mortars) or platoon weapons.

The RMR frequently detaches officers and men to the regular Corps and occasionally to units of the Royal Netherlands Marine Corps and US Marine Corps for exercises. Training has recently been carried out in Belize, Canada, Cyprus, Hong Kong, The Netherlands and Norway. There are opportunities for Staff College training and,

indeed, senior officers must pass a Staff College course before taking up their appointments.

In 1976, following the Defence Review, RMR units were affiliated to Commando Forces RM as follows:

City of London 41 Commando Group; 42 Commando, RM; Commando Logistics Regiment, RM.

Scotland 45 Commando Group; Commando Logistics Regiment, RM.

Bristol 3 Commando Brigade HQ and Signals Squadron, RM; Commando Logistics Regiment, RM.

Merseyside 40 Commando, RM.

Tyne 45 Commando Group; Commander Logistics Regiment, RM.

THE MARINES AND FOREIGN NATIONS

The Royal Marines have a series of arrangements with overseas marine formations and now provide the following military training teams:

Baltic States A 14-strong Royal Marines team began training the future UN peacekeeping battalion of the combined Baltic States Battalion (BALTBAT) in September 1994. This work will continue until at least October 1995.

France Anglo-French co-operation is now to be an important feature of the Corps' European

Co-operation – for nearly two decades, the Royal Marines and the Royal Netherlands Marine Corps have co-operated, with a company of Dutch Marines under command of 45 Cdo. (Paul Beaver)

operations following the formal exchange of letters between the respective British and French defence ministers in February 1995.

The Netherlands Some years ago a Memorandum of Understanding was agreed between the British and Dutch governments for the operational and training deployment of elements of the Royal Netherlands Marine Corps (RNLMC) under the command of Commando Forces RM for NATO purposes. Two elements are usually earmarked for such duties – 1 ACG and Whiskey Company, both based at Doorn in the Netherlands. The combining of these elements has resulted in the UK/NL Amphibious Force, whose joint training is often held up as a good example of NATO co-operation.

In addition, the Royal Marines has seconded and training officers with the forces of Brunei, Nigeria and Oman, and is involved in exchange programmes with the United States Marine Corps, RNLMC and the Australian Special Forces.

MARINE SPECIALISTS

Although all Royal Marines except those of the Band Service are Commando-trained, it is possible for a Marine to undertake training for a Specialist Qualification (SQ) or to undergo trade training with Technical Training Company (TT Coy) at RM Poole. The Marines have three levels of specialist: Grade 3 (ordinary Marine); Grade 2 (usually a Corporal); Grade 1 (usually a Sergeant or Colour Sergeant). In addition, there are artificers who are usually Warrant Officers, but their training is progressive because, unlike the RN, the Corps does not recruit direct into the artificers grade.

NCO and Marine specializations are:

General Duties Branch Air Crewman; Assault Engineer; Drill Instructor/Leader; Helicopter Pilot (SNCOs); Heavy Weapons Instructor; Landing Craft; Provost/Marine Police; Physical Training Instructor; Platoon Weapons Instructor (weapons up to and including 84 mm); Mountain Leader (M&AW); Swimmer Canoeist/Parachutist; Driver; Signaller; Radio Operator; Groom.

Technical Branch Bugler; Clerk (CQ, equipment); Clerk (CPR, pay and records); Musician (Band Service).

Tradesmen Illustrator; Carpenter; Metalsmith; Printer; Armourer; Vehicle Mechanic; Artificer (Vehicle); Telecom Technician.

The Mountain Leader SQ is to provide a cadre of Border Patrol Troop personnel for long-range patrol, leadership and training tasks. Most of the technical training is carried out at Poole, or administered from there but actually carried out with the British Army at Bordon, Hampshire, where armourers are trained, or Netheravon, Wiltshire, for support weapons, whilst Royal Marines cooks are trained with the army at Aldershot, home of the British Army. Aircrew training takes place at Middle Wallop, Hampshire, home of the Army Air Corps.

ROYAL MARINES EQUIPMENT

Over the years, the Corps of Royal Marines has depended on the mainstream of British Army equipment for all but the most specialist roles. Today, after many years of involvement in Northern Ireland, the Royal Marines have been equipped for internal security duties as well as the Commando Forces role.

The Royal Marines are unique in the armed forces of the United Kingdom and therefore there are various elements of their equipment which have no place elsewhere.

Personal weapons

9 mm Pistol Automatic L9A1

Calibre 9 mm; **Length** 0.196 m; **Length of barrel** 0.112 m; **Weight empty** 0.88 kg; **Weight loaded** 1.01 kg; **Muzzle velocity** 34 m/s; **Magazine capacity** 13 rounds; **Rate of fire** Single-shot; **Maximum effective range** 40–50 m.

This is the officer and special duties pattern pistol which has been standard since the 1940s. It is also known as the Browning 9 mm. The pistol is worn on the hip in a canvas holster or in a shoulder holster for those on special duties. It has an unusually large magazine capacity and can be used accurately by relative newcomers to the weapon because of the long grip which can help to steady the user's arm. The butt is also a fine combat weapon in its own right.

Sub-Machine Gun 9 mm L2A3

Calibre 9 mm; **Length (butt folded)** 0.482 m; **Length (butt extended)** 0.69 m; **Length of barrel** 0.198 m; **Weight empty** 2.7 kg; **Weight loaded** 3.5 kg; **Muzzle velocity** 390 m/s; **Magazine capacity** 34 rounds; **Rate of fire (single-shot)** 40 rpm; **Maximum effective range** 200 m.

This is the universally known Sterling SMG, the replacement of the equally well-known Sten gun of the Second World War. It is the third modification of the standard 1945 pattern Sterling and is used by support units and for infantry house clearing and associated work. It is possible to fix a bayonet to the muzzle. In service, many users tape two magazines together for quick changes.

SA 80 Individual weapon 5.56 mm

Calibre 5.56 mm; **Length overall** 0.77 m; **Weight loaded** 4.28 kg; **Muzzle velocity** 900 m/s; **Magazine capacity** 20 or 30 rounds; **Rate of fire** 700/850 rpm; **Maximum effective range** 400 m.

This is the British forces' new weapon system, designed to replace the 7.62 mm SLR system and primarily for ease of use. It can be carried in confined spaces, such as helicopters, assault craft and snow vehicles. Service introduction for the Royal Marines began in 1986 and continued until 1990 when all Commando and logistical units were fully equipped. It has been criticized by many users, but the sighting system is said to be second to none, making 'a poor shot into a good one, a good one into a marksman'.

Light Support Weapon 5.56 mm

Calibre 5.56 mm; **Length overall** 0.9 m; **Weight loaded** 4.88 kg; **Muzzle velocity** 945 m/s; **Rate of fire** 700/850 rpm; **Combat range** 1,000 m.

The bipod-mounted support weapon intended for troop use, it will replace the GPMG in certain roles, although not totally. Trials began in 1984 and service introduction for Royal Marine Commando units began in 1986.

Sniper Rifle 7.62 mm L42A1

Calibre 7.62 mm; **Length** 1.181 m; **Length of barrel** 0.699 m; **Weight empty** 4.43 kg; **Weight loaded** ? kg; **Muzzle velocity** 838 m/s; **Magazine capacity** 10 rounds; **Rate of fire** Single-shot only; **Maximum effective range** 1,200 m.

This is a classic sniper rifle which would be used in many battle areas to pick off special targets, such as enemy commanders. It is the result of rebarrelling the old Lee Enfield Service Rifle and is most commonly seen with a telescopic sight, known as the Sighting Telescope (L1A1). Various types of ammunition are used as well as several types of grip and sling.

Replacement by the **Accuracy International Model PM** is thought to have been completed.

Rifle 5.56 mm M16

Calibre 5.56 mm; **Length** 0.99 m; **Length of barrel** 0.508 m; **Weight empty** 3.1 kg; **Weight loaded (20-round magazine)** 3.68 kg; **Weight loaded (30-round magazine)** 3.82 kg; **Muzzle velocity** 1,000 m/s; **Magazine capacity** 20 or 30 rounds; **Rate of fire (cyclic)** 70–960 rpm; **Rate of fire (practical)** 40–60 rpm; **Maximum effective range** 400 m.

The Armalite (or M16 or Ar-15) is a small-calibre assault rifle used in the British Armed Forces primarily for close-quarter and jungle warfare, and it was in this role that the Royal Marines first became familiar with it. It is now used by the Corps for special operations (SBS) and by reconnaissance troops. It is well liked by those who operate it and is a good close-quarters weapon.

7.62 mm Light Machine-Gun L4A4

Calibre 7.62 mm; **Length** 1.133 m; **Length of barrel** 0.536 m; **Weight empty** 9.96 kg; **Weight loaded** 10.68 kg; **Muzzle velocity** 869 m/s; **Magazine capacity** 30 rounds; **Rate of fire (cyclic)** 500–575 rpm; **Rate of fire (practical)** 120 rpm; **Rate of fire (single-shot)** 40 rpm; **Maximum effective range** 800 m.

This is the Light Machine-Gun (LMG) which the Corps use mainly in the jungle and Arctic for light anti-aircraft and anti-personnel operations. It is basically a modified Bren gun of Second World War vintage and was replaced at section level by the GPMG in the 1960s.

7.62 mm General Purpose Machine-Gun (GPMG) L7A2

Calibre 7.62 mm; **Length as LMG** 1.232 m; **Length as HMG** 1.049 m; **Length of barrel** 0.629 m; **Weight empty (LMG role)** 10.9 kg; **Weight loaded (LMG role)** 13.85 kg; **Weight of tripod** 13.64 kg; **Muzzle velocity** 838 m/s; **Type of feed** 100-round belt; **Rate of fire (cyclic)** 625–750 rpm; **Rate of fire (LMG role)** 100 rpm; **Rate of fire (HMG role)** 200 rpm; **Maximum effective range (LMG role)** 800 m; **Maximum effective range (HMG role)** 1,800 m.

The L7A2 GPMG is based on the FN MAG and is used by the RM as a section weapon in all areas of operation. It is particularly valuable as a sustained-fire machine-gun (GPMG SF), when it is fitted with a tripod mount. It is fully automatic, air-cooled, belt-fed, gas-operated and can continue firing for considerable periods. The gun is fed from left to right using M13-type disintegrating linked belts. There is a gas regulator and a flash-hider attachment to aid concealment.

The GPMG SF is designed to give sustained fire for effective infantry cover and control, day or night, on a range of predetermined targets. The SF kit is easily portable and can quickly be in action. It is normal to have at least two Marines in the SF location – the aimer/firer and the loader; in addition, whenever possible, a third man acts as the gun controller. Spare barrels are necessary in this role.

SF kit specification: **Overall folded dimensions** 190 x 190 x 810 mm; **Weight** 13.4 kg; **Traverse** 360°; **Elevation** –11° to +22°; **Tripod type** L4A1; **Sight for SF role** Sight Unit C2; **Magnification** 1.7.

Northern Ireland special equipment

As the Royal Marines operate in the Province as a British Army battalion, they use the standard army anti-riot and IS equipment, including grenade discharger (L1A1); anti-riot gas dischargers (L6A1, L9A1 and L11A1); 1.5-in anti-riot cartridges (L3A1) and baton rounds – plastic and rubber bullets.

Support weapons

Unlike the United States Marine Corps (USMC), the Corps goes into action with only the essentials. Support weapons can be carried as troop weapons up to the size of the 84 mm Carl Gustav, however. Mortars are operated by mortar troops within a Support Company of a Commando, but are transported in half-ton Land Rovers or broken down into man-portable loads. The same applies to the Milan-equipped anti-tank troop of each Support Company, but they are more mobile, making use of 1-tonne Land Rovers. All RM support weapons are air-portable for flexible deployment.

51 mm Light Mortar L3

Calibre 50.8 mm; **Length of barrel overall** 0.7 m; **Length of bore** 0.515 m; **Weight of barrel** 1.5 kg; **Weight of breech piece** 0.99 kg; **Weight of sight unit** 0.65 kg; **Weight of monopod** 0.48 kg; **Weight of base plate** 0.76 kg; **Weight complete in action** 4.6 kg; **Maximum range** 800 m; **Minimum range** 150 m; **Bomb weight (HE L1A1)** 0.68 kg; **Bomb weight (smoke L1A1)** 0.68 kg; **Bomb weight (illuminating L1A3)** 0.85 kg; **Rate of fire (maximum)** 8 rpm for 2 minutes; **Rate of fire (normal)** 3 rpm for 5 minutes.

This is a man-portable light mortar which is designed to: provide rapid and accurate smoke screen up to 750 m from the mortar; bring down quick, accurate and lethal neutralizing or protective fire on the section front; provide target illu-

mination for 'Charlie G', LAW 80 and Milan anti-tank systems; be capable of direct or indirect fire when manned by only one individual; and overlap in range with the 81 mm mortar.

The 51 mm has increased range, lethality and accuracy over the old 2-in mortar, but the latter's ammunition can be used if required.

This mortar will fire explosive, smoke and illuminating bombs which have an aluminium casing and are fitted with plastic rings to prevent damage to the barrel. There are also drill and practice rounds.

Round	Weight	Filling	Remarks
HE	1.025 kg	TNT	272 mm long; with fragmentation effect
Smoke	0.95 kg	HCE	Time delay of six secs; duration 120 secs
Illuminating	0.825 kg	Various	Maximum range to light-up 750 m; burst height 250 m; duration 70 secs

A rate of fire of three rounds per minute for five minutes (15 rounds) can be achieved, but it is more usual to require eight rounds per minute for two minutes in most tactical situations. The mortar is manufactured by the Royal Ordnance Factory.

Rocket 66 mm HEAT L1A1

Calibre 66 mm; **Length extended** 0.893 m; **Length closed** 0.655 m; **Length of rocket** 0.508 m; **Weight complete** 2.37 kg; **Weight of rocket** 1 kg; **Muzzle velocity** 145 m/s; **Maximum effective range** 300 m; **Armour penetration** Up to 270 mm steel plate.

This is the American M72 HEAT (High Explosive Anti-Tank) weapon designed to give anti-tank protection at section level. Basically, it is a man-portable, disposable system which can be used against most modern AFVs. This weapon is in service with Commandos and Royal Marine Reserve units but is currently being replaced by the LAW 80. It is essentially an extendable tube with primitive sight.

Light Anti-Armour Weapon 80

Projectile calibre 94 mm; **Launcher length extended** 1.5 m; **Weight overall** 9.5 kg; **Weight**

of projectile 4 kg; **Maximum range** 500 m;
Combat range 300 m.

Formerly called MAW, the Hunting Engineering
light anti-armour system is designed for defence
against modern main battle tanks and other
armoured vehicles. It has an integral spotting rifle
to give high kill probability and the operator
requires minimal training. Service introduction
began in 1990.

84 mm Carl Gustav L14A1

Calibre 84 mm; **Length of barrel** 1.13 m;
Weight complete 16 kg; **Muzzle velocity** 160 m/s;
Weight of HEAT round L40A4 2.59 kg; **Weight
of HEAT projectile** 1.7 kg; **Range, anti-tank
(mobile)** 400 m; **Range, anti-tank (stationary)**
500 m; **Range, HE and smoke** 1,000 m; **Rate of
fire** 6 rpm; **Armour penetration (HEAT at 60°)**
228 mm.

This is the Swedish-made 'Charlie G', which is
the largest weapon carried at troop level.
Replacement by the LAW 80 commenced in 1988.
It is designed as an anti-tank weapon which is
shoulder-held in action; it is recoilless and capable of knocking out any known tank.

81 mm Mortar L16A1

Calibre 81 mm; **Length of barrel overall** 1.27 m;
Weight of barrel 12.27 kg; **Weight of
mounting** 11.8 kg; **Weight of sight unit** 3.4 kg;
Weight of base plate 11.6 kg; **Weight complete
in action** 39.6 kg; **Muzzle velocity (maximum)**
255 m/s; **Maximum range** 5,660 m; **Maximum
range (HE L31E3)** 5,800 m plus; **Minimum
range** 180 m; **Elevation** 45° to 80°; **Traverse** 5°
left-right at 45°; **Bomb weight (HE L15A3)**
4.47 kg; **Bomb weight (smoke L19A4)** 4.49 kg;
Rate of fire 12 rpm.

Although of medium calibre, this mortar is considered to be a lightweight type. It is accurate,
portable and reliable and has an extensive range
of ammunition available. It is equivalent to a
medium artillery piece in some roles, when using
a bipod mount. There are usually six in a mortar
troop.

The main feature of this weapon is its high
accuracy, being 0.5 per cent in any range setting.
It is broken down into a three-man load with the
heaviest part, the barrel, weighing 12.28 kg. It is
also capable of a high sustained rate of fire.

The ammunition is specially made and HE, WP
and illumination rounds are available to match the
mortar's own considerable characteristics. Three
basic rounds are British-made – HE, WP and

practice (the illumination round for the 81 mm is
currently under development).

HE round (L15A3): **Weight** 4.45 kg; **Filling**
TNT/RDX; **Overall length** 0.472 m; **Range**
180–5,660 m. *Smoke (L19A4)*: **Weight** 4.45 kg;
Filling White phosphorus (willie peter); **Overall
length** 0.46 m; **Range** As HE. *Practice (L21)*: A
reusable round with a range of 25–75 m.

Milan

Weight of missile 6.65 kg; **Weight of missile
and container** 11.5 kg; **Weight of launch unit**
15.5 kg; **Length of missile** 0.769 m; **Body
diameter (minimum)** 90 mm; **Span** 0.225 m;
Weight of warhead 2.98 kg; **Weight of warhead
charge** 1.45 kg; **Velocity** 75–200 m/s; **Maximum
range** 2,000 m; **Minimum range** 25 m; **Rate of
fire (maximum range)** 3–4 rpm; **Time of flight
to 2,000 m** Up to 13 seconds; **Armour
penetration** Up to 352 mm.

The Milan (*Missile d'Infantrie Leger Anti-Char*)
is a second-generation wire-guided ATM. It
replaced the Aerospatiale SS 11 in French Army
service and was ordered for the British Armed
Forces in 1978; it is now manufactured under
licence by British Aerospace. The standard Milan
team consists of one man acting with the support
of one or two others with extra missiles, and in
the Royal Marines the weapon equips the anti-
tank troop of a support company within a
Commando. The usual complement of a Troop is
one officer, 48 Marines and 14 launchers, plus
nine vehicles for transportation. The usefulness of
a Milan depends on how mobile the team is
because, once spotted, the Milan emplacement or
position is bound to come under attack, such is
the effectiveness of the weapon.

The system comprises a launcher on a tripod
with clip missiles in sealed containers. The missile is fin-stabilized and powered by a rocket
motor which ignites away from the launcher.

Javelin

Length 1.39 m; **Diameter** 760 mm; **Weight
(missile)** 11 kg; **Weight (warhead)** 0.6 kg HE;

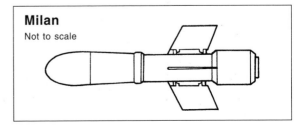

Milan
Not to scale

Maximum range 4,000 m; **Guidance** Semi-automatic command to line-of-sight.

This man-portable, two-stage air defence missile system is a development of the Blowpipe and was introduced into Royal Marines service to meet the evolving requirements of ground force defence (particularly as an effective stand-off range system against helicopter attacks). Deliveries began in 1986 but the missile is now obsolescent, although it is still used by Royal Marines units defending warships against low-flying aircraft and helicopters in the Armilla and Sharp Guard (Adriatic) patrols.

Heavy weapons

The Corps does not have its own heavy weapon support, but relies on 29 Commando Regiment, Royal Artillery, to provide batteries of the 105 mm Light Gun for service with the Corps at Commando Brigade level. The model used is the L118, which is air-portable (1,862 kg) by Sea King HC 4 as a single load. The normal towing vehicle is the 1-tonne Land Rover with gun crew, plus another Land Rover as ammunition carrier. Each Commando Regiment Battery would have six 105 mm Light Guns in wartime; a Territorial Army battery (No. 289) provides additional support.

Specialist equipment

Although the Mountain & Arctic Warfare (M&AW) cadres have special weapons for their environment, and it is presumed that the Special Boat Service (SBS) would be similarly equipped with whatever equipment was thought necessary, the Royal Marines has very little special equipment.

Mines and detectors

A large number of mines are available in the modern world and they have become a favourite weapon of terrorist groups, even though it is never possible to predict who will be killed or maimed as a result of detonation. More often than not it is the innocent civilian who is hurt. On the battlefield the mine can be used as an offensive or defensive weapon, depending on tactics. It is not known whether mines are particularly effective in snow conditions.

Claymore Anti-Personnel Mine M18A1

Weight 1.58 kg; **Length** 0.216 m; **Height** 0.083 m; **Width** 0.035 m; **Weight of charge** 0.68 kg; **Range** 50 m (16 m rearward).

This is an American-made device which is used to

Starstreak – the next generation of air defence weapon is due to enter service with the Corps soon. (Shorts)

disrupt enemy patrols. It consists of a curved box which contains 700 'nasty' steel balls; these balls are propelled upon detonation by an explosive charge to a height of 1 m and a range of 50 m. Detonation is by remote control or trip wire. The device is carried in a bandolier.

Horizontal Action Anti-Tank Mine

Weight 12 kg; **Length** 0.26 m; **Diameter** 0.2 m; **Range** 80 m.

This French-made device is used against heavy vehicles such as armoured personnel carriers (APCs) and armoured fighting vehicles (AFVs). In similar fashion to the Claymore, it is positioned at the side of a route used by vehicles and is exploded to cause as much damage to tracks and the softer parts of vehicles as possible. The charge is propelled against the armoured fighting vehicles and can penetrate 70 mm of armour.

Mine Detector No. 4C

Weight in use 9.15 kg; **Weight in transit box** 14.4 kg; **Search head length** 0.286 m; **Search head height** 0.108 m; **Search head width** 0.184 m; **Amplifier depth** 0.216 m; **Amplifier height** 0.108 m; **Amplifier width** 0.108 m; **Handle extended** 0.127 m; **Handle collapsed** 0.38 m; **Detection depth (soil)** 0.51 m; **Detection depth (pave)** 0.305 m.

This is the standard metal mine detector used by the RM for sweeping paths and other areas where enemy mines may be located, and has been in service since 1968.

It is possible to use this device whilst walking or, if in action, in the prone position, because the handle and search head are adjustable. Various anti-sweep devices such as iron filings can be overcome using the special selector for pave material. Like all detectors of this type, it works on the principle of electromagnetic induction when two coils are in balance; any metallic object coming into the field is usually strong enough to put the balance out and so register.

P6/2 Sweep Metal Detector

Weight complete 4.5 kg; **Length of long probe** 1.016 m; **Length of short probe** 0.4 m; **Length of open loop probe** 1.143 m; **Length of personnel probe** 0.4 m; **Dimensions of electronic unit** 0.25 x 0.08 x 0.25 m.

The P6/2 Sweep metal and mine detector is a militarized version of the Plessey P6 pulse indication metal detector. In military use the Sweep is issued

with four different probes which can be used to fulfil almost any detection role from conventional mine detection to personnel body searches. The probes are an open loop probe for normal ground searches, a ferrite rod for searching foliage and water locations, a short probe and the personnel search probe. Using the ferrite probe, an object the size of an automatic pistol can be detected up to 0.28 m away.

Selected specialist vehicles

The Royal Marines and the Royal Navy operate a

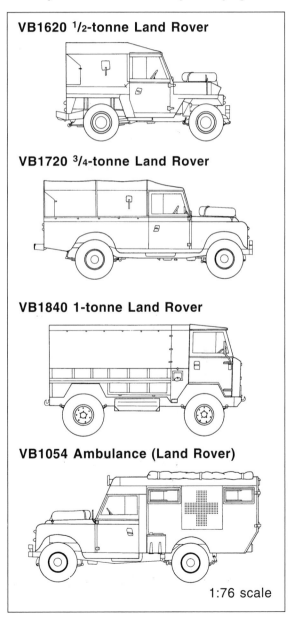

VB1620 ¹/₂-tonne Land Rover

VB1720 ³/₄-tonne Land Rover

VB1840 1-tonne Land Rover

VB1054 Ambulance (Land Rover)

1:76 scale

series of specialist vehicles, especially in the Norwegian theatre and for amphibious landings. A selection of current types is described below, but as this is a constantly changing inventory, this is not an exhaustive listing.

Landing craft

The landing craft is the fundamental delivery vehicle for men and equipment in the Royal Marines and the craft are operated independently or as part of the complement of an assault ship or other amphibious vessel.

Landing Craft Utility (LCU) are embarked in *Fearless* and *Intrepid* and operated by the landing craft training company and 539 Assault Squadron. Originally, they were designed to carry a main battle tank, but today, their role includes logistic support. In *Fearless* and *Intrepid*, two LCUs are carried in the dock. There are 12 LCUs in service.

Landing Craft Vehicle & Personnel (LCVP) are smaller and used for confined waters and are carried on the davits or decks of amphibious ships. To a certain extent, the LCVP has been supplemented by the hovercraft, but not replaced, and trials continue with new types of

landing craft. There are 21 LCVP Mk 4 craft in commission.

LCU data: **Length** 25.7 m; **Beam** 6.5 m; **Draught** 1.7 m; **Displacement** 178 tonnes fully loaded; **Crew** SNCO + 6; **Capacity** 100 tonnes cargo; **Speed** 10 knots.

LCVP data: **Length** 12.7 m; **Beam** 3.1 m; **Draught** 0.8 m; **Displacement** 14 tonnes fully loaded; **Crew** NCO + 2; **Capacity** 35 Marines; **Speed** 10 knots.

Griffon Hovercraft (LCA)

In 1994, the Royal Marines re-adopted the hovercraft as a prime mover of forces to supplement the LCVP, even in sea state 3. Initially trials were carried out in February 1994 in the Outer Hebrides. The craft were found capable of travelling 300 nm at 25 knots.

Length 8.4 m; **Beam** 3.8 m; **Draught** Zero; **Displacement** 2 tonnes fully loaded; **Crew** NCO + 1; **Capacity** 16 Marines; **Speed** 25 knots.

Rigid Raiders

A new type of Rigid Raider was developed for the

An LCU offloading a Bv 206 transport across a beach in Norway. (RN/CPO Chris North)

The Griffon LCA – on its first major Royal Marines exercise in February 1994. (Paul Beaver)

Royal Marines and eight were delivered to Poole in 1992, followed by another 16 in 1993. These are the standard raiding craft of the Royal Marines and can carry 10 Marines.

Rigid Inflatable Boat (RIB)

Arctic 22 This 40-knot boat can carry 15 Marines for 30 nm.

Pacific 22 A larger and heavier version, it has a range of 85 nm at 25 knots, carrying 15 Marines or 2 tonnes of cargo.

Fast pursuit craft Six were built by Watercraft for the Hong Kong Squadron and are used for anti-smuggling operations.

SBS water craft

A variety of specialist water craft are used by the Royal Marines' Special Boat Service for covert

Fast pursuit craft – the Royal Navy operates six RIBs in Hong Kong with RM coxswains as part of the operations against illegal immigrants and smuggling. (Paul Beaver)

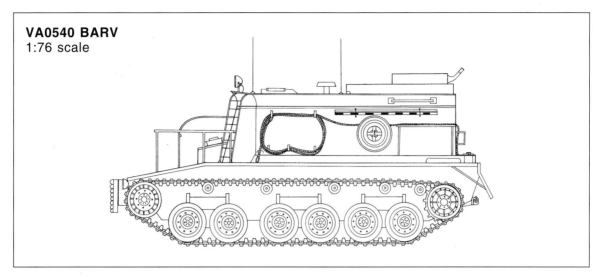

VA0540 BARV
1:76 scale

reconnaissance and other operations, including:

Klepper Canoe This is the traditional SBS swimmer/canoeist craft. Built to carry two swimmers, it can be launched from a landing craft, submarine, hovercraft or helicopter. It is 5.56 m long and weighs 51 kg dry.

Beach Armoured Recovery Vehicle
To aid amphibious operations, the Royal Marines have a beach armoured recovery vehicle, based on an old Centurion tank chassis, which has been specially modified for beach operations. A new version is currently being developed, which could have a more operational role, including fitting a mortar.

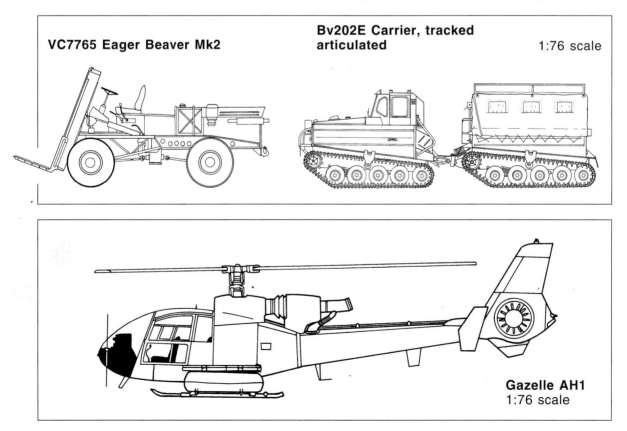

VC7765 Eager Beaver Mk2

Bv202E Carrier, tracked articulated   1:76 scale

Gazelle AH1
1:76 scale

Snow Cats

Over-snow transportation is difficult in Norway. Initially, the Royal Marines used the Aktiv Fischer Snow Cat, and although this has been replaced, it began a close relationship with Swedish equipment. The replacement was the Bv 202 which entered service in 1968 and was used in the Falklands (Malvinas) campaign. It remains

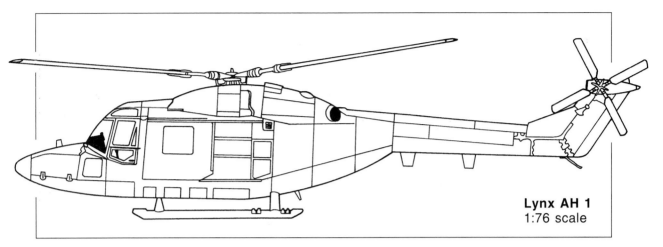

Lynx AH 1
1:76 scale

Fire team – Royal Marines Gazelle and Lynx/TOW helicopters during an exercise in the Outer Hebrides. (Paul Beaver)

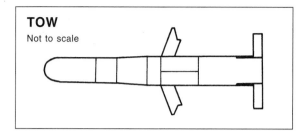

TOW
Not to scale

operational in Bosnia-Herzegovina with the UNPROFOR mission. The latest Snow Cat in service is the Bv 206, which can carry 2.3 tonnes of equipment over almost any terrain. Manufactured by Hagglunds of Sweden and powered by a Mercedes-Benz engine, it replaced all other Royal Marines snow vehicles from 1990. In 1996, a new armoured version, the Bv208S, will be brought into service.

Royal Marines helicopters

Although the Fleet Air Arm provides the basic lift capability for the Royal Marines, the Commando Brigade Air Squadron (847 Squadron) has been equipped with its own helicopters for nearly three decades. The helicopters have seen active service around the world, including during the Falklands (Malvinas) campaign and in Northern Ireland.

The Brigade Air Squadron, currently at Yeovilton, has been developed in parallel to the Army Air Corps' battlefield squadrons with the Gazelle and Lynx/TOW. However, because the helicopters are frequently embarked in amphibious shipping, they are specially configured for overwater operations.

Gazelle AH 1 This is the reconnaissance and liaison helicopter which can carry a crew of two and three passengers. It has a range of 650 nm and an endurance of 2.5 hours. It is generally unarmed but carries an observation aid mounted over the aircraft commander's seat.

Lynx AH 7 Equipped to fire the 2.8 km range TOW anti-tank missile, the Lynx AH 7 is the latest British Army version of the battlefield Lynx which has been configured to fire the wire-guided missile by day or night. It has a range of 650 nm and can also carry eight Marines if required.

CHAPTER NINE

Personnel matters

THE ROYAL NAVY and the Royal Marines play a major role in protecting the United Kingdom and British interests around the world. They have done so for more than 300 years.

Since the infamous Nott Defence Moratorium in 1981, the Senior Service has been increasingly under fire from the government as they have looked for defence cuts but without a review of defence commitments and needs.

The three main roles of the Royal Navy are:

* Provision of amphibious forces and shipping;
* Provision of carrier air support and escorts;
* Provision of submarines, including the United Kingdom's strategic nuclear forces.

The Royal Navy is charged with deterring aggression against the United Kingdom, its 14 depen-

Women at sea – mixed training in small boats at Raleigh, *the Royal Navy's latest training establishment on Plymouth Sound.* (HMS *Drake*)

dent territories and allies in a world where there are fewer and fewer foreign bases. The Royal Navy is a key part of the North Atlantic Treaty Organization (NATO).

The running costs of the Royal Navy take up about a quarter of the United Kingdom's annual defence budget of £21.72 billion (1995/96).

The April 1996 figures are:

	Royal Navy	*Royal Marines*
Officers	7,500	700
Ratings	33,600	6,200
Total	**41,100**	**6,900**

This includes the Queen Alexandra's Royal Naval Nursing Service.

There are now 650 female sailors at sea. Over 500 of them were on their second sea draft in 1995 and 65 were officers, including Officers-of-the-Watch. Females, formerly called Wrens, went to sea in 1991 and so far it seems that women are better at some sea-going jobs because of their dexterity, voice and powers of concentration. It will be another 10 to 12 years however before there is a female officer who is high enough on the promotion ladder to command a warship.

Recruitment

Officers are recruited between the ages of 17 and 26, with Supplement List (short service) officers requiring five UK GCSE passes and General List (career) officers needing at least two UK A-level passes. About 70 per cent of the officer candidates are now graduates and all train at the Britannia Royal Naval College, Dartmouth.

In 1995, the Royal Navy recruited 200 officers, including 50 Royal Marines, 100 seamen and 50 specialists, including dentists and doctors. From 1996, the officer selection will require 450 candidates to pass and go to Lympstone or Dartmouth.

UNIFORMS AND INSIGNIA

The Senior Service has always had the smartest uniform of any of the British Armed Forces. Men and women no longer have a distinction in their dress or rank insignia.

The Royal Fleet Auxiliary Service has a distinctive marine uniform dictated by their merchant status, whilst the Royal Maritime Auxiliary Service wears a mixture of civilian work dress and marine reefer jacket.

The Royal Marines have adopted British Army dress to suit their combat needs, but their dress uniform remains distinctive.

Naval rank badges

The use of the nautical gold ring and curl is an ancient tradition in the Royal Navy, and today

Young Officers training in navigation as Second Officer-of-the-Watch in the patrol craft Plover. (Paul Beaver)

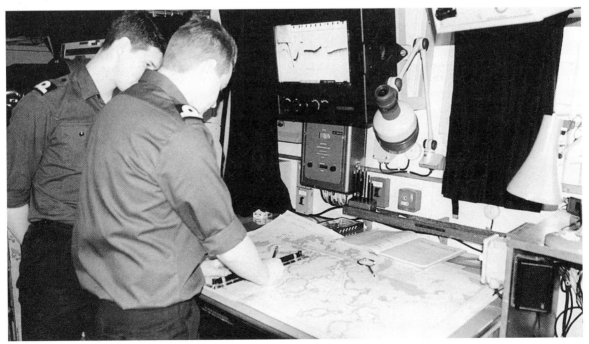

they are not only worn on the sleeve of the blue tunic/jacket but also as shoulder straps on jerseys, Disruptive Pattern Material jackets and flying suits.

Flag Officers
Admiral of the Fleet A broad gold ring with four quarter-width rings above; on certain ceremonial dress, a crown over crossed batons within a wreath over the royal cipher is worn on a shoulder strap.

Admiral A broad gold ring with three quarter-width rings above; on certain ceremonial dress, a crown over a crossed baton and sabre over three pips (triangular formation) is worn.

Vice Admiral A broad gold ring with two quarter-width rings above; on certain ceremonial dress, a crown over the crossed baton and sabre and two pips is worn on the shoulder.

Rear Admiral A broad gold ring with one quarter-width ring above; on certain ceremonial dress, the shoulder badge is a crown over crossed baton and sabre, over a single pip.

Flag Officers' caps have the Naval cap badge (anchor surmounted by crown in a wreath) with two rows of gold oakleaf embroidery to top and edge of naval cap with white cover. (The white cover on all naval caps is retained irrespective of location, climate or season.)

Naval Officers
Commodore A broad gold ring on sleeve or shoulder flash.

Captain Four gold rings on sleeve or shoulder flash.

Commander As for Captain RN, except that only three gold rings are worn.

(Cap peaks: the above three have a single row of gold oakleaf embroidery to top and peak of the Service cap; the badge is the same for all Naval officers.)

Lieutenant Commander As for Captain RN, except that rank is denoted by two gold rings with a single thin gold ring interposed.

Lieutenant As for Captain RN, except that only two gold rings are worn.

Sub-Lieutenant As for Lieutenant, except that only a single gold ring is worn.

Midshipman A white lapel flash with gold/brass/anodized naval button is worn.

Medical and Dental Officers
The medical and dental branches of the RN have corresponding ranks to their brother officers from Vice Admiral (Medical) and Rear Admiral (Dental) downwards. There is no equivalent to Commodore in the dental branch. All medical and dental officers have their ranks prefixed with 'Surgeon' and dental officers have (D) after their rank. There are rarely Surgeon Sub-Lieutenants in the active list and there are no Midshipmen in the medical and dental branches.

Examples of corresponding ranks:

General List RN	Medical Officers	Dental Officers
Rear Admiral	Surgeon Rear Admiral	Surgeon Rear Admiral (D)
Commander	Surgeon Commander	Surgeon Commander (D)

Medical and dental officers are recruited post-qualification, although they may be university cadets of the RN previous to that. Many use Service life as a unique opportunity to obtain medical training before returning to the National Health Service much enriched by their experience.

The medical officers (including dental officers) of the Royal Navy are to be found in establishments and HM Dockyard sickbays, in the naval hospital, aboard larger ships, and attached to frigate and destroyer squadrons. Women are recruited directly into the dental branch of the Royal Navy and have never been considered to be members of the former Women's Royal Naval Service. Medical research is carried out at INM Alverstoke where entrants to the branch are also sent following a course at Britannia Royal Naval College, Dartmouth. Medical and dental students are given the rank of Surgeon Sub-Lieutenant until pre-registration, when they become Acting Surgeon Lieutenants and, on registration, they are commissioned as Surgeon Lieutenants RN.

The Royal Navy's medical and dental branches are responsible for the health and general well-being of the Royal Navy, Royal Marines and the other branches. Several naval doctors and dentists are Commando-trained and serve with the Royal Marines.

Medical and dental uniforms are identical to those of the Royal Navy's other branches except that the gold rings are laced with intermediate red (medical) and orange (dental); pink intermediate rings signify a Medical Service Officer.

Seaman Officers
The executive branch is the backbone of the Royal Navy at sea, in that it provides sub-specializations which give variety to the branch's activities: aircraft control; aviation – pilot and observer; mine warfare and clearance diving (MCD); submarines; and hydrographic surveying. It is important to remember that only Seaman Officers are eligible for command at sea, but the

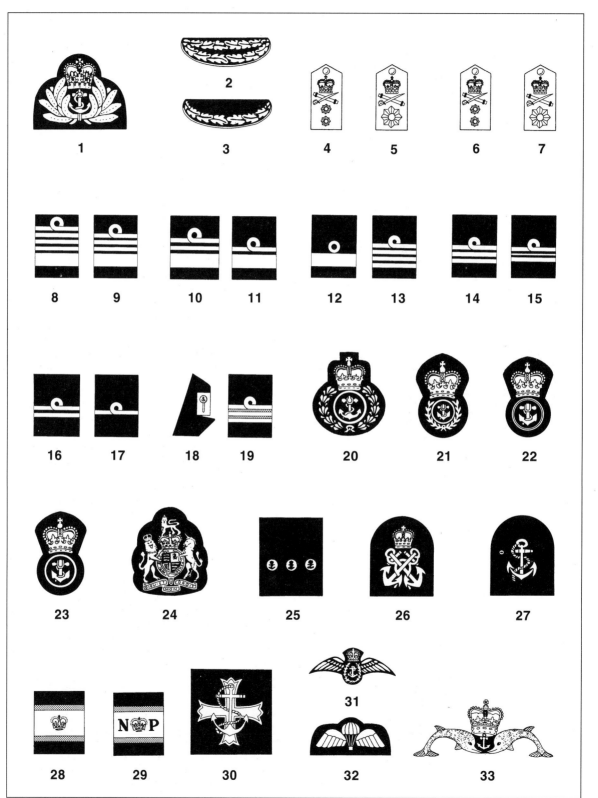

1

2

3

4

5

6

7

8

9

10

11

12

13

14

15

16

17

18

19

20

21

22

23

24

25

26

27

28

29

30

31

32

33

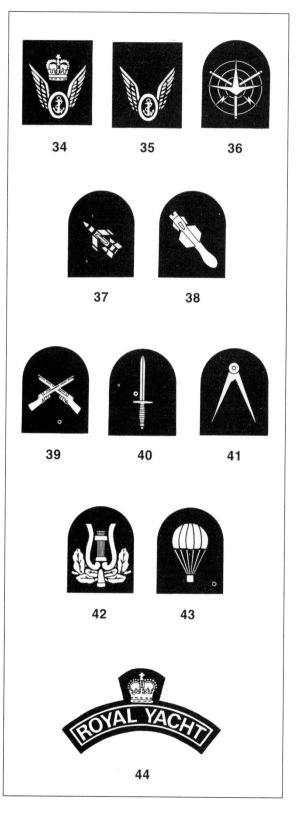

34   35   36

37   38

39   40   41

42   43

44

1 *RN Officers' cap badge, gold with silver anchor and red centre to crown.* **2** *Flag Officers' cap peak, gold on black.* **3** *Commodore's, Captain's or Commander's cap peak, gold on black.* **4–7** *Admiral of the Fleet's, Admiral's, Vice Admiral's and Rear Admiral's shoulder boards, gold base, silver insignia, red centre to crown.* **8–11** *Admiral of the Fleet's, Admiral's, Vice Admiral's and Rear Admiral's sleeve lace, gold on navy blue.* **12–17** *Commodore's, Captain's or Commander's, Lieutenant Commander's, Lieutenant's and Sub-Lietenant's sleeve lace (duplicated on shoulder boards), gold on navy blue.* **18** *Midshipman's lapel distinction, white with gold button.* **19** *Distinction cloth, see text: Medical Officers, scarlet; Medical Service Officers, pink; Dental Officers, orange; Instructors (now rarely worn) white.* **20–22** *Petty Officer's cap badges, gold and silver anchor and red centre to crown: WO, Chief PO.* **23** *Other ratings' cap badges (worn when not dressed as seamen), red.* **24** *WO rate badge, predominantly red, gold and blue with white unicorn.* **25** *CPO's gold cuff buttons.* **26** *PO's rate badge, gold with red centre to crown.* **27** *Leading Rate's badge, gold.* **28** *PO's armlet, blue/white/blue stripes, dark blue crown with red centre.* **29** *Naval Patrol armlet, colours as above.* **30** *Chaplain's cross with fouled anchor superimposed.* **31–44** *Specialist badges, normally gold on No 1s, blue on working and tropical dress and otherwise red.* **31** *Pilot's wings;* **32** *Parachutist (gold wings, white parachute);* **33** *Submariner (red centre to crown);* **34** *Observer;* **35** *Aircrew;* **36** *Aircraft controller;* **37** *Missile aimer;* **38** *Airborne missile aimer;* **39** *Marksman;* **40** *Commando;* **41** *Navigator's Yeoman;* **42** *Volunteer bandsman;* **43** *Subsunk parachute assistance group;* **44** *Seaman assigned to duties on the Royal Yacht* Britannia.

individual sub-specialization does affect the selection process.

Aircraft controllers are trained at Yeovilton and are responsible for the guidance and safety of the Fleet's aviation assets, either afloat or based at a Naval Air Station ashore. Pilots and Observers, however, have an intensive and costly (about £1.5 million) course which takes them from elementary flying with the RAF and teaches the operational skills of a front-line helicopter or Sea Harrier flyer (pilots only). Training would begin before the Seaman Officer's 23rd birthday. Supplementary List (SL) officers often join the Royal Navy to fly, but all Naval aircrew officers are Naval officers first and foremost, having spent time at sea, usually as Young Officers (YOs). At some time in their careers, they will have undergone watchkeeping training.

Medically fit officers are able to train to

An artists impression of the Helmets Ltd Rescuer system for SAR aircrewmen; includes remote radio system for cliff rescues.

oceanographic survey, but unlike the others, this branch retains those who have trained through their service careers. Many hydrographic officers are members of the Royal Institution of Chartered Surveyors, the world's leading professional body in this field.

The Chaplaincy

The Royal Navy is conscious of the needs of men and women for spiritual and community guidance. For many hundreds of years, ships at sea have borne 'men of the cloth' and the major warships of the RN still do. There are Chaplains in the Service from the Church of England, Church of Scotland, the Free Churches, the Jewish faith and the Roman Catholic Church. They all wear the cross of their calling on a suit-like uniform jacket, or No 5J, and the traditional 'dog collar'. Several Royal Navy Chaplains have successfully completed the Commando training course at Lympstone and are thus entitled to wear the green beret.

Chaplains are members of the Wardroom Mess, holding ranks for administrative purposes, and are thus considered officers; nevertheless, they are capable of reaching all ranks and their families, taking on the rank of the person to whom they are speaking.

Instructor Officers

The Royal Navy's 'Schoolies' are one of the four specializations of the General List (GL). They are distinguished by the white intermediate rings of their rank insignia and are both carried at sea and based ashore. They offer technical advice and meteorological and oceanographical services to the Fleet as well as teaching the trainees of the Service.

After initial training at Dartmouth, the Instructor Officer attends the School of Education and Training Technology at *Nelson*. At sea, the 'Schoolie' may well double up as a Flight Deck Officer (FDO) and those serving with the Royal Marines can take the Commando Course.

Supply and Secretariat Officers

The 'Pussers' of the Royal Navy provide support to the Fleet and the RN/RM in general. The Branch provides Supply Officers (SOs) afloat and ashore (Base Supply Officer – BSO) and also the Assistants and Secretaries to Captains and Admirals. Pussers also deal with legal, promotion and welfare matters. Aboard ship, the Pusser can be the Public Relations Officer and may undertake secondary duties, such as FDO. Supply Officers look after pay, wardroom staff, stores

become ships' divers and later, if selected, to go on to mine and explosive ordnance disposal courses. Many such officers are selected to command the Royal Navy's Minor War Vessel flotilla units of mines countermeasures vessels or patrol craft.

The officers who volunteer for the Submarine Service have the right to wear the coveted 'double dolphin' badge. The Submarine Command Course is often called the 'Perishers Course' but is now undertaken with a submarine from the Royal Netherlands Navy rather than a British boat, following the paying off of the 'Upholder' class.

The final sub-specialization open to the Executive branch is that of hydrographic and

and catering. Like Instructor Officers, they are often trained for bridge watchkeeping and as Officers-of-the-Day (OODs).

Examples of Supply and Secretariat specializations:

Rear Admiral Director General Naval Manpower and Training; Area Flag Officer; Admiral President, RN College, Greenwich.
Commander Supply Officer, DLG; Naval Attaché; BSO Royal Yacht.
Lieutenant Captain's Secretary, Destroyer; Section Officer, Admiral's Staff; Lieutenant to Admiral, General or Air Officer.

Engineering Officers

The modern Royal Navy is a complex working place with many high-technology systems which require competent engineering skills. The Royal Navy had a university-equivalent training college at Manadon (*Thunderer*) at Plymouth in which to train Engineering Officers until the 'Options for Change' defence cuts.

There are still four sub-specializations: Marine Engineering (Submarine); Weapons Engineering (Surface Ship); Weapons Engineering (Submarine); and Air Engineering, including Maintenance Test Pilots.

The Marine Engineering Officer is responsible for the hull and general structure of ships, their main propulsion, associated systems, power generation, ventilation and control for all systems, including fuel and water. The MEO (Submarine) has similar duties aboard submarines which also include the reactors and specialist sub-surface systems. The Weapons Engineering Officer (Surface Ship) is primarily tasked with ensuring that weapons are effective at all times. This includes computers, mountings, electronic warfare and sonar. The WEO (Submarine) has a similar function in undersea boats, but he includes watchkeeping and Trident missile systems within his area of responsibility. Finally, the Air Engineering Officer (AEO) ensures that all aircraft perform as required, both fixed and rotary-wing types. All avionics and weapons for aircraft come under the AEO's aegis.

Royal Naval Reserve

In recognition of the way officers of the Reserve, then called the Royal Naval Volunteer Reserve, now the Royal Naval Reserve, answered their country's needs during the Second World War, King George VI granted them the right to wear the gold bands of the Royal Navy, the only distinctive mark being the tiny 'R' in the curl of the rings. This move, in 1951, abolished the use of 'Wavy Navy' stripes. Further integration took place in 1976 when the Royal Naval Reserve and the then Women's Royal Naval Reserve came under central command.

Male and female ratings wear the shoulder badge 'ROYAL NAVAL RESERVE'. In all other respects, the badges and uniform of the Royal Naval Reserve are identical to the regular equivalent.

Special Duties List

SD officers have been commissioned from the ratings of the Fleet and are special in that they have a great wealth of technical expertise and experience of Service life. A large number of Naval Officers are now commissioned this way. They attend Dartmouth but can only rise in normal events to the rank of Lieutenant Commander (SD), many remaining at Lieutenant for up to a dozen years. They are found in specialist branches, such as Photography, Naval Provost, and where technical skills are all-important, such as Engineering. They cannot be distinguished from GL or SL officers on commissioning, except that their beards tend to be greyer.

Other distinctions

Chaplains wear a gold cross of Christ with naval anchor (fouled) superimposed. Submarine officers and ratings are entitled to wear the Submarine Badge of two gold dolphins, naval crown and anchor. Officers of the Fleet Air Arm wear either the double wings of the Naval pilot or the wings of the Observer. These awards are worn on the lower sleeve except on tropical dress and flying suits; the latter often have name/wings/squadron flashes on the left breast.

Naval ratings

Warrant Officers The Royal Crest of lion and unicorn is worn on the lower sleeve of cuffs on jacket, or on a shoulder flash. The cap badge is the Naval crown with anchor surrounded by an oak wreath. WOs are holders of the Sovereign's warrant.

Chief Petty Officers They wear three gilt buttons on each cuff to denote rank. The cap badge is a more compact WO badge. Chief Regulating Officers are known in certain circumstances as Masters-at-Arms, and are very often the senior rating in a ship. These much-respected men (and women) are allowed to wear their anodized metal branch badges (a crown) on a white strap above the right cuff on the Jersey Wool Heavy. There is a further graduated pro-

45–63 *Branch badges. Stars and crowns are added to denote appropriate standards of qualification.* **45** *Missile.* **46** *Sonar.* **47** *Radar.* **48** *Mine warfare.* **49** *Diving.* **50** *Surveying recorder.* **51** *Seaman.* **52** *Electronic warfare.* **53** *Coxwain.* **54** *Radio operator.* **55** *Communications (tactical).* **56** *Master-at-Arms.* **57** *Regulating.* **58** *Physical training.* **59** *Naval airman (MET = meteorological recorder. Other letters beneath the badge are: AH = aircraft handler, P = photographer and SE = survival equipment). The air engineering mechanic's badge is identical but carries different lettering: M = mechanical, R = radio/radar, WL = weapons electrical, W = weapons, L = electrical and O = ordnance.* **60** *Marine engineering mechanic; letters under are M = mechanical or L = electrical.* **61** *Weapons engineering mechanic; letters under are O = ordnance or R = Radio.* **62** *Supply and Secretariat; in this case, letters are carried within the circle: CA = caterer, C = cook, S = steward, SA = stores accountant or W = writer.* **63** *Missileman.* **64** *Medical (red and white); letters under are: N = State Registered male nurse, R = radiographer, P = physiotherapist, H = health inspector, L = laboratory, M = mental nurse or HP = health physicist.* **65–67** *Good conduct badges – 4, 8 and 12 years respectively.*

motion to Charge Chief which has no military equivalent.

Petty Officers wear two crossed and fouled anchors below the Naval crown. The cap badge is a fouled anchor in a circle below a Naval crown.

Leading Rates wear a fouled anchor on the left arm. Leading Rates and below, when not dressed as seamen, wear the fouled anchor with single circle and a simpler crown on caps and berets.

Good conduct and service

Royal Navy and Royal Naval Reserve ratings are permitted to wear chevrons denoting good conduct, with a single stripe for each four years up to a maximum of 12 years.

Royal Naval ratings wear gold badges on No. 1s, red badges on No. 2s and blue badges on other dress.

Special Dress

In the late 1970s, Special Dress regulations were issued to cover the appointment of Royal Naval and Royal Marines officers to NATO, North American and hot climate positions. The Royal Navy have noted this as No. 1W White Full Dress whilst the Royal Marines call it No. 4W Stone Coloured Service Dress; basically it is a cap or beret (RM) with stone-coloured tunic and trousers, tie, shirt and boots/shoes. Royal Marines officers wear Sam Brownes and may be required to wear the white helmet as well.

Mountain & Arctic Warfare

The Commando Forces are mountain and arctic warfare (M&AW) trained for operations in Norway and other regions with a similar climate. The Royal Marines have specialist dress for these operations which are not mirrored by the Royal Navy.

Any naval officers or ratings who go to Norway, for example as members of Naval Air Commando Squadrons, wear Royal Marines issue clothing.

Naval officers attached to Royal Marines units wear the Marine's dress for working with 'ROYAL NAVY COMMANDO' shoulder flashes and the naval crest in the beret, as opposed to the anodized or bronze Corps crest. Naval rank badges will also be worn on Royal Naval uniform as required. RM officers wear either cloth or bronze rank badges (Army pattern) as applicable to the style of dress. Some aircrew from the Commando Brigade Air Squadron will wear Army Air Corps pattern flying suits or camouflage (DPM) suits and Army pattern boots as required.

Naval Air Commando aircrew also wear DPM suits in certain situations. The latter are more comfortable than certain Naval aircrew dress garments.

In hot climates, the Royal Navy and Royal Marines have adapted their dress accordingly. Officers wear white dress (No. 2W) for mess functions as per No. 2s. Whereas Royal Naval officers continue to wear white (including 'safari' jackets) with long or short trousers, the Corps have adopted stone-coloured bush jackets (No. 5W) – equivalent to Nos 1, 4 and 5 Dress. The navy has a speciality in its No. 10W Red Sea Rig which consists of white dress shirt, navy blue trousers, black cummerbund and shoes; this is worn in the evening for normal mess dress. The Corps has a similar dress for hot climates which is made up of white tropical shirt, blue trousers, scarlet cummerbund and black shoes – this is known as No. 10W as well.

While in action in hot climates, the Marines wear No. 11W Tropical Combat Dress, which consists of beret, combat shirt, lightweight trousers, puttees, DMS boots and web belt; tropical DPM combat smocks may be worn if ordered. RN officers on bridge watchkeeping wear a form of rating action dress, and at sea in tropical climates wear blue short-sleeved shirt and blue shorts with sandals.

Marines and ratings have special clothing for hot climates including stone-coloured bush jackets (RN – No. 2A/6/7; RM – No. 5W) or shirt-sleeve order (RN – No. 7A/7N; RM – No. 8W) which consists of shirt and trousers. Sea-going tropical routine dress of shirt and shorts, known to both Services as No. 10s, is stone-coloured or No. 10W, which is blue (e.g. Hong Kong Squadron). Royal Marines wear No. 11W Tropical Combat Dress: this is in place of No. 11 Combat Dress.

No. 8A Arctic Working Dress Winter hat; windproof jacket; lightweight trousers; combat shirt; jersey; ski march boots; snow gaiters; wool mittens and windproof outer gloves. In addition, arctic overalls are worn by technicians and thermal overboots are issued to ranks on static duties.

No. 11A Arctic Combat Dress Winter hat; windproof jacket; windproof trousers; white camouflage suit; ski march boots; snow gaiters and mittens/gloves as required. Underneath combat shirt and Jersey Wool Heavy are worn. The same additions of overboots and overalls apply.

Rating aircrew No. 3A Aircrew blouse and trousers; red badges; shirt/tie or vest; heavy navy jersey; beret; and boots/shoes may be worn during working hours at sea, in harbour and on Royal Naval Air Stations, but only by aircrew.

In the 1980s, the traditional rough serge items of clothing were replaced by lightweight polyester materials. This gear is easier to wear, and stands up to washing in the automatic laundrettes which now equip ships and establishments, replacing the Chinese laundries of the old Fleet (the last Chinese laundryman was paid off in 1995).

From mid-1980, the familiar ratings' cap was altered to give the wearer better service: it is now two-piece consisting of a peak and frame with a detachable white top. The naval rating still wears 'Square Rig' on all semi-formal and formal occasions and this tradition is very unlikely to change, other than for convenience, the regulations about pressing them in the normal onshore fashion (rather than horizontal creases) being an example of this change. In 1994, the Admiralty Board ordered the phasing out of the bell-bottom trouser.

The 1970s saw the introduction of the Jersey Wool Heavy – the 'Woolie-Pullie' – which has revolutionized Naval and Marine dress. Not only officers wear the garment, with rank tabs on the shoulders, but ratings and other ranks now also wear them for routine dress and as part of combat clothing. Wrens have a V-neck pattern jersey. Shoulder flashes are worn, including 'ROYAL NAVY COMMANDO', 'ROYAL NAVAL RESERVE' and 'ROYAL MARINES COMMANDO'. In 1979, it was announced that a Commando Skills badge would be introduced for ratings who are Commando-qualified, the design being a representation of the Commando fighting knife.

Royal Marines' rank badges

The Royal Marines, although very much a part of the Royal Navy, make use, where appropriate, of the British Army dress, badge and uniform system. RM officer rank badges are gold, grey or black, depending on circumstances.

General Officers

Lieutenant General A crown over crossed baton and sabre.
Major General A pip (four-pointed star) over a crossed baton and sabre.
(Cap badges: various forms of globe and laurel badge of the Corps.)

RM General Officers are usually mounted for the review and ceremonial inspection of Marines. There are no Brigadiers in the Corps of Royal Marines.

Field Officers

Colonel A crown over two pips all in line.
Lieutenant Colonel A crown over a pip.
Major A crown.

Junior Officers

Captain Three pips all in line.

Lieutenant Two pips in line.
Second Lieutenant One pip.
Officer Cadet A white stripe across the shoulder or white patch with gold button.
Warrant Officer Royal Coat of Arms.

NCOs

Colour Sergeant A crown over three chevrons worn on the upper arm.
Sergeant Three chevrons.
Corporal Two chevrons.
Lance Corporal One chevron.

Colours are altered to suit dress; the Corps cap badge is also worn on the green beret (signifying Commando-qualified) or blue new intake beret (also worn by Band Service), when the badge is worn on a red patch.

Queen Alexandra's Royal Naval Nursing Service

Officers of the QARNNS wear a complex insignia of rank which was reviewed in 1982–83; the following system is currently operating:

Matron-in-Chief and Director of Defence Nursing Staff A crown, over the QARNNS badge, over a gold-surrounded red cross on a white background, over the Sovereign's cypher, all on black surrounded by one gold line.
Principal Nursing Officer As for Matron-in-Chief but with the Sovereign's cypher (unless Matron-in-Chief at the same time) replaced by a gold horizontal bar and a thick gold line rather than two thin ones. The two gold cap lines are also not worn.
Chief Nursing Officer As for Principal Nursing Officer but without the gold bar. One gold band on hat.
Superintending Nursing Officer As for CNO but with a red surround to the rank badge. One red line on hat band.
Senior NO The cap is blue with red badge area surround: the insignia is as for Superintending NO but is rectangular and has no red surround. A red bar is also worn under the red cross badge.
NO As for Senior NO but without the red bar.
WO Wear grade badges on the cuff consisting of vertical red bars; three, two and one respectively. HNN (and Head CQA) and AHNN (and Assistant Head CQA) wear tie pins: the QARNNS' badge with a wreath and crown above, and the same without the wreath respectively.
Clerical and Quarters Officers Wear the same basic badge as Nursing Officers but without the red cross device. The C&Q branch will be

phased out in due course.

Cap badges The hat badge is the traditional Naval pattern, except that the wreath is red and the Naval crown is replaced by the baton/fouled device of the QARNNS in red and gold.

Rating badges QARNNS ratings wear the red batons outlined in gold; CQA ratings wear the former Women's Royal Naval Service pattern red circle with CQA inside, the 'C' above the 'QA'.

Corresponding ranks

Today, the Royal Navy and Royal Marines work closely with their colleagues from other Services and it is important for efficiency and for discipline that everyone knows exactly who is senior to whom. In addition, in bi- or tri-Service situations, it is important for command to pass smoothly and to the next senior. From the Naval point of view, the controlling apparatus is the Naval Discipline Act 1957, to which all the members of the Royal Navy are subject. Corresponding ranks are noted in Queen's Regulations and are summarized in the table over the page.

When Royal Marines officers are carried on the 'books' of warships and auxiliaries, the rank system

68 QARNNS cap badge, red leaves, red/gold crown and symbol. 69 QARNNS hat and beret badge, red and gold. 70–71 QARNNS tie pins: WO, CPO and PO nurses. 72 Arm badge. 73 Clerical and Quarters Assistant. 74–79 Officers' cape and rank badges; 74 Matron-in-Chief, 75 Principal Matron, 76 Matron, 77 Superintending Sister, 78 Senior Sister and 79 Sister. Capes blue for Sister and Senior Sister, red for higher ranks. 80–82 Cuff grade badges, red: 80 Head Naval Nurse, 81 Assistant Head Naval Nurse and 82 Senior Naval Nurse. 83 Royal Naval Reserve (example). 84 Temporary Officer (example). 85–87 Sea Cadet/CCF officers: 85 Lieutenant Commander, 86 Lieutenant and 87 Sub-Lieutenant.

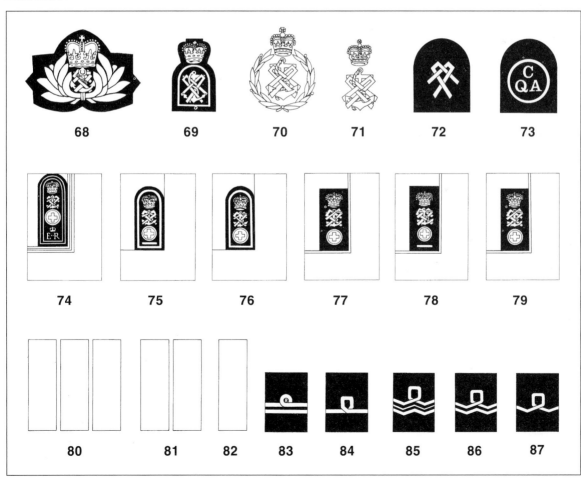

Naval	RM and Army	Royal Air Force
Admiral of the Fleet	Field Marshal*	Marshal of the RAF
Admiral	General*	Air Chief Marshal
Vice Admiral	Lieutenant General	Air Marshal
Rear Admiral	Major General	Air Vice Marshal
Commodore	Brigadier	Air Commodore
Captain	Colonel	Group Captain
Commander	Lieutenant Colonel	Wing Commander
Lieutenant Commander	Major	Squadron Leader
Lieutenant	Captain	Flight Lieutenant
Sub-Lieutenant/Acting	Lieutenant	Flying Officer
Sub-Lieutenant†		
Midshipman†	Second Lieutenant	Pilot Officer/Acting PO

* No equivalent in the Royal Marines.
† Junior to military and RAF ranks of the same level.

is altered slightly because the Corps is then considered to be subject to the Naval Discipline Act rather than the Army Act 1955. This also applies to Corps officers attached to Naval establishments.

Special clothing

The Royal Navy has developed clothing to suit its specific needs over the years, including the now familiar white hood and gloves of anti-flash gear, worn with action dress aboard ship. On the flight deck, there are various special dresses for fire-fighters and other personnel, including heavy weather jackets, protective caps with integral ear-defenders and life-jackets with face protection. In the engine room, machinery control room or boiler room, members of the Engineering Department usually wear as little as possible, frequently just a white overall with cap. This can be considered to be their working rig, which is navy blue shirt and tough trousers elsewhere on the ship.

Standard Temperate Combat Dress is made up of jacket, trousers and occasionally hat in DPM (disruptive patterned material) and worn with DMS (directly moulded soles) boots. The Denison smock of the parachutists is also worn but this is no longer issued. Tropical combat gear is more lightweight and suited to climatic conditions near the equator, whilst Cold Weather Clothing is equally as complete for operation in Norway.

The former standard helmet is now being replaced by a glass-reinforced plastic variant for the Royal Marines, whilst the RN still wears the American-style curved and round helmet for action duties. More often than not, both RN and RM action dress head gear is the beret.

Royal Fleet Auxiliary Service

Officers of the RFA are technically on contract to the Service, being merchant seamen. Their marks of distinction are shown below, and are worn on reefer jackets and jerseys, Naval pattern:

Commodore Master Broad gold ring with the gold square of all officers (cf. Commodore RN).

Commodore Chief Engineer As for Commodore Master but with purple ring below broad gold.

Master Four gold rings.

Chief Engineer Four gold rings with purple between.

Chief Officer Three gold rings.

Second Engineer Three gold rings with purple between.

Ship's Surgeon Three gold rings with red between.

First Officer Two gold rings with smaller one between (cf. Lieutenant Commander RN).

Senior Radio Officer As for First Officer, but light green between.

Senior Electrical Officer As for First Officer, but dark green between (hence the term 'greenie' for the personnel of this branch).

Senior Purser As for First Officer, but with white between.

Second Officer Two gold rings.

Third Engineer As for Second Officer, but with purple between.

First Radio Officer As for Second Officer, but with light green between.

Purser As for Second Officer, but with white between.

Uncertificated Second Officer Two thin gold rings.

First Electrical Officer As for Uncertificated Second Officer, but with dark green between.

Uncertificated Third Engineer As above, but with purple between.

Third Officer Single gold ring.

Fourth Engineer As for Third Officer, but with purple ring below.

Second Radio Officer As above, but with light green below.

Rating structure of the modern Royal Navy

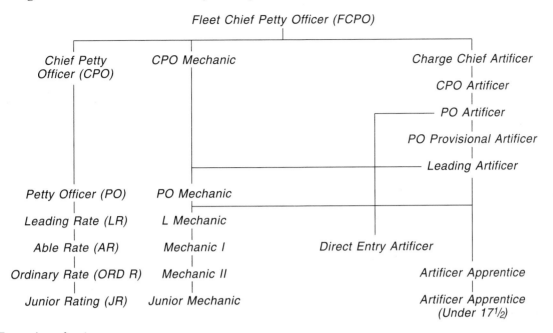

Examples of category:
WEM(R)	Weapon Engineering Mechanic (Radio)
LWEM(O)	Leading Weapon Engineering Mechanic (Ordnance)
LNAM	Leading Naval Air Mechanic
LCK	Leading Cook
CPO(D)	Chief Petty Officer (Diver)
CPO(Phot)	Chief Petty Officer (Photography)
LREG	Leading Regulator
LWREN	Leading Wren (Women's Royal Naval Service)

Assistant Purser As above, but with white below.

Uncertificated Third Officer/Fourth Officer Single narrow gold ring.

Uncertificated Fourth Engineer/Junior Engineer As for Uncertificated Third Officer, but with purple narrow ring below.

Second Electrical Engineer As above, but with dark green narrow ring below.

Note: Uncertificated Third Engineer's rank mark is also used for Senior Refrigeration Engineer; Uncertificated Fourth Engineer's mark is used for Junior Refrigeration Engineer.

NBC clothing

Nuclear, Biological and Chemical warfare is not new to the Royal Navy or the Royal Marines, and today's methods of protecting personnel are based on high technology and experience. It is not possible to give more than an indication of the current clothing available to the Royal Marines and Naval ratings ashore as a Naval party, but the reader will gain an insight into the real world of NBC.

Basically, a two-piece suit is used and the current system is Suits Protective NBC No. 1 Mark 3 manufactured by Remploy Limited of London. The smock has two layers of materials: the inner, anti-gas, layer and the outer nylon layer, complete with integral hood which fits in with the standard Service (S6) Respirator. A detector plate is carried to give warning of hazards being experienced. Quick adjustments to the neck, wrists, etc., are important. The trousers also have two layers of material and gloves and special overboots to complete the 'noddy suit'. NBC No. 1 Mark 2 is the Naval equivalent of the RM suit. Weight: smock 0.8 kg; trousers 0.66 kg.

Aircrew have the benefit of a special inner NBC Mark 1 Undercoverall Flyers NBC which is designed as an inner garment to be worn under a flying suit, on top of 'long johns'. A special hood is worn over the standard Type 'G' Aircrew helmet and it can be used with the AR5 Respirator.

Weight: inner coverall 0.6 kg; hood 0.12 kg; socks 0.09 kg.

The standard non-aircrew respirator is the Haversack Respirator (Anti-Gas) S6 Mark 2 which is carried in a 26 x 21 x 13 cm haversack which weighs 0.4 kg. Casualties are cared for in Casualty Bags, either Whole or Half.

FLAGS AND PENNANTS

The White Ensign – the red cross of St George with the Union Flag in the top left-hand corner, against the hoist – is carried by all vessels of the Royal Navy, including the small craft. In harbour or at anchor it is customary for the Ensign to be worn at the Ensign Staff on the quarterdeck, but at sea it is more usual to see a warship with the Ensign at the gaff (the fore- or mainmast). In the morning and at sunset, the 'colours' are hoisted and struck respectively, whether the 'vessel' is a ship or shore establishment. The Alert is sounded by pipe or bugle (larger ships only) and all officers and men on deck face aft and stand at the salute until the 'carry on' is sounded. At establishments, officers and men in the open stand at the salute facing the Ensign. One warship will also salute another when passing at sea or on entering/leaving harbour. The full rules are complex and outside the scope of this book.

Squadron command ships of the Royal Navy now wear pennants denoting authority. Until 1984, black bands were painted on funnels but they have been removed in order to improve all-grey camouflage. All Captains (D) and (F) and Commanders (MCM), (FP), (HK) and (NI) wear the short white swallow tail, with a red border top and bottom. It is worn on the starboard yardarm but does not displace a distinguishing flag or broad pennant.

Flags

Royal Standard This is the personal flag of the Sovereign, the Lord High Admiral, and is only hoisted when the Sovereign is actually present; it is struck when the Sovereign departs. HMY *Britannia* wears the Royal Standard at sea and in harbour whenever the Sovereign is aboard.

White Ensign As described above; came into full and complete use in 1864.

Union Flag The flag of the United Kingdom of Great Britain and Northern Ireland is worn at the jackstaff (bow) of all RN vessels at anchor or alongside, unless escorting the Royal Yacht or another vessel in which the Sovereign is present. It is also the flag of an Admiral of the Fleet. This flag is only called the 'Union Jack' when used as a jack from the jackstaff.

Admiral's flag A red cross of St George against a white background; like all flags worn at the mainmast or foremast or flown from the establishment flagstaff.

Vice Admiral's flag As for Admiral but with a red ball in the upper left corner next to the hoist.

Rear Admiral's flag As for Admiral but with two red balls next to the hoist.

Pennants

Commodore's pennant A red cross of St George against a white background with a red ball next to the hoist.

Senior Officer's pennant A white/green/white/green/white pennant worn at the yardarm of the ship bearing the most senior officer when warships are in harbour.

Commissioning pennant Worn from the day a ship commissions until she is decommissioned. It is not struck until that day, unless temporarily replaced by a Royal Standard or appropriate flag.

Paying-off pennant When a ship is nearing decommissioning, she wears a paying-off pennant – a red cross of St George against a white background – which is proportional to the length of the commission. It is apparently a custom rather than a requirement in the Royal Navy. It is only worn when entering or leaving harbour, and on Sundays, during this time.

Pennant number This is the group of letter(s) and number(s) worn on the hull and stern of British warships and auxiliaries; it is made up of a 'flag superior' letter denoting type and a hull number. The characters are carried in black with a white outline, or white on black hulls. Certain vessels, including submarines and survey ships, do not carry them.

A   Auxiliary (also Y, which is not carried)
C   Helicopter cruisers
D   Destroyers
F   Frigates
K   Helicopter support ships/diving vessels
L   Assault vessels
M   Mines countermeasures vessels
P   Patrol vessels
R   Carriers
S   Submarines

Some landing craft carry what appear to be pennant numbers but these denote their parent ship (e.g. T4 is an LCU from *Intrepid*).

Note From 1 November 1993, the Women's Royal Naval Service (WRNS) was fully integrated with the Royal Navy proper. In fact, integration had been underway since 1970, but now there is almost full equal opportunity and career opportunity.

Index

General Index